Thomas Aquinas

DENYS TURNER

Thomas Aquinas

A PORTRAIT

Yale UNIVERSITY PRESS/NEW HAVEN & LONDON

Yale University Press books may be purchased in quantity for educational, business, or
promotional use. For information, please e-mail sales.press@yale.edu (U.S. office) or
sales@yaleup.co.uk (U.K. office).

Designed by Mary Valencia.
Set in Adobe Caslon type by IDS Infotech Ltd.
Printed and bound by CPI Group (UK) Ltd, Croydon, CR0 4YY

The Library of Congress has cataloged the hardcover edition as follows:
Turner, Denys, 1942–
Thomas Aquinas: a portrait / Denys Turner.
p. cm.
Includes bibliographical references (pages   ) and index.
ISBN 978–0–300–18855–4 (alk. paper)
1. Thomas, Aquinas, Saint, 1225?–1274.
I. Title. B765.T54T87 2013
230'.2092—dc23   2012044497

ISBN 978-0-300-20594-7 (pbk.)

A catalogue record for this book is available from the British Library.

For Marie

". . . the onlie begetter . . ."

Contents

Acknowledgments ix

Introduction 1

One A Dominican 8

Two A Materialist 47

Three The Soul 70

Four God 100

Five Friendship and Grace 145

Six Grace, Desire, and Prayer 169

Seven Christ 189

Eight The Eucharist and Eschatology 230

Epilogue The Secret of Saint Thomas 267

Notes 271

Further Reading 285

Index 293

Acknowledgments

I have not until undertaking this work ever given more careful consideration to an intended readership for what I write than to think in terms of the needs of the students I have taught professionally in theological schools in the United Kingdom and the United States. Those students alone have truly mattered to me as a teacher and writer. And on the whole, after many years of teaching them I have imagined myself to have a pretty good idea of their needs. For this work, though, Jennifer Banks at Yale University Press called for availability to a wider and less specialist readership, and I have had the good fortune of being able to rely heavily on the advice as to how this might be done forthcoming in the first instance from Jennifer herself, from Philip King, the

Press's sensitive and tactful copy editor, and then from a large number of readers from a diverse range of theological and nontheological disciplines. Of necessity I could not take all the advice offered, even if in the course of revision I have ignored none.

In the first place, I am as grateful as only that teacher is who is lucky enough to have the sort of class that I taught on the life and thought of Thomas Aquinas at the Yale Divinity School in the fall of 2011 and to benefit from their feedback. I am especially grateful to six Ph.D. students in that class working in a variety of academic fields, not all theological: to Bradley East, Andrew Forsyth, Ryan McAnnally-Linz, Ross McCullough, John Stern, and Eric Weiskott. I set them the task of commenting on the version to hand, which they did, much to the enhancement of the text's clarity of focus.

I am grateful to three others who have had an important impact on the genesis and completion of this book. From the very outset of my writing of this work through to its completion Elizabeth Trang has been generous and perceptive in her provision of comments line by line. Her influence was transforming, especially at an early stage. Emily S. Kempson was the first of two graduate student copy editors who took turns at making of my rough drafts a publishable book, she with a challenging gusto that caused me much rethinking. It is, however, to Courtney Palmbush that, once again, I am chiefly indebted, for as with my previous book on Julian of Norwich she saw this text through several stages to its final form with the same combination of meticulous scholarship, conceptual rigor, and sensitivity to the reader's standpoint that, in conjunction with the prior work of Elizabeth and Emily, have made this book what it is, a matter now for others to judge.

I am grateful to Wm B Eerdmans for permission to reprint on pages 119–28 here a slightly revised version of pages 26–32 of my contribution to their collection of essays *Do We Worship the Same God?* edited by Miroslav Volf (2012).

This is certainly the last monograph that I will write as a full-time teaching professor of theology. It is therefore time to acknowledge an unpayable debt, the size of which has been accumulating for over forty years of married life, to my wife Marie. Throughout those decades I wrote, and taught, and got the credit. Marie namelessly provided the conditions without which that work would have been impossible, taking no credit for any of it. This book, then, is hers, hers not by virtue of its author's gift, but because it stands symbolically for what by right is due to her in justice on account of her selfless generosity as its "onlie begetter."

Introduction

What follows in this short book is a portrait in outline of a man and a mind, and, insofar as it is possible, of a soul. They all belong to Thomas Aquinas. It is a profile sketched out in thin strokes of the pen, exaggerating a few features out of all proportion and omitting many more altogether. It is therefore a caricature. But caricatures do not always distort. At best they reveal the prominent features of a character unobscured by excess of detail. My caricature, I hope, is no more distorting than any other work on Thomas Aquinas, just differently so. For I have not attempted any sort of comprehensive survey of Thomas's thought, even in summary. What herein I offer is more a point of entry into the man's thought obstructed by as little of the technical jargon of the medieval philosophers and theologians as is consistent with accuracy of exposition.

This work, then, is specifically not intended for professional theologians and philosophers. It is an invitation extended to those of whatever academic background or none, to find a way into one of those few minds in the history of writing that contains not any one great leading thought, nor only a mind large enough to "contain multitudes" of them, but something nearer to a cogently worked through universe of thought—and without question Thomas is in that company to which Dante, Plato, Shakespeare, Homer, and perhaps a few others belong.

Tasks such as the composition of such a work ought not to be undertaken by those not scared out of their wits at the prospect, strewn with so many pitfalls as the path is. The main danger is that of supposing that the thing to do is get a mind on the scale of Thomas's into your head, a task of compression that will be achieved only at your head's peril, so vast being the difference in scale between his head and yours—inevitably the result is but to cramp the one and cause splitting headaches in the other. The only safe thing to do is to find a way of getting your mind into his, wherein yours has room to expand and grow, and explore the worlds his contains.

There the reader of Thomas might just get a glimpse of the place in the man where the very visible public teacher, preacher, and theologian have the same source as the almost wholly invisible saint. There are more reasons than one why this is so hard to do, the main reason being that Thomas, who as a teacher was on more or less permanent public display, deliberately hid that place from anyone else than his confessor. The man indeed was a saint. But he made it his business to ensure that you would not get to know about it. In any case, he had little to hide that would arouse suspicions of exceptional holiness on the standard models of his time. He prayed, for sure, early in the day and long, but most of the time he taught, and when not teaching he read and he wrote, often late into the night. Otherwise he traveled frequently within and between Italy, Germany, and France, fulfilling conventional duties as a Dominican friar, and apart from the fact that he often forgot to eat and was somewhat overweight, that was pretty much it. His Franciscan contemporary and friend, gentle Bonaventure, is easier to get to know, and is the more obviously likeable saint, if just as obviously the lesser theologian. As for the life of Thomas, theological genius he may have been. But there is not a lot of material on the record making for an exciting hagiographical read.

The evidence of Thomas Aquinas's holiness is invisible, then, simply because he himself made sure of it. Consequently what I have done in this little book is the only thing you can do with such an impossible man, and that is write about that invisibility itself as the form and evidence at once of his holiness, of his pedagogical style, and of his writing as a professional theologian. In their different ways, all three consist in a disappearing act, an act of self-effacement that is itself so discreet that you could well spend your life reading the man without noticing that all along *he* has been missing. His life is a sort of hoax, the hoax of the genuinely humble who will not make a fuss even out of persuading people that he is not worth making a fuss of. He just disappears, unannounced, and his texts appear, as if authorless.

It is against the odds, therefore, that I have tried to write about this man, his mind, and his soul. What you miss when you fail to advert to the trick that Thomas plays on you is, in fact, the whole point, the whole point of the teacher, the whole point of the theologian, and (you might as well say) the whole point of Thomas. Thomas is a saint so that theologians might have at least one model within the membership of their guild of a theologian without an ego to promote or protect, who knew how to make holy disappearing into a theological act. Of course there are other theologians who are saints, in his own times Bonaventure, as I say, being one. Bernard of Clairvaux, a century earlier, is worth mentioning in Thomas's connection by way of the extreme contrast between them. Bernard is spectacular. Thomas is unremarkable. Then too there is Augustine, rather more obviously a sinner and then dramatic convert, but he is the last person from whom one would learn how to disappear—much like his theological mentor, Paul, he writes himself prominently into nearly every work of theology he composed. Paul and Augustine represent the fortunate possibility of sainthood for all, even for the ego-obsessed. Then again there is Meister Eckhart, a fizzing show-off, just a little bit too self-indulgently enjoying his own talent for paradox to be an entirely convincing preacher.

Of Thomas's contemporaries, then, perhaps it is only Albert the Great, famously the teacher of both Thomas and Eckhart and otherwise largely ignored, who shares with Thomas the virtue of allowing words to speak for themselves, which you can safely do if it is the work that your words effect that you want make count whether for your students in the classroom or for your reader in the study, rather than the impression you yourself make on either. Both Albert and Thomas make unlikely saints because both devote themselves principally to the business of teaching and writing. And when as a teacher he writes, Thomas makes sure that he himself is the least of your worries when learning how to do theology. He doesn't really have a personal style; you have the feeling that for him nothing he writes is his, a personal possession, so you do not have to negotiate a deal with an intruding person-ality in order to make his theology your own. Here, then, is the paradox: it is of just such a man that you most want to know how he did it. What sort of man is he, who leaves you with so much written material and so little of it for the biographer, let alone the hagiographer, to work on?

This is the Thomas of this short work, a caricature, of course, which attends less to the exaggerated visibility of an overdevel-oped cerebellum than to those features of his life and thought and personality that led his fellow students in Cologne to nickname him "the dumb ox." The Thomas I have come to know over some fifty years undoubtedly agreed with those students, and did so sincerely. A dumb ox is what he himself thought he was, and we can know that this was no false humility, because believing he was a dumb ox did nothing to hold back his study, or his teaching or his writing, the sheer energy of which is prodigious. You know when humility is a pretense, because false humility is the excuse of the lazy and uncommitted, or of those who are too daunted by the demands made on them by a truthful assessment of their abilities to get on with what they ought: so they imitate an unchallenging form of modesty and pretend not to be up to it. Albert famously rebuked those fellow students of Thomas for misjudging him. But perhaps we should admit that unwittingly those students in one respect got Thomas right. Though not a great conversationalist, he was certainly not dumb, at any rate on paper. But he was a sort of ox. He plods.

Thomas refused to be scintillating. His style is deadpan. There are academics who love to scintillate; they will make anyone (but themselves) pay the price of a particularly fine scintillation, though the effect is, like lightning, of a flash of excessive brilliance draining the world of color, followed by a darkness all the deeper as a result. Thomas's, by contrast, is a steadier light that is seen, not in itself, but in what it illuminates, in the dense and polychrome colorations it elicits from the surfaces it strikes upon, so that it is the natural world, it is the human person, it is Christ, it is God, that you see, not Thomas. Everyone loves to quote the Thomas who says that it is better to cast light for others than merely to shine for oneself, and truly the Dominican motto, *contemplata aliis tradere*, the passing on to others what one has encountered in contemplation, is nearly as good as it gets as a précis of Thomas's holiness. But Shakespeare's words in *Measure for Measure* (1.1) have the sharper edge, and were you to read Thomas Aquinas with Shakespeare's words in mind, you would not need this book, or anyone else's, in order to find your way to that point of intersection where the teacher, the theologian, and the saint all meet: "Heaven doth with us as we with torches do / Not light them for themselves. For if our virtues / Did not go forth of us, 't were all alike / As if we had them not . . ." That is my Thomas Aquinas. That is the Thomas Aquinas caricatured herein, Dominican friar, preacher, teacher, theologian, and saint, each of these severally only because of all the others, and all of them serving the one purpose of his life, which was the service of the knowledge and love of God.

ONE

A Dominican

FAMILY MATTERS

In April 1244, Thomas Aquinas stunned his parents and family by taking the habit of the Dominican order from the hands of the prior in Naples, Thomas Lentini. Apart from the prior, the Dominican community there consisted of but one other friar, John of San Giuliano, so in a manner typical of the Thomas we will later get to know, the ceremony must have been an under-stated and low-key affair. Thomas was nineteen or twenty years old at the time, and Dominic, the founder of the Order of Preachers (as he had called his band of followers) was dead only some twenty-three years. It seems that Thomas had not prepared his family for his drastic decision—drastic, because it drove a coach and horses through the plans his parents had long had for him. In consequence, anticipating opposition from his family—and as it turned out, with good reason—fait accompli evidently seemed to Thomas the wiser course: get the deed over and done with and only then sort out how to get his parents on board.

By any standard, Thomas's action was dramatic and radical. His decision to throw in his lot with the Dominicans would have verged on the incomprehensible to any parents who, like his, were of aristocratic (if only of a relatively minor) standing, and were correspondingly ambitious for the future career of their child. Thomas was their youngest son, with consequently no prospects of a significant inheritance in title, money, or property, and, as so frequently was the case in upper-class families, he was destined for the highest ecclesiastical office that diplomatically cultivated connections in the right quarters and an appropriate education could buy. In fact, Thomas's parents had years before set him on the path to ecclesiastical preferment, in 1229 having placed him and his education at age five in the hands of the Benedictine monks of the abbey of Monte Cassino. No doubt they anticipated his taking the habit there in due course and, as befitted his aristocratic status, eventually holding senior office in, perhaps even the abbacy of, that most prestigious of all Benedictine communities. There in the abbey of Monte Cassino, perched atop a steep hill some eighty miles southeast of Rome, Thomas remained for ten years, receiving a basic education and living in part the Benedictine rule without any long-term, full commitment to the monastic vocation.

His mother, Theodora, and Landolpho his father could understand the Benedictines. Long-established, conservative, wealthy, fully integrated into the systems of power and patronage of the Middle Ages, Benedictines formed part of the accepted cultural landscape of their world. Monte Cassino, the first of Benedict's own foundations established in 529, was in the Ivy League of medieval monastic communities; his parents would be doing well for Thomas by finding him a place within such a prestigious community of monks. It was a career trajectory of the kind that any responsible parents could wish for a youngest son, not least because of the extension of family influence that would accompany his involvement there. By Thomas's time the renowned abbey represented that peculiarly medieval conflation of genuine piety and sociopolitical ambition that Benedict's communities had achieved—a mixture of motivations that came naturally to a distinguished family like Thomas's. But to the extent that they understood such motivations were they ill-prepared for their son's abrupt and inexplicable abandonment in 1244 of the career path they had mapped out for him fifteen years earlier.

That Thomas's choice of a Dominican vocation profoundly shocked his family cannot therefore be a surprise. It seems to have come to his parents out of the blue, which couldn't have helped them understand a vocational option that, as ecclesiastical career trajectories go, was so distinctly unpromising as to be practically suicidal. Founded by the Spaniard Domingo de Guzman (or, as Latinized, Dominicus) in the early years of the thirteenth century and granted papal approval in 1216 (just eight years before Thomas's birth), the Order of Preachers turned the ecclesiastical world of the early thirteenth century upside down. Most were at a loss to know what to make of Dominic's band of street preachers, committed to keeping preaching and poverty inseparable and living outside the orderly and closely governed precincts of economically self-sustaining monastic communities typified by that at Monte Cassino.

The problem Thomas's parents would have had in accepting their son's decision to join these Dominicans was compounded by the difficulty they, and many genuinely honest and respectable Christians of their times, had in distinguishing these itinerant preachers from mere vagabonds. The new preaching orders, including also and perhaps even especially the Franciscans— founded in the same decade by Dominic's friend, Francis of Assisi—were genuinely hard to discern from the multitude of groups and individuals that proliferated in the late twelfth and early thirteenth centuries likewise claiming to imitate the poor Christ. Though often justifiably organized in protest at the venality of an over-powerful, excessively wealthy, and frequently corrupt established Church, too many of such groups and move-ments were themselves marginally orthodox in doctrine at best, and at worst were little more than self-serving anarchists. Christians of high and low degree alike wondered if many of these movements were not simply bands of vagrant beggars making a career out of the pretense of imitating the poor Christ. Were they not but idle malingerers, layabout bums, who in the name of poverty refused to work for a living, while doing well enough for themselves out of the charity of others? How were Thomas's parents to know the difference between the mendicant Dominicans and such gangs of self-promoting tramps?

And so it was that upon hearing in May 1244 of Thomas's peremptory decision, the reaction of his family was instant and determined. No doubt with the encouragement of Landolpho, Theodora traveled to Naples with plans to dissuade Thomas from his decision, only to discover that he had already left. Undeterred, she organized Thomas's brothers into a raiding party to retrieve him by force from the hands of the Dominican confreres with whom he had fled, after which he was placed in effect under house arrest in the family castle in Roccasecca. There Thomas remained for about a year before the family relented and allowed him back to the friars at Naples, his mother being the first to give way. The rest of his family followed in due course, though not before having made a foolish attempt to seduce him from his Dominican calling by sending a naked prostitute into his room—a maneuver suggesting how little his kin knew their brother. Furious, Thomas chased the terrified woman out of his room with a brand seized from the fire and scored the sign of the cross on the locked door with the charred stick. As we will see, this other-worldly academic was more than once capable of swift and decisive action when his vocational ministry was called into question.

We know, then, what provoked his family's opposition. If indefensible, it was at least understandable. But what about Thomas himself? There is no evidence that he had made any permanent profession as a monk when he left Monte Cassino sometime in 1239 to pursue further studies in Naples, though being fourteen or fifteen years old he was of an age when he could have done so. In fact it seems that when at his father's behest, and apparently with the agreement of the abbot, Thomas left the community of Monte Cassino for the University of Naples, he did so with every intention of returning to the monastery once his studies in Naples had been completed. Moreover, temperamentally Thomas was no adolescent rebel anxious to free himself of parental influence. In particular he valued family loyalties, believing, as he would later explain at length, that in the order of indebtedness that anyone owes to others, the debt owed to one's parents comes first and was in principle impossible to repay, for parents gave you life itself, and nothing *in* life could match the gift *of* life. For which reason, in the order of charity toward one's neighbors, Thomas tells us, you are to love your parents before all others, including even one's partner in marriage.[1] What was it, then, that caused Thomas to defy his parents' wishes for him so radically?

Herbert McCabe, a great Dominican teacher and preacher of our own times, used to say that Dominicans exist not to pray, but to preach. We cannot say what Thomas's personal motivations were for so uncharacteristically throwing caution to the winds and against all the odds joining up with what seemed to his family to be little more than an ill-dressed rabble of pathetic underachievers with no proper career prospects. But what we can say is that underlying this decision was the same perception that had inspired Dominic himself twenty-eight years earlier to found the Order of Preachers: that there is a form of holiness achievable within the practice not of monastic contemplation, but of mendicant preaching. In short, he threw in his lot with the Dominicans and with a rule that made a way of life and of holiness out of speaking the word of God with that kind of effectiveness that can come only from the preacher's own imitation of the poverty of Christ, the poverty of the "son of man who had nowhere to lay his head."

MONKS AND FRIARS

Such a shift in vocational mentality was radical. Thomas's early education was monastic. The men from whom he first learned how to read and write were vowed to stability of place: their life-long vocational commitment was not that of the friars to an ideal of Christian living lived out wherever the requirement to preach took them, but rather to living the Christian life of poverty, chastity, and obedience within the constraints of a particular and contingent community. Even its buildings formed a confining precinct—the monk's world for life, spiritual and physical, was contained in a single, unchanging physical space. Moreover, inside the perimeter of that space the monks' rule required of them that they spend a good proportion of their time engaged in an entirely useless (though not for that reason pointless) activity, namely singing before God. The monks, in fact, sang their hearts out—their whole day, every day, was punctuated by seven sessions of collective choral praying known as "the hours." They sang the scriptures, especially the Psalms, all 150 of them each week, so that in a monk's lifetime he could have sung the whole Psalter some 2,500 times, or 52,500 psalms in total. Singing was how they prayed, thereby "praying twice," as Augustine had said; otherwise they read, and meditated on what they read—again, mainly scripture—and engaged in manual labor, above all in self-subsistence farming.

Benedict, the sixth-century founder of the western Christian monastic tradition, had warned against the chief spiritual risk of the monastic life: idleness, aimlessness, and consequent depression—*accidia* as the medievals called it. Following Saint Paul,[2] therefore, he ordered that all those capable of working to support themselves but who did not should be left to starve.[3] But all that complex mix of singing, reading, meditating, farming, was for the monk one form or other of a single activity: prayer—for even "to work is to pray," *laborare est orare*, as Benedict had said. And if, as they did at length, monks also wrote, their texts were hardly more than extensions of their meditative reading set down on paper. Writing, for the monks, was just one more rung on what Guigo the Carthusian in the twelfth century had called "the ladder of monks," which, like Jacob's ladder in the book of *Genesis*, reached from earth to heaven—from reading, through meditation and prayer, to contemplation[4]—a journey that arises from and ends in that most characteristic monastic activity, the silence of the study, the silence of manual labor in the field, the silence from which all prayer arises, and to which it leads. At any point of the day the monk was to be found standing on one or another of these rungs, or else, like the angels in Jacob's dream, moving between them, ascending or descending, as the spirit, or more commonly and imperatively the monastic *horarium*, took them.[5]

For ten of the first fifteen years of his life, this, then, was the world—social, spiritual, and theological—that Thomas knew. There in Monte Cassino he not only learned how to read and write, he learned a particular culture of reading and writing; there he first acquired theological learning, only no one in Monte Cassino would have spoken of their monastic learning as "theology" in the sense that Thomas himself later helped define the term, as a distinct academic discipline, since for the monks the "love of learning" was indistinguishable from the monastic form of the "desire for God," the Latin word *studium* meaning both things at once. Doubtless Thomas would have heard the abbot preach in chapter, but it is likely that impressed upon him more vividly than any words of his abbot's sermon at Monte Cassino were those of another abbot of the preceding century of a similarly prestigious, if less ancient, monastic foundation, Hugh of the Abbey of Saint Victor in Paris, who insisted that neither preaching nor teaching was any business of monks; rather what was properly theirs was to "mourn," to "weep," for his monastery was a place of sorrowful reparation for the sins of the world, a "vale," therefore, "of tears."

The contrast could hardly be starker between what Thomas learned from those two Dominicans with whom at some stage he joined company in Naples and everything he had brought with him to Naples from his upbringing in Monte Cassino as a temporarily professed Benedictine monk. If the monks sing, the friars—especially the Dominican friars—talk. Dominicans preach and teach, the monks weep; Dominicans engage in no economically productive activity, the monks farm; Dominicans are beggars, the monks are economically self-supporting; Dominicans can count on no permanence of place, and if they preach, they preach to all comers off the street, whereas the monks are vowed to stability of place and belong to settled communities; Dominicans are city dwellers, the monks commonly rural; Dominicans are university men, their learning that of the schools; the monk's *schola* is the cloister. But above all, the Dominicans for the most part talk, and the monks, when not singing, are for the most part weeping those silent tears.

Perhaps today it is not easy to grasp, never mind sympathize with, an ideal of holiness that is acquired and exercised through the disciplines of good speaking. But it does say something about how seriously Dominic took the business of words that he could conceive of a community of preachers whose holiness would be won or lost in the success or failure of their pursuit of the *bon mot*. Of course Dominic did not reduce holiness to mere rhetoric. But this was not because he thought words do not matter. On the contrary, it was because he thought they matter supremely, and that rhetoric is *never* "mere," never idle, for if words are not doing good they are doing harm. Dominic knew this, for he had learned in the course of his travels from his native Spain through the Languedoc on his way to Rome how counterproductive were the words of the worldly Cistercians whom he had observed attempting to convert the rigorously ascetical Albigensian heretics by preaching from the saddles of fine horses and backed up by impressively well-funded retinues. It was in his observation of the contradiction of word and life in the Cistercian mission in Languedoc that Dominic discovered the genius of the Dominican vocation to lie in the essential connection between poverty of spirit and the effectiveness of the preached word, the first being the condition of the second. Dominic saw that if words always have an effect, for good or for ill, the result depends on how those words stood to the life lived by their speaker. So he conceived of a community that would be at once a training ground of preachers and a school of holiness, a place where learning how to enflesh the word was the same thing as learning how to live by the Word made flesh, particularly in imitation of the poor Christ. Within that distinctive combination of preaching and poverty lay the possibility of "holy teaching." And that, *sacra doctrina* as he called it, was what Thomas devoted his life to when in 1244 he abandoned the stability of the monastic life of Monte Cassino for the life of the wandering preacher with those two newfound companions, Thomas of Lentini and John of San Giuliano.

THE TEACHER OF PREACHERS

Not that Thomas himself was ever particularly famous for his preaching, though we do possess a few sermons of his whose impassivity would put to shame some purveyors of a self-referring histrionic homiletic of our time—and in the best Catholic tradition his sermons are mercifully short. Although his life's work being that of a teacher of preachers it should be obvious, it has somehow become easy to forget how *Dominican* a theologian Thomas is, how distinctively predicated on the training of preachers is his conception of theology. While by instinct no revolutionary himself, Thomas participated with enthusiasm in a theological revolution that had been taking hold of the Western Church throughout the twelfth and thirteenth centuries, in the success of which the Dominicans had a major stake. And that revolution was so complete by the time Thomas died that even now it is hard for us to imagine any other meaning for the word "theology" than that which Thomas and his like in the thirteenth century have bequeathed to us.

For the theologians of our times (the majority of whom occupy professorships in the modern equivalent of that twelfth-century invention, the university), most of what Thomas does by way of theology is in its external lines perfectly familiar. What he studied in Naples, and subsequently in Cologne and Paris, would likewise seem perfectly familiar to a student preparing for ordination in a professional divinity school in an American private university (though Thomas would have had no conception of what could be meant by "theology" in the academically detached ethos of a state university's department of religious studies). Of his early studies we need say little except that Thomas served his term as the medieval equivalent of a research and teaching assistant to Albert the Great both in Cologne and in Paris, and it was not until 1256 that Thomas the theologian was installed as a *magister* at the University of Paris, a professor, a trained academic. By then his career was set as an academic theologian, a trainer of preachers and teachers, and above all as a teacher and wordsmith, both written and oral.

He went on to write systematic expositions, or *summae*, of theology. And though his writings in this genre are not unprecedented in the history of the Church, in the distinctive form that Thomas wrote his, they are distinctly a product of the environment of the schools of the twelfth and later centuries. Those schools created a demand for the sort of books that a school needs, classroom texts of more than one kind—although Thomas's most famous work, the *Summa theologiae*, reads more as a handbook for university teachers than as a textbook for students, his earlier *Compendium theologiae* serving the latter purpose. By 1256, then, Thomas was a professional teacher; and that points to another innovation bearing on the character of the new theological style: he had been able to gain the qualification he needed for appointment to a university professorship only by writing a commentary on the *Sentences* of Peter the Lombard.

The innovative character of Thomas's theology is unintelligible except against the background of his twelfth-century predecessor.

In fact, the distinctive character of the theologies of all the great masters of the thirteenth-century universities, not only Thomas himself but also Alexander of Hales, Albert the Great, Bonaventure, Henry of Ghent, Giles of Rome, and Duns Scotus, can be understood only against the background of principally two ground-shifting theological earthquakes of the twelfth century. Peter's *Sentences* did for the twelfth-century study of university theology what only decades earlier in the twelfth century the *Glossa ordinaria* had done for the high medieval study of the Bible. Sometime between 1110 and 1130 a team of scholars in the school of Laon in northern France compiled extracts of commentarial texts on books of the Bible accumulated across the range of patristic and earlier medieval authorities, placing them between the lines and in the margins of every single verse of scripture. The resulting *Glossa* presented what the medieval theologians called the *sacra pagina*, each page interweaving the text of scripture with a compendious summary of a thousand years of continuous reception of it in the Church. The *Glossa* was scripture as received and read, written about and preached upon, by the community that at once owned it and was formed by what it owned. It was an indispensable tool of the new theological learning that the universities inaugurated in the late twelfth century and progressively made their own in the first decades of the thirteenth.

Compiled on wholly different principles but equally encyclopedic in scope were Peter's *Sentences*. Written in the mid-twelfth century, this was a four-volume assemblage of scriptural texts and theological opinions gathered from equivalent sources in the tradition, arranged topically in the form of responses to questions of theology. The styles of the *Glossa* and of the *Sentences* could not be more different. Whereas the *Glossa* gave the (false) impression that the Church's reception of its scriptures had achieved the seamless, coherent, hermeneutical uniformity of an uncontested tradition, in the *Sentences* Peter gave the opposite, but equally false, impression that every theological question was up for grabs. But there was fidelity to method in Peter's dialectical promiscuity. It mattered not to him whether the topics that he assembled were genuinely open questions continuing to be disputed in his day or whether they were by then regarded as having already been authoritatively settled. Hotly disputed in his day was whether charity in the Christian soul was the created work of the Spirit working its grace through the soul's natural powers, or the uncreated Spirit itself displacing human agency. Undisputed was the existence of God. But either way, whether it was the case that everyone, or the case that no one, denied a theological proposition, disputed or established, every topic was to be subjected to the same rigors of debate. For the method of the *quaestio* that Peter formalized in his *Sentences*, with the presentation of answers either way together with arguments for and against each, was essentially not a method of theological inquiry so much as pedagogical in intent, a method of teaching and learning—or, at any rate, so it became by the thirteenth century.

For by the thirteenth century, aspirant masters of theology were required to cut their theological teeth commenting on Peter's text, such *Sentences* commentaries being therefore, roughly in today's terms, Ph.D. dissertations. The comparison is not entirely fanciful. After all, the commentarial genres, whether on theological texts such as the *Sentences* or on scriptural texts themselves, and the practices of formal disputation of theological questions, were but medieval means devised to serve a conception of theology as a subject to be taught; and not only taught, but also examined in a university degree course. But then a degree course that is to be examined required a curriculum of study, the teaching of which in turn required institutions offering qualifications acquired over a fixed period of years, whether as a condition of entry into the higher ranks of a professionalized clerisy, or else with a view to recycling them through an academic career, or, sometimes, both. Such was the medieval university. It emerged with a task to perform: to teach theology (among the other disciplines of the humanities, especially philosophy, medicine, and law) in fixed-time degree courses offering a portable set of skills to be used by the Church's priesthood in the liturgical, pastoral, and homiletic service of the Church.

Thomas himself compiled his own *Sentences* commentary with a view to taking up in 1256 the officially established chair of theology designated at the University of Paris for a Dominican master. As we will see in the next chapter, it was not without fierce opposition from the established secular masters that he, and together with him his Franciscan colleague Bonaventure, eventually did so, and only insistent papal pressure succeeded in forcing hostile colleagues to accept the two friars within the university community. In due course, however, both Thomas and Bonaventure took up their respective professorships, and though the successful completion of a commentary on the *Sentences* was normally a condition of election to a full professorship, Thomas had not completed his when he began teaching in the Parisian schools, finishing it perhaps a year later. It is a complex, brilliant work, and though the myth needs to be dispelled that Thomas's thought fell fully formed from his pen consistent from his earliest to his last work—there is no doubt that there are major developments and revisions of his theology between his earliest and his latest writings on key issues of philosophy and theology—his *Scriptum* on the *Sentences* remains an important and underconsulted source for his theology as a whole.

Nonetheless, within fewer than ten years, Thomas was evidently considering writing a completely new commentary. He abandoned that project in due course, however, for a very different schema, one that would become his most famous work—the *Summa theologiae*. The change of plan is certainly significant. Thomas's reasons for envisaging the composition of a new commentary on the *Sentences* would presumably have had to do with dissatisfaction with the quality of his own earlier *Scriptum*, whereas the reason he began work on the *Summa* instead seems to have had more to do with dissatisfaction with the *Sentences* itself and with commentary on it as a vehicle of systematic theological exposition. It seems that Thomas concluded that the *Sentences'* deficiencies of structure were too radical, especially as to the ordering and sequencing of theological topics, to serve either his developing theological or pedagogical purposes. In any case, sometime in 1264–65, Thomas made the decision to embark on an entirely new theological project that, nine years later, he still had failed to complete, the *Summa theologiae*.

THE SUMMA THEOLOGIAE

The context of Thomas's composition of the *Summa theologiae* is distinctly Dominican. He left his chair in Paris in 1259, after which he was engaged in a number of teaching positions in the Dominican order in Italy; in 1265, when he began writing the *Summa*, he was in Rome teaching his Dominican brethren. What sparked the composition of the *Summa theologiae* was a very specific request by his superiors to undertake the wholesale reform of Dominican theological education. Especially on his home ground of Italy, Thomas's superiors—and doubtless Thomas shared their view—judged the provision of theological training to be in a parlous condition, and Thomas was given the task of running a personal school of theological education more or less with a free hand to reorder the curriculum of studies as he thought fit. All the evidence seems to point to this experience's having been decisive for the next stage of his theological development, for it was when presented with the responsibility of rethinking the theological curriculum from the point of view of the best pedagogical principles that Thomas saw clearly the curricular deficiencies of Peter's *Sentences*. Hence the *Summa theologiae*.

In too many ways to enumerate the *Summa* is different in structure and organization from the *Sentences* of Peter the Lombard. Different as they are, it is possible to mistake the significance of those differences, too much having been made of a theological nature of the particular sequencing of topics that constitutes the structure and division of Thomas's later work. In fact, if we are fully to understand Thomas's value as a theological innovator we must take all the evidence together, including the fact that he devised a number of very different structures of theological exposition—three mainly: one in the *Summa contra gentiles*, another in the *Summa theologiae*, and a third in the likewise incomplete *Compendium theologiae*. Each of these works offers a different way of setting out coherently and compendiously the whole business of theology as a linear sequence of topics forming a sort of curriculum of theological education.

The *Summa contra gentiles* is principally a work of apologetics, designed to equip Dominican preachers with the sort of arguments and persuasions they would need in conversation with heretical Christian and non-Christian disputants—in three of its four books it rarely appeals to anything but rational arguments in support of Christian beliefs, only in the fourth book showing how the conclusions of those arguments square with revealed biblical truth as Christians know it. Wholly different in purpose, and because of that, also in structure, is the incomplete *Compendium theologiae*, which is organized in three parts based on the specifically Christian theological virtues of faith, hope, and charity, stopping short in the middle of the discussion of hope. Yet again, the sequencing and ordering of topics in the likewise incomplete *Summa theologiae* differs from both the *Contra gentiles* and the *Compendium*, and just because Thomas clearly thought the structure of Peter's *Sentences* to be deficient the reader should not suppose that he thought there was only one successful organization of theological material possible on systematic lines, namely those represented by the organizational structure of the *Summa theologiae*. He happily worked with three very different models (and some scholar ought to make the case in full some day that pretty much the whole of Thomas's theology could be taught from a fourth completely different genre of writing, his *Reportatio* on the gospel of John). The theological conclusions would be much the same. But how different would be the feel of Thomas's theology, how different its texture!

Undoubtedly, then, Thomas was a pluralist when it came to questions of systematic theological exposition. He evidently thought there was more than one way of setting out the topics in an orderly and cogent sequence. But by 1265 he had come to believe that the *Sentences* was not one of them. For in the general prologue to the *Summa theologiae*, Thomas claims his own work satisfactorily to have described, in a way that he had by now decided Peter Lombard's *Sentences* failed to do, a distinctly productive and creative theological learning curve. And in doing so he perhaps does not go far enough when he says that he is engaged in a work merely of curricular reform, or even of curricular innovation: he is saying a lot more than that the teaching of theology needs to be emancipated from the grip of the *Sentences* upon the theological curricula of the universities. His critique extends to the university curriculum of theological study as a whole. He is saying that theology is so haphazardly taught in the schools as to not even be a "subject" at all, just a set of ad hoc teaching practices amounting to little more than a disorderly theological casuistry. So in the general prologue what Thomas in fact claims to have achieved, though he pretends not to be claiming any such thing, is the reinvention of a subject called theology—"subject" in the sense that we today recognize history or English literature or physics to be "subjects." That is to say, Thomas says it is a true *disciplina*, it has a teachable curriculum, it requires training in specific skills you can acquire and carry about with you, it covers a defined range of issues and texts that are studied over a fixed period, it carries a standard bibliography of authorities, and you can examine students so as to test how good they are at it. You can pass or fail them. It is a context of learning in these ways so familiar to us today that forms the background to Thomas's prologue to the *Summa*, where he states his purpose to be decidedly pedagogical:

> [In structuring this work] we have taken into account how those new to this teaching are in so many ways held back by the writings of various authors, partly because of the prolif-eration of pointless questions, articles and arguments, partly because what such newcomers need in order to progress

in knowledge is set out not in obedience to the structure of the discipline itself, but in accordance with the exigencies of textual commentary or of set-piece disputations; but also because repetitiousness has bred boredom of spirit in the students.

Thomas is manifestly reacting to standard pedagogical practice as he knew it, and the chief target of his critique of the standard theological teaching of his times is that the sequencing of topics in the texts used lacks rationale, is ill thought out, and does little justice to the inner nature of theology as a teachable subject. It is hardly an exaggeration to say that Thomas's solving of the problem of a creative linear sequencing of theological issues is among the work's chief merits. It is easy to forget that the meticulously structured linearity of the *Summa* is in fact a solution. And because the difficulty of the problem that it solves is forgotten, most readers today fail to understand how astonishingly good that solution is, or even that it *is* a solution at all. But that there is a problem to be solved is obvious: one has only to think of the number of ways in which it is possible to string along in a sequence the approximately 4,500 theological questions the *Summa* addresses, and it is clear that the way Thomas keeps control shows him to be a master of the sequential ordering that makes for the best learning curve. The man is a *magister*, a master-compiler of the syllabus for a degree course in theology—designed, as we will see, especially for mendicant preachers.

We should, moreover, remind ourselves that if what Thomas does is Dominican, it is also an entirely academic sort of thing to do. For to construct a syllabus for a course to be studied and examined over a fixed period for a qualification in a subject makes sense only within the sort of institution that eventually becomes what we call the university. It makes no sense in a monastery. To repeat: some commentators have made more than is justified of the theological significance of the *Summa*'s particular ordering of topics, and less than is required of the priorities of either Thomas the university teacher or, more specifically, Thomas as a major player in the formation of Dominican preachers. Correspondingly, too little attention has been paid to the specific purpose of the *Summa* as a work of theological pedagogy, as a university text. It is principally the design of a university degree course—at any rate that is what *Thomas* says it is meant to be.

It is clear, then, that while some of Thomas's criticisms of the current state of theological teaching were general, motivated both by his experience of university teaching in Paris and by his experience of internal Dominican theological training, the immediate motivation for the composition of the *Summa* was a principally Dominican task undertaken in fulfillment of his superiors' commission in Rome, specifically, to reform the theological training of Dominican preachers. It is a striking fact, not often commented on, that fully two-thirds of its pages are devoted to what a later age would call "moral theology." Mark Jordan

speculates[6] (in my view rightly) that in undertaking the reform of
the curriculum of Dominican theological training, Thomas was
principally concerned with advancing it beyond the level of practical (indeed casuistical and piecemeal) pastoral instruction in how
to deal in sermon and confessional with standardized lists of cases
of conscience—-in which, as he had found it, Dominican semi-
nary training in Italy principally consisted. From this point of
view, the grand structure of the *Summa* as a whole reveals itself to
have, once again, a primarily pedagogical purpose, and, once again,
a distinctly Dominican one. That structure itself speaks theologically and pastorally, as if to say: "For us, friar preachers, the
pragmatism of the homiletic *exemplum*, or of the casuistical solution to problem of conscience, is not enough. We are not just
confessors mechanically dispensing absolution to sinners, we are
preachers of a holy life for all, and if we are to give water to others
to drink, we must drink from our own wells first; if we are to
preach to others from the book of life we must first read from
the book of our own experience. Therefore, if you novices want
to be friar preachers and confessors ever on the move, carry
with you no spare sandals; if in your imitation of Christ you can
accept having no place to lay your head, and within predominantly
mobile and urban ministries you wish to eschew all reliance on the
security of fixed capital—if, in short, you wish to be a mendicant
friar and out of this witness to the poverty of Christ you want to
preach the word of Christ on the street—then carry nothing
with you but the vision of God and the word of God which

Christ preached, the desire to preach it yourself, and the knowledge required to preach with effect." In short, Thomas says—and here I paraphrase his own words—better than merely to shine for oneself is to cast light for others; and so the better form of life than the merely contemplative is *contemplata aliis tradere*, to hand on to others what they have drunk from their own wells of contemplation. The *Summa* is friars' theology, the one scrip that mendicant preachers must carry with them; it is a poor man's theology, the poor Christ *as* theology. Friars must carry that theology with them, as poor people do, in their heads, in their skills, in their training—books are too heavy to be carried very far on the back.

So it is that Thomas brackets that enormous second part of the *Summa*, devoted to the practice of the Christian life that Dominicans are to preach, with a profound meditation at the front end on the meaning of the God to whom Jesus prayed, and the meaning of the Christ who thus prayed at the back end. For the moral life comes from God as its source and returns to God through Christ alone. Typically, Thomas's source for this recasting of Christian moral theology is that ill-assorted pair of bedfellows, the Gospels and Aristotle. For Aristotle had said that if you want to know what the good life is like, all you need do is see how the good man lives. But Thomas, unlike Aristotle, knew what a truly good man looked like—from the Gospels. These are the theological, or, one might say, contemplative wells from which

Dominicans must drink; this is the *disciplina* of the Dominicans' theology, the theology of the migrant preacher, the *imitatio Christi* on the hoof.

What Thomas effects in the *Summa* is therefore the conversion of the theological project into a discipline of training. He makes it into a "subject" that may be distinguished methodologically from other subjects; he reconceives theology as a teachable, examinable, portable, intellectual skill; and he disengages the practice of theology from its enclosure within the secluded and specifically prayerful practices of the cloister, liberating it for a multitasking practice in the street. In that sense, or perhaps better, in those senses, theology is for Thomas a discipline, a rule-governed intellectual practice with a purpose: *contemplata aliis tradere*, which is a Dominican conception of theology through and through.

To put all this in other words, Thomas's conception of the theological task is inseparable from his vocation to follow the poor Christ as a friar preacher, inseparable, that is to say, from Dominic's experience of revulsion as he observed the failures of Cistercian preaching in Languedoc. In a later chapter we will see just how shockingly irresponsible this peculiarly Dominican conjunction of theology, poverty, and preaching seemed to the establishment academics in Paris, and why. But for the time being we should note a particular aspect of this conjunction which seems very distinctive of Thomas as a person, and so to the profile, to the particular form, of his holiness.

A DISAPPEARING ACT

Thomas, I have said, is all Dominican teacher, and it is a paradoxical feature both of his teaching and of his holiness that it consists almost entirely in a disappearing act. Whether or not he was as physically obese as legend has it, there is yet no personal bulk at all, no personal mass, in his teaching. In fact if anything is massive about Thomas it is his modesty. And it is this that presents a problem for the writer who wishes to track down the precise point at which Thomas the saint, Thomas the theologian, and Thomas the teacher intersect. For the fact that he deliberately hid that point of intersection from us and made a secret of it makes Pope John XXII's canonization of Thomas in 1323 seem more like the canonization of a library than of a man. And that might seem absurd, except that there is just one important sense in which that is exactly what John XXII had done. It is a lovely paradox, one that gets to the heart of what Thomas seems to have wanted to hide from us behind the bulk of his writings, that there is something intensely holy about his absence from them. It reveals a lot about Thomas the man that his writings tell you nothing about Thomas the man. Thomas gets himself entirely out of the way of the act of communication. In short, Thomas is all teacher—a holy teacher, and a professor of theology as holy teaching.

If, then, so little does Thomas as a person appear in his writings that one is tempted to conclude that it was not the speaker but the speech-*act* that was canonized, this is, in fact, a truth—but only a half-truth. We do know a little about Thomas the man. He was evidently tall, fair-haired and balding from the front, physically fit (Torrell calculates that over his lifetime he traveled at least 15,000 kilometers on his journeys between Italy, France, and Germany, much of it on foot, perhaps some of it by sea); he was taciturn, not much given to chatter, forgetful of mealtimes and prone to disappear into fits of abstraction, all of which sounds a little daunting, until the witnesses report that he seems to have had a talent for friendship, and a willingness to spare any amount of time for the needs of his brethren. All witnesses tell of the sense of peace that he radiated. Given his intense preoccupation with writing and teaching and a punishing work rate, that is pretty convincing evidence of his personal priorities. Apparently if you needed his attention when he was lost in thought, you just tugged on his sleeve, and he was all yours. For Thomas, in life as in thought, charity trumps all. And, as we will see, there are perhaps two occasions when even in his writings Thomas the man breaks through the impassive objectivity of his prose in an outburst of indignant rage. But even on such occasions, the exception proves the rule, as when, at the end of a polemical work directed against some philosophers in the Faculty of Arts in Paris, Thomas angrily demands that they come out into the open in a fair fight over their plainly heretical reading of Aristotle on the nature of the intellect, accusing them of abusing their professorial power over the young by whispering to them unchallenged in corners.[7] Only very rarely would Thomas the teacher come out into the open personally, and then when the defense of his students, or the integrity of the teaching role itself, demanded it. On such occasions he was fully prepared to come out fighting, gloves off.

All the same, there is nothing we know of in Thomas's personal life that tells of what gets called "heroic virtue" in the circles of the canonizing bureaucracies—except his teaching and writing theology. In consequence, if one is reduced to searching for the nature of Thomas's holiness in his default mode as a teacher, it is in just that role that he disappears into a sort of canonizable absence. And one way into the discovery of that holiness's nature, hidden as it is, is, paradoxically, through the aspect of his writing that is its most obvious and visible feature, namely its lucidity.

That lucidity is truly exceptional. By comparison Duns Scotus throttles thought in an entanglement of complexity, Augustine is dense, Bonaventure imprecise, Meister Eckhart elusive. Thomas is transparent. As a general principle, whether of teaching or writing, lucid exposition requires that its author gets out of the way, because authors who stand in the way of the light obstruct it and cast a shadow. The shadow is the teacher, or, as the case may be, the author. Any teacher, especially any university teacher, knows the ever present temptation to obstruct the light of teaching with an over-present selfhood, to prize performance at the podium above the elucidation of the minds of students. At any rate, if there is any teacher who does not know of this temptation in himself, he will have students enough who could if they dared tell him of the signs indicating how far he has, in fact, succumbed to it.

As to lucidity of theological style, it is inseparably connected in the medieval mind with the topic of light as a substantive reality, physical and spiritual. It is true that the phenomenon of light was, perhaps, more an Augustinian than an Aristotelian trope. It was Bonaventure, that other great friar theologian and friend of Thomas, who put one aspect of this Augustinian light motif (as one might say) most succinctly. We know all things, Bonaventure says, in the divine light of truth; everything is illuminated by the divine. But the light *in* which we see cannot itself be one of the things seen, for we can see the light only insofar as it is reflected off opaque objects. Therefore, he argues, if light were itself an object of sight then we would be able to see nothing in it, just as, if the eye's seeing were itself colored, then we would be unable to see any variations of color by means of it: to see colors, the act of seeing itself has to be color-neutral.[8] Just so, we can see in creation the multiple variations of shade, and density, of texture and luminosity, because of the different properties of the surfaces the light is reflected by. And it is the same with the divine light: the light which is God we can see only in the creatures which reflect it. Therefore, Bonaventure says, when we turn our minds away from the visible objects of creation to God, whose "eternal art" is the source of their visibility, it is as if we see nothing. The world shines with the divine light. But the light which causes it so to shine is itself like a profound darkness.[9]

Nowhere does Thomas put the matter in quite that Augustinian way—profoundly indebted theologically as Thomas is to Augustine, his rhetorical styles are quite different—but there is one connection in which Thomas constructs a closely parallel argument. All Thomas's imagery of knowledge is that of light, as we will see in the next chapter. Were we brute animals equipped with bodily senses and imagination alone, our relation with the world would be as if we were bumping around in a darkened room, able only to register the immediate impacts of the objects it contains. And even if we were to become very skilled in the negotiation of unobstructed routes in the room, we would still know nothing of what sort of place we were in. We would be like the team of blind people trying to reconstruct the shape of an elephant by reporting to one another their separate sensations of touch alone. But when the intellect turns toward what the bodily senses present it with, it is, Thomas says, like switching on a light, and the objects are revealed in context, and so in their meanings. We are "present" in and to the room through the light intellect sheds on it, but only, Thomas adds, in what we might call a pre-reflexive way.

For my act of experiencing the sitting room is not in the same way an object of experience as the sitting room is: or, as we might say, in Bonaventuran spirit, the intellectual light *in which* we now see the illuminated space to be a sitting room is not itself an object of our seeing. In fact, Thomas says, in exact parallel with Bonaventure, when we turn our gaze back upon the act of gazing itself, it is as if we see nothing. Try to catch *yourself* in the act of experiencing the world, and that self performs a disappearing act, like an infallible sleuth who, however quickly you turn round to catch him in the act of sleuthing, is always behind you, haunting your experience but never captured within it. For Thomas, the thinking self systematically eludes the self that thinks.

What as a professional philosopher Thomas says about knowledge is a sort of theoretical précis of his practice as teacher and writer. He disappears as light-obstructing subject, appearing only in the lucidity of his object, the theology he teaches and writes. To teach, he says, is to cast light for others, which you can do only insofar as your *act* of teaching is invisible and does not stand in the way of the light that you cast: there is a sort of necessary self-denial required of the teacher who wishes *contemplata aliis tradere*, a self-denial which is a condition of true lucidity.

His contemporaries most frequently commented on Thomas's humility, a virtue little prized in our times, since we seem unable to distinguish the humble person's self-evaluation from what we call low self-esteem. In consequence, self-assertion takes on the appearance of a virtue, merely by way of contrast with that mistaken conception of humility. Humility, in the sense that his contemporaries observed its presence in Thomas, had more to do with that peculiarly difficult form of vulnerability, which consists in being entirely open to the discovery of the truth, especially to the truth about oneself. One might say, likewise, that what humility is to the moral life, lucidity is to the intellectual—an openness to contestation, the refusal to hide behind the opacity of the obscure, a vulnerability to refutation to which one is open simply as a result of being clear enough to be seen, if wrong, to be wrong. We might well say, then, that Thomas was fearlessly clear, unafraid to be shown to be wrong, and correspondingly angered by those among his colleagues, especially in the University of Paris, who in his view refused to play the game on a field leveled by lucidity and openness equal in degree of honesty to the requirements of the intellectual life. And yet, even in Thomas's anger there is nothing personal. His is the anger of a true teacher observing students to have been betrayed by colleagues. It has no more to do with self-assertion than his humility has to do with lack of self-worth.

THE SILENCE OF THE SAINT

Thomas's lucidity, then, draws on deeper sources than those of a plain, unfussy, unselfconscious, and meticulous literary style. It draws upon his core vocation as a Dominican teacher, above all on his commitment to mendicant poverty not only respecting material goods (which appeared to mean little or nothing to Thomas anyway) but even respecting what he valued most, the goods of the mind, his theology and his writing. And we know this because of something that happened to Thomas on December 6, 1273.

We do not know what actually happened that day in any detail, except that at the height of his powers qualitatively, and when his output of writing and teaching had reached almost superhuman levels of productivity and creativity, Thomas's pen at last fell from his exhausted hand. Early legends have it, with what historical accuracy is impossible to determine, that he said to his secretary and amanuensis, Reginald of Piperno: "After what I have seen today I can write no more: for all that I have written is but straw." Perhaps the story is apocryphal as to fact. It hardly matters, because whether or not Thomas said any such thing to Reginald, the legend, if that it be, contains an important truth about the meaning of the silence of Saint Thomas in those last three months of his life.

What happened? Did he have some kind of mystical experience? Or, was it, more simply, nervous collapse and depression as a result of over-work?—a very plausible explanation, considering that, on a rough calculation, Thomas's output had been the equivalent in volume to two or three average-length novels per month between the beginning of 1269 and December 1273. In any case, there may be no good reason to think that it could not have been both. What is fact is that from that day in December 1273, Thomas left everything he had been working on unfinished, and some explanation is required especially concerning the *Summa theologiae*, the text of which breaks off midpoint in the discussion of the seven sacraments. Is it unfinished because, exhausted and ill, he *could not* finish it? Or was not finishing it a decision that in so doing, a better purpose was served?

We cannot know for certain the cause of Thomas's peremptory decision simply to stop writing, leaving not even a hint as to how he might have finished his work had he chosen to do so. The disputed comment to Reginald apart, Thomas himself leaves the unfinished condition of his work to speak for itself, and perhaps we should see the incompleteness of his life's work as itself a theological statement. For what we do know is how much Thomas made of silence theologically—not just in those last three months of writer's block, but throughout his twenty-five or so years as writer, preacher, and teacher. Nowadays, we call this theological silence his "apophaticism." We refer thereby to a powerful medieval theme of the relationship in theology between speech and silence, of how there is an interpenetration between that of which theology can speak and that "whereof it must be silent." And therefore we refer in Thomas to his conviction that all theology *emerges* from silence, whence all faith and all "holy teaching" emerge, in the way that, as a student musician once explained to me, the silent up-beat immediately precedes the first note of a musical performance. And as they emerge from silence, so do all those millions of words of theology that Thomas wrote *proceed*, because they are the articulation of that same silence, in the way that the massive structures of the medieval cathedral articulate the spaces they enclose. And, all those words *end* in silence because, as he said, it is through the Son who is the Word that we enter into the silence of the Father, the Godhead itself, which is utterly beyond our comprehension. For Thomas, silence is not the absence of speech. It is what the fullness of speech demonstrates—namely that, even at its best, speech falls short; indeed, it is only speech at its best that truly discovers this silence. And theology at its best discloses but the name of that silence from which the Word proceeds, and to which it returns. Its name is God.

This is how Thomas the teacher conceived of teaching itself, as he explained when in 1256 he was "incepted" as a theological master in the University of Paris. That day he preached one of the few sermons of his that we still possess in full. He preached on a text of Psalm 103,[10] which tells how the wisdom of God falls upon the earth like the rain, refreshes the earth, and returns to its source, itself enriched by its movement through that trajectory away from, and back to, its origin. That sermon served for Thomas the purpose that is served by a senior professor's inaugural lecture in the European universities of today: it was his personal manifesto, the creed of Thomas the teacher inaugurating a mastership that is nothing but the service of the Word, the *Verbum supernum prodiens*, the "supreme Word breaking out," as he puts it in one of his Eucharistic hymns.[11] What thereafter his students recognized amid their university teacher's profusion of words was no self-referential prolixity, but selfless lucidity; they heard the words, but perhaps more so they heard the silence from which those words emerged and to which they must ever return. As Josef Pieper so eloquently argued decades ago, when in December 1273 Thomas was finally lost for words, he was simply returning home to his Father's house, to the house of contemplative silence, to the source from which all his words had proceeded, because from there alone proceeds the divine Word, the *sacra doctrina*, to which he had dedicated his life.

This intertwining of word and silence is, therefore, the default position of Thomas's theology from beginning to end. Early in the *Summa theologiae* he tells us in the dry, laconic style to which he resorts, especially when dropping theological bombshells, that words fail the theologian all along the line—their all being "but straw" simply goes with the theological territory. "In this life," he says, "we do not know what God is, even by the grace of faith. And so it is that by grace we are made one with God *quasi ei ignoto*, as to something unknown to us." There is no doubt at all that for Thomas all theological speech is in principle grounded in that silence from which it first emerged, and into which it then inevitably falls helplessly back.

All that is true, then, but it does not explain the unfinished *Summa*. It explains something important about how Thomas wrote when he did, the *Summa* that we have, not the *Summa* that we don't have. To grasp fully the significance of that unfinished condition of the *Summa* one has to imagine the courage it took to resist the temptation to complete it. Having got so far with it, seven-eighths of the way through, he must desperately have wanted to finish it—which author would not have felt the power of the imperative to complete? It is difficult to exaggerate the power that that temptation must have exerted on Thomas when one considers the investment of energy, intellectual and physical, the demands made on his powers of intellect and imagination, and the sacrifices of personal need of food and sleep that had gone into writing the *Summa*; when one considers the personal satisfaction that Thomas must have gained from what he would have known by the time he got to question 90 of the *Tertia Pars* to be a masterpiece of theological writing; and finally, when one considers how easy it would have been to finish it, at his work rate, in a matter of months. But something theologically important to Thomas, some sense of fidelity to his Dominican vocation, held him back. Consequently, supposing that Thomas was in a state of health such that he could have finished it, one is forced to ask why he did not do so. What is the meaning of his "I can write no more"?

It would be far too easy to suppose that, after all is said and done about how his Dominican way of life is a form of holiness to be found not in spite of, but by means of, the practices of preaching and teaching, Thomas in the end was compelled to concede that only in *monastic* silence, the form of which he had years before abandoned in Monte Cassino, was true holiness to be found. But if one is not to make nonsense of his life as a Dominican, one has to suppose that what Thomas the teacher saw on December 6, 1273, was that the elected incompleteness of the *Summa* could itself teach something theologically that could never be taught by the *Summa* completed. In short, in failing, or in refusing, to complete the *Summa theologiae*, Thomas was still a devoted Dominican theologian, teaching to the end—this time, however, by knowing when to stop. The silence of Thomas in those last three months of his life was a final response to the demands of mendicant poverty, for on that December day he laid down the one scrip that as a Dominican he could legitimately carry and call his own, his personal work as a theologian. That elected incompleteness of his life's work was, therefore, a form of silence that was Thomas's last word as a Dominican theologian, his response to the last and ultimately self-denying demand that the poor Christ could make on him. For Thomas to be the theologian he was it was necessary that he should rate poverty of spirit above theology. And in that final silence of Thomas we at last see fully exposed that place within him where the Dominican, the theologian, and the saint intersect, and can no longer be told apart. When, therefore, in 1323 Pope John XXII canonized Thomas, what he canonized was the *aliis traditio*, the "handing on to others"—not, that is, the *theology*, but the theological teaching *act* itself, both the millions of words of selfless speech and the final, ultimately unselfing, silence. For that indeed was Thomas's whole life, a holy life of "holy teaching." Better said, then, is that the Pope canonized both the words and the silence of Thomas—that great but quiet, friendly mass of a man, for whom the life of poverty was that of the Dominican teacher who to the end preferred to stand out of the light so that others might see.

TWO

A Materialist

TROUBLE WITH BISHOPS

Thomas's theological identity is all Dominican, even if by no means are all Dominicans recognizable from a common profile, theological or spiritual. Meister Eckhart, who shared a teacher with Thomas in Albert the Great, could hardly differ more from Thomas in spirit, in style, and in some important matters of theological substance. To say that Thomas Aquinas is "all Dominican" is therefore not to say that he is stereotypically Dominican. There is no Dominican theological stereotype, the Dominican rule being a positive encouragement to diversity, personal and theological. Moreover, though today Thomas stands out as the greatest of the theologians of the Dominican tradition, in his own lifetime, and for some decades thereafter, his standing as a theologian was far from unrivaled, whether inside or outside his own Dominican community. Duns Scotus seemed the cleverer, Meister Eckhart the more energetically radical, Henry of Ghent the more traditionally "Augustinian," Bonaventure the more spiritual.

Of course it was hard on Thomas that so soon after his death his reputation was dragged into an increasingly ill-tempered feud between Dominican and Franciscan theologians, and within decades he had become at once a trophy possession for the former and an object of bitter hostility among the latter. But if historical fortunes not of Thomas's own making had this polarizing effect on his reception in the early fourteenth century, such is not the way his fortunes turned out immediately after his death. Franciscans were not alone among those who first took issue with Thomas's theology. It was, after all, a fellow Dominican and archbishop of Canterbury, Robert Kilwardby, who with the support of the faculty of theology at Oxford on March 18, 1277, published a list of propositions condemned as heretical, including a number manifestly intended to target views of Thomas.

In fact, 1277 was a bad year for the posthumous fortunes of Thomas's theology and its reception. Coincidence being unlikely, it is probably significant that it was eleven days earlier and therefore on the third anniversary of Thomas' death, March 7 of that year, that the bishop of Paris, Stephen Tempier, had already launched a frontal attack on the theology faculty in his own city, indiscriminately condemning as heretical 219 propositions that he believed were being widely taught in the university schools. In fact, none of these condemned propositions specifically identify Thomas's teachings. But inseparable from Tempier's general strategy of assault on the university's faculties of theology and of arts was his revocation but three weeks later of the license to teach of the Augustinian master, Giles of Rome, for the offense (among others) of promoting fifty-one theological opinions, thirty-one of which were recognizably those of his own former teacher, Thomas. There is no doubt that, one way or another, Tempier saw heretical risk in some key propositions of Thomas's theology, lumped together with others as a job-lot of typically unbridled and theologically frivolous university speculation.

There is, therefore, a shotgun character to Tempier's catalog of condemned propositions, and its promulgation witnesses more to Tempier's investment in a power struggle with university theologians and philosophers than to any particularly subtle theological insight on his part. The strategy seems to have been to scatter the shot wide enough to hit targets good and bad theologically, thereby creating maximum risk of being caught in the episcopal line of fire—a classic fear-inducing strategy of the censorious designed to ensure that all keep their heads safely down when the next target of condemnation is so unpredictable. But two propositions included in both the Parisian condemnation of Giles and in Kilwardby's English list stand out as particularly relevant to our concerns, which are with what in Thomas's intellectual profile struck contemporaries as being distinctively his, and as being distinctively problematic. Condemned was the proposition, clearly maintained by Thomas, that God could not create matter without form, Thomas having argued that no stuff could exist that was not stuff of some *kind*, because to exist at all was to exist *as* something or other. In consequence, for Thomas the term "formless existence" was the nonsensical description of an impossibly existent nothing-in-particular. Even God, Thomas thought, cannot create anything that isn't something.

More immediately relevant to our concerns—though if indirectly, still importantly connected with the first—was the condemnation of a second proposition, again clearly defended by Thomas, that "in human beings there is only one substantial form, namely the intellectual soul." In due course we will examine the significance of both these propositions in detail, as also the importance to Thomas of their connection. In the meantime it is important to look behind the scholastic formulas peculiar to the times, and not alone at the political motivations inspiring their condemnation. For it is important to understand what it was that genuinely, and, as far as we can tell today, sincerely, troubled Tempier and Kilwardby theologically about these propositions, especially the second. The reason why they, and some of the theologians at Oxford, were in common bothered by Thomas's view that human beings possess but one soul and that it is intellectual in nature is that, to them, it sounded like a plainly materialist and unspiritual view of the human person, puzzling as such an interpretation of Thomas's meaning might at first blush seem.

THE MIND OF A MATERIALIST

Misguided as they were, Tempier and Kilwardby were nonetheless on to something important about Thomas's intellectual profile, something that can be missed if one treats late-thirteenth and early-fourteenth-century anxieties about the orthodoxy of Thomas's theology only with the contempt of historical hindsight. As we begin the inquiry into the distinctive character of Thomas's intellectual and theological profile, a single word suggests itself as aptly describing it: true enough Thomas's is the mind of a materialist, a description requiring qualification only in light of the philosophically myopic materialisms of our own times, which, in their stronger forms, Thomas very sensibly rejects. For he could see no good reasons, and certainly he had heard of no good arguments, why anyone should maintain that nothing but matter *could* exist, nor why in advance of any particular issue of explanation it should be decided that only appeals to material causes should ever be permitted. Of course, then, to call him a "materialist" in today's sense of the term would be to do an injustice to Thomas, not only because for him there is more to the world than matter, but perhaps even more because for Thomas, there is a lot more to matter itself than meets the eye of today's average materialist. Less anachronistically, the chief defect of the standard forms of materialism known to him (mainly those of the later classical Greek philosophers, such as Empedocles, or, in the Latin tradition, Democritus) is not that they are bad on the subjects of mind and spirit—that criticism Thomas reserves for the Platonizing Christians of his day. Thomas's criticism of the materialists of whom he had knowledge was that they were simply not very good on the subject of matter.

In terms of relative philosophical positions, Thomas stands in a variety of relationships of similarity and contrast with his own contemporaries and with later philosophers. But by comparison with most of them, Thomas seems just a lot earthier, and in no connection does he stand out more clearly as materialistically inclined than in his account of the natural object of the human mind. Thomas thought that the mind's natural object—as it were, what the mind settles on as a matter of course and without having to extend itself in any of the many ways it is able to lengthen its natural reach—is the world of material objects into which, by way of their bodies, human beings are inserted. Of course he does not deny that human beings can think of and understand all sorts of things that are not material, for after all they can be easily enough taught that 2 + 2 = 4. In fact, Thomas was a keen student of all the devices that language provides for the stretching of thought and experience beyond the material—metaphor, allegory, analogy, and all forms of trope. He studied them specifically for the purposes of working out the rules for their systematic employment in the philosophy of mind, in the hermeneutics of biblical texts, and in his account of the logic of language about God. But in exploring these possibilities of language he knew that what he was asking of language was a stretch beyond its natural range, for non-material things do not come to the human mind, or to its powers of description, with the naturalness that material things do. And Thomas was acutely aware that nearly the whole dictionary of terms for mental acts and for talk about God is derived by trope from vocabularies whose literal meanings refer to the material world.

Early in the *Summa theologiae*, however, Thomas notes an objection to this earthbound understanding of theological language in the words of Jesus himself. Addressed by a member of the crowd as "good master," Jesus responds with some asperity, "Who is it that calls me good? None is good but God alone" (Matthew 19:17), thereby giving heart to all those Christian theologians of a Platonist persuasion for whom the primary meaning of all such words is not derived from a principally worldly reference, but from their reference to the ideal and divine. Thomas is not disconcerted. Distinguish, he says, between what a word means and that on account of which we are justified in attributing it to some object.[1] Of course the primary meaning of the word "good" is in its reference to God, from whom all the goodness of all creation flows, and naturally Thomas says, along with all medieval theologians, goodness exists primarily in its uncreated cause, secondarily in its created effects. Indeed, no goodness at all could exist in its created effects did it not exist first in its creating cause. In that respect his Augustinian-Platonist colleagues were correct. But, Thomas adds, if that is how things are in themselves, it is not how it is with us. For we can know God's goodness only by extrapolation from what our minds are naturally attuned to, namely the goodness of creatures.[2] In short, he insists that we know God from his effects, natural and revealed, above all of course from that revealed effect that is the human nature, human life, and death of Christ. For "he who knows me knows the Father who sent me." Our natural language is worldly, and for Thomas, the human mind by default faces outward to the material environment. Language and mind alike have to be stretched to reach above and beyond it.

By contrast, the Franciscan Bonaventure, his contemporary, friend, and briefly (in 1256–57) his fellow professor in the faculty of divinity at Paris, thought that in the same sense of the word "natural," the natural object of the human mind was God, and that "ideas" of created things exist first in the divine mind—hence, it is from the existence of their "exemplars" in the divine mind that human minds can know the natures existent in the material world. There is an Augustinian idea at work here. Augustine had argued that the human mind, being itself an unstably changeable creature, would be unable to judge the changeable things of the world as to "good, better, and best" by any unchanging standard (which, as we know, it can and does do) unless it were illuminated by the unchanging light of eternal truth which, though not *of* it as its own possession, is present *within* the human mind.[3] Likewise, Bonaventure knew that of course the human mind could in fact possess such genuine knowledge of the material world. But, following Augustine, he thought we could possess that genuine knowledge only by way of the divine light of eternal truth, the divine ideas of created things, and that they were the mind's natural object. For Bonaventure the human mind is thus turned upward to God and the ideal. From there it has to be stretched downward to creation.[4]

More than three centuries later, Descartes thought that the natural object of the mind—that is, again, what the mind did not have to work at to gain access to, but just knew in its default mode—was itself. For him the mind faced inward first, there to find present its own innate "ideas." And, as the ensuing history of Western philosophy witnesses, if it is from its own "ideas" that the mind is naturally disposed to start, you have your work cut out to show anything to exist outside the mind to which those ideas correspond. For what part of the mind not already connected with objects in the "external" world could demonstrate the correspondence between its ideas and those "external" objects? And if the mind is already thus connected, who needs the demonstration? If the correspondence can be shown, then it does not need to be. And if the correspondence needs to be shown, then it cannot be done—otherwise, that is, than by appeal to God as the guarantor that some of our ideas, those that Descartes calls "clear and distinct," do correspond with the way things are.[5]

Between these three, then—Thomas, Bonaventure, and Descartes—are philosophical differences of a more than merely technical kind across common territory of assumptions; nor do they differ merely as divergent routes setting out from a common starting point. There are fundamental differences of moral and spiritual orientation, differences concerning how in general human persons relate to a world. For Bonaventure, we know the world and the self from the standpoint of God; for Descartes, we know the world and God from the standpoint of the self. For Thomas, we know both God and the self from the standpoint of the world. In this sense, then, Thomas is by a long way the more materialistically disposed by any measure, at any rate as to the mind's natural object. For Thomas that natural object is the material world.

HUMAN BEINGS ARE ANIMALS

These differences concerning the basic orientation of knowledge toward its natural object, whether the created world, God, or the self, ramify into many other differences, one of the most significant manifesting in the corresponding accounts of the nature of persons themselves. Again, Thomas, relative to the majority consensus of his times, was the earthier. Plato had thought that I *am* my soul, or more precisely, I am my mind, on which my body exerts a gravitational pull downward from which only death can release me, and Bonaventure, so much more of a Platonist than Thomas, was of much the same view. Thomas dissented. As we will see in the next chapter, emphatically he denies that I am my soul—the "I" that I am does not consist in the soul that I have, and a bodiless soul is no person. So emphatic is Thomas in insisting that no human person can exist without a body that you may well find yourself asking why he needs to speak of the soul at all, since all he seems to mean by "soul" is whatever it is that accounts for a body's being alive. In consequence, the first surprise for many modern readers is the discovery that for Thomas there is nothing special about human beings in that they have souls. For Thomas, God and the angels apart, anything alive in any way at all has a soul, so that "has a soul" seems to him to be no more than a synonym for "is alive."

And then it is clear that there is yet another sense in which Thomas may fairly be described as a materialist. For Thomas, the study even of how human beings are alive begins with the recognition that a human is a kind of animal, alive with an animal's life. And like any animal I am a being essentially *situated*, set within a complex of relationships with other beings that are alive, at a number of different levels. As an animal I cannot exist without an organic world, a world full of other sorts of life, animal and vegetable. Volcanoes and black holes have no such needs. They need other physical objects with which to interact and impersonal physical laws to govern their interactions. But they do not need company, as animals do. Black holes have no family life. Neither, at the other end of the scale of things, do angels—each of whom, Thomas believed, realizes all the possibilities of its species, and needs no others to be the kind of spiritual being that it is.

Unsurprisingly, then, it worried Augustinian-Platonists about Thomas that he seemed scarcely to need a special account of the human soul at all, and therefore would seem to have no basis for an account of what is "spiritual" about human beings. Conversely it worried Thomas about Bonaventure and the majority Augustinian-Platonist opinion of his times that by their account, the identity and existence of human beings were "spiritualized" to the point of neglecting the material context within which they lived. And it certainly seems as if it was principally by contrast with an excessively spiritual account of human nature of an Augustinian-Platonist kind that his account seemed "materialistic" to his contemporaries. What Thomas does insist upon is that human beings are *essentially* world-dependent. Human beings are a form of life requiring the existence of not only other persons male and female of the same nature as themselves, but also forms of life other than their own. What is more, they need also the deaths of such other forms of life as are edible. To stay alive, animals have to eat formerly alive now dead matter, vegetable or animal. Minerals make no meals. In short, for Thomas, a human being requires a living world structured ecologically, an ecology of which it is itself an integral, and interacting, part. Human beings are animals and as such are at home within the living systems of natural reciprocity that characterize essentially, even uniquely, a world of animals and vegetables. It does not follow for Thomas that human beings do not have souls, or even that they lack distinctively human souls. It is just that when it comes to an account of human life, you should begin with the fact that human life is essentially a form of *animal* life.

BODY AND SOUL

Thomas, however, goes further still. He does not say merely that human beings are animals living at home in a world made for animals. He says we are *wholly* animal, animal from top to toe.

We are not, as the Platonizers thought, partly animals, animals up to the neck. A human being is not an intellect connected to an animal body, not for Thomas. This was the issue over which he got his fingers burned by the authorities in Paris and Oxford. The disagreement can seem to us merely technical, if not downright trivial and academic, but in fact it was stark, and as we will see, theologically critical. Moreover, both parties, Thomas and his opponents (some of whom, like Bonaventure, were friends), knew just why it mattered so much.

As to what hangs on it we will see later. As to the disagreement about the soul, the proposition condemned by Stephen Tempier in Paris in 1277 got it right if it is indeed true that Thomas was the intended target. In that condemnation Thomas is correctly described as having maintained that there is for each human person but one soul and that its nature is intellectual. Thomas is therefore not targeted by that condemnation for denying that human beings have souls, for manifestly he never denied that. Nor is he targeted for saying that human beings have intellectual souls—for that is exactly what his theological opponents them-selves believed. Thomas is targeted for saying that human beings have only *one* soul and that its nature is intellectual. That proposi-tion profoundly disturbed his contemporaries, because it seemed to them to imply a form of materialism. How so?

The issues in Thomas's time are a complex tangle (though scarcely more so than they are today when, in fact, they are not much different from what they were in the thirteenth century).

The first knot to untangle concerns what Thomas meant by "soul" in general, for what he meant is hardly at all what today most people assume the word "soul" to mean, whether they believe that human beings possess one or deny that they do. For *eadem est scientia oppositorum*, as Thomas liked to quote Aristotle as having said, meaning, roughly, that opponents are truly opposed only when in agreement as to what they disagree about. Thomas's position on the soul is not much like what either today's soul-affirmers or their corresponding soul-deniers in common affirm or deny. For example, Thomas did not accept—indeed, he specifically rejected—the teaching accepted by most of his contemporaries that human beings "have" a soul that is "united to their bodies." For that is pure Platonism, and at this point, if nowhere else, Thomas is pure Aristotelian. In consequence, as to that Platonic account of soul, Thomas was indeed a firm soul-denier.

Plato thought that a human being is a soul *attached to* a body, and his medieval Christian followers agreed. Aristotle's response is typical: by contrast with what seemed to be Plato's counterintuitive and unnecessarily complex philosophical conceit, he offers a more plainly intuitive and, one would have thought, more obvious account. What you mean by "soul" is nothing more than that which accounts for a thing's being alive in a certain kind of way— the way a spider is alive, or the way a fly is alive, it is the spider's soul, or the fly's, that accounts for it. Hence, whenever you have a living body, its being a living body just is its having a soul, for it would not be alive without a soul, and it would not be a body if it were not alive. Thomas agrees. A word of advice might profit modern readers wishing to understand how different Thomas's position on the soul is from that not only of medieval Platonists but also of a lot of Christian believers in our own times: You just have to try and stop thinking of *any* soul, a cabbage's or a king's, as a sort of *thing*. The way Thomas puts it is that for a cabbage's living body to be a body at all it needs a soul as its "form," for the soul of a thing is that thing's form of life. And it is no different with human persons. A human soul is what makes this body a living body of any kind, and specifically a human body, alive as human beings are alive.

Thomas could see no harm, then, in the form of words, "the body needs a soul to be alive," so long as one is not misled concerning the logic of the expression "needs a soul to be alive." For the form of words, though unavoidable, can seem too easily to lend support to the Platonist error of supposing that there is something or other, namely a body, and that it, the body, "needs a soul to be alive." It is on this point that the error of the Platonists, for Thomas, is pinned down. The statement "a body needs a soul to be alive" is logically on a par with the expression "a human being needs a brain to be alive"—which of course it does. But this is not to be understood as meaning there is such a thing as a human being who, lacking a brain, needs one, because it goes without saying that without a brain there is no human being to do any needing whatever. Likewise, Thomas maintains, there cannot be any such thing as a body that "needs a soul," because a body without a soul is no body at all—without a soul it is just dead, a corpse, a fortiori having no needs. As Aristotle said, a dead body is only a "body" in a manner of speaking. Thomas agrees. A dead person is not a person in the unfortunate condition of being dead. A dead person is what once was a person, but now is not: that is why Thomas says that even though human souls survive death, souls thus separated from their bodies are not persons. Likewise, an animal body is what the corpse *was* before it died. Thomas's position, then, comes down to this: a human being is a body alive in a particular kind of way; and what accounts for the body's being alive in just that way is, for Thomas, what you mean by its "soul" being the body's "substantial form." Nothing else.

ONLY ONE SOUL AND IT IS INTELLECTUAL

It was on account of this Aristotelian philosophical anthropology that in the eyes of many of his contemporaries Thomas was seen to pose a materialistic threat. Appearing to put him beyond the pale of orthodoxy was his insistence that for every living human being there is just one "intellectual" human soul, and that one soul accounted for a person's whole life—not, as his Platonizing opponents maintained, that persons "have" three souls: a vegetative, an animal, and a rational or intellectual. It is true, Thomas thought, that human beings are alive in three formally distinguishable ways: we are alive in that we feed and grow as any cabbage does; we are alive in that we can move ourselves from one place to another, feel warmth and cold, hunger and pleasure, pain and the relief of it, we see and we hear and we smell, we hunt some other animals as prey, and with others we identify danger and fight them or flee; all those things that all animals do, we humans do. And being alive in all these ways we are driven by natural inclinations, biologically and without consciousness, or psychologically and therefore consciously.

For it is a natural property of living things that they tend to act or to resist being acted upon so as to stay alive, as animals out of hunger search for food or in fear flee danger. Hence, Thomas says, these activities answer to natural animal tendencies and so are good for their agents, serving their interests for survival. But when it comes to human beings, they not only possess these tendencies as all animals possess them, nor only act on them as all animals act. These activities are good for human beings not merely as a matter of natural fact. Human beings can engage in them choosing to do so *because* they are good for them. Human beings characteristically, if not always, do what all animals do, but they do them for *reasons*, while non-human animals do what they do because naturally *caused* to do so by inclination. Reasons are good or bad, they justify actions or fail to justify them. Causes are blind to such distinctions: they cannot bring about what they cause "rightly or wrongly"—they cause what they cause, like it or lump it. Causes are dumb masters, and their effects mutely follow: reasons, on the other hand, are articulate, they narrate the course of action. In short, if for Thomas human beings are animals, they are animals of a particular species: they are *rational* animals; that is to say, they are animals that act for reasons, and these actions can tell, or be told by, stories. Human lives are narratives, they have plots.[6]

There is little doubt that what in all this caused trouble for Thomas, both after his death and in his lifetime, was that it seemed to his more Platonizing readers to be just too materialist an account of human nature to be properly Christian. Thomas, of course, was far from intending to deliberately scare his readership with a polemical materialism. Indeed, unlike his younger fellow Dominican Meister Eckhart, who regularly used scare tactics as a homiletic method, Thomas, knowing as well as anyone how his readership would react, made every effort to scare no one and intentionally cultivated a reassuringly relaxed and deadpan style to that end. Eckhart often says more than he means as a sort of shock tactic. But once you get used to his rhetorical devices the effect of his hyperbole wears off. Thomas almost always means exactly what he says, but the voice is so low-pitched that it is sometimes hard to credit how shocking he can be. To those for whom it is a matter of Christian belief to maintain that human beings are a higher species than brute animals, and that it is by virtue of a non-animal part of our souls that we are thus "higher," it *is* shocking to say, as Thomas does in an early monograph, *De ente et essentia*, that human beings are *wholly*, not partly, animals. His reasoning is simple and clear: you could not say of a human being that it is an animal at all if being an animal were merely what Thomas calls an "integral" (or, as we might say, "constituent") part of what it is to be human.[7] My being an animal is not a bit of me, like a leg or a brain, for an "integral part" is not predicable of the whole whose part it is. I have, but you cannot say I am, a leg or a brain or a heart—surgery can remove or replace "integral" parts. By contrast, you do and must say I *am* an animal, you cannot say I *have* an animal part of me that surgery could excise. A human being is an animal all the way through, all the way up, and all the way down. No human being is all leg. And even Thomas is not all brain.

Moreover, cast as it is in the technical language of his time, Thomas's meaning is unmistakable. How does the genus "animal" stand to the cat owner and her two cats? First, all three are wholly animal, and being an animal is not "part of" what the cat owner is, a part that she shares with her cats, her being rational adding another "part" to the cat owner that her cats do not share with her. For it is not thus that a human person's animality and her rationality stand to one another, not as Thomas saw it. For Thomas, both the cat owner and the cats are wholly animals: the difference between them falls *within* their common animality—it is an *internal* differentiation, a *differentia* as Thomas puts it, within the genus "animal."[8] For nothing that is not an animal can be rational.[9] Rationality is a specifically animal way of being alive.

It is here, however, that Thomas and Bonaventure are furthest apart from each other. For though Bonaventure, like Thomas, thought that human beings are alive in three generically different ways (as vegetative, as animal, and as rational), he also thought, unlike Thomas, that these different ways of being alive were to be accounted for by three different formal principles, or "souls"—a vegetative soul, an animal soul, and a rational soul, each really distinct from the other, each accounting for some of the living functions of a human being. To use the terminology of their times, Bonaventure, along with the majority opinion, maintained that these multiple expressions of human life showed that there must be in human nature a "plurality of forms" or "souls," each accounting for some "part" of what it is to be human. And for a number of reasons, principally two, Thomas could not accept this.

The first reason is technically metaphysical, having to do with the nature of existence and of individuation. Three individualized forms, each determining a different kind of life independently of the other, would just for that reason entail that a human being is a composite of three distinct existents. For if the soul that accounts for my having the life of a vegetable (growing and feeding) is really distinct and independent of another soul accounting for my having the life of an animal (sniffing, hunting, and having seasonal sex), and if each of those souls is really distinct from and independent of the soul that accounts for my rational life (celebrating birthdays, getting married, emailing my friends, and writing books), then each soul must actually exist in its own right. But, Thomas says, that destroys the unity of the person: for it would follow that I am, by virtue of my three souls, three existents: I am a plant, plus an animal, plus a rational agent. Bonaventure, of course, tried to evade this conclusion, unacceptable as it was also to him. But Thomas will allow no evasion, pointing out that the unacceptable conclusion is inescapable, for, on this account there is no possible way of explaining how I am also just one person, just one existent, just one source (albeit generically multiple) of agency.

The second reason is more empirically grounded. Nonetheless, it follows from the first and, as we will see, is of enormous consequence for Thomas's theology as a whole. Were it the case that a human being possessed an animal soul really distinct from a rational soul, then a human being's animality would be indistinguishable from a non-rational animal's animality in such a way that my exercising animal powers of perception of danger, for example, or reaction to the stimulus of the smell of food, would be interchangeable cognitively with those of my dog. Thomas thinks this is simply untrue. Of course, if, both of us being distracted by a loud noise, I and my dog turn suddenly to look in the same direction, no doubt (since we share similar nervous systems) we may both be described as having been startled by the noise; and (possessing physiologically similar auditory apparatus) we will both be correctly described as having heard the direction of it; and, having both turned our attention to its source, both will correctly be said to see much the same objects at a distance, and by means of the same kind of physical organ, our eyes. We are both animals. But otherwise than at this rudimentary level of description, everything else is different. For in me, this sensory input is mediated by a universe of meaning available to me by virtue of language, and unavailable to my dog for the want of it. Both of us sense danger. But only I can sense the danger and fear it under the description "terrorist threat." And I can describe the danger that particular way because I live in a world of language out of which and in which that description is made. Being linguistic animals is, Thomas says, what chiefly characterizes us as rational animals; and while it is true that for the materialist Thomas my animality goes all the way up through my rational nature, it is also true that my being rational goes all the way down through my animal nature.[10] As one might put it, fear of terrorists goes all the way through me, coming out as my hairs standing on end when I anxiously observe the unaccompanied suitcase at the airport. In fear of threatening animals, including men, my dog bristles too. But it is not *as* terrorists that her hair thus responds to them, even when she smells the explosive in the case and is trained to sense danger upon doing so. My dog knows no such descriptions because dogs do not know *any* descriptions. Indeed, for Thomas it is not even as human beings that her hair responds to them, but only as present threat, present danger. My being an animal means, for Thomas, that when threatened by danger my hair stands on end. My being a rational animal means, for Thomas, that my hair can stand up on end not only in response to, but at the very thought of, a very specific threat, a *terrorist* threat from Al-Qaeda. The difference is simply this: my sensations are mediated by language. My dog's sensations are not.

Like my dog I am, then, wholly animal. But unlike my dog I am also wholly rational. As Thomas puts it, neither my animality nor my rationality are "integral parts" of anything else: I am one living being, I exist and am alive by virtue of one "intellectual" soul, that form of intellectual soul that is distinctive in being wholly vegetative, wholly animal, and wholly rational in nature, all of them all the way through, a single form, a single form of life. And *that* is where the problem was that made Thomas seem too materialistic for Augustinian tastes. For in saying that human beings have only one soul and that it is intellectual is to say that the human intellect is deeply rooted in, not separable from, the animal and vegetative life of a human person. And that is Thomas's firm conviction, albeit that it seemed—and he knew it—too unspiritual an account of human nature to be tolerable to theologians of a Platonist cast of mind. But that is the reason for describing Thomas as a materialist. It does justice to the way his account of human nature was perceived by his Augustinian-Platonist opponents. And for his part, Thomas the theologian was wholly undisturbed so to be perceived.

THREE

The Soul

SOUL, INTELLECT, AND IMMORTALITY

Souls are not angels. Angels are not souls, nor do angels "have" souls. Only embodied beings have souls, for any soul is the life of some body, a body alive in the characteristic ways of humans, dogs, cabbages, and cats. It is of the greatest importance to get this much clear if we are not to mistake Thomas's account of the soul for other accounts much more familiar than his—accounts much easier to understand and to some much more plausibly consistent with Christian beliefs, especially with Christian beliefs regarding human persons' survival of death. Thomas, believing as firmly as anyone in personal survival of death, is nonetheless sure that Platonizing accounts of the soul are mistaken. The human soul, Thomas says, is the "substantial form" of the body. Put negatively, and at its most straightforward then, Thomas means that the human soul is not a complete entity, is not an actual *anything*, any more than a cat's life is an actual cat. Of course we can give an account of what a cat's life is like without reference to any particular cat, for we can place the life of a cat in its general features on a continuum of animal species. But we cannot cuddle Felix's life. We can cuddle only the living Felix.

In the same way we can give a general account of "soul" as Aristotle does in his *De anima*, but, according to both Aristotle and, following him, Thomas, there cannot be an existent soul that is not the soul *of* some body, making it to be a body alive with a certain kind of life. That is why for Thomas there should be no *general* problem about how the soul is related to the body. At any rate, you should not find yourself having a problem of the kind that you would have if, like Plato, you thought that the human soul was in itself a complete entity naturally existing without reference to a body. That the soul somehow and for some reason got joined up with a body is, for Plato, some kind of catastrophe of birth, a disaster that caused the soul whose natural habitat is the world of universal "ideas" or "forms" to be plunged into the cognitively obfuscating conditions of the particular and changeable objects of the material world. That's Plato in the ancient pagan world, and as early as the late second and early third centuries his influence was being felt in the first formulations of Christian teaching. The doctrines of Plato's *Phaedo* are those also of that erring and erratic genius, the early Christian Origen.

Of course, by the thirteenth century, body-soul dualisms of so extreme a kind were rare, largely because of the authority of Augustine, who early in his post-conversion writings had entertained the doctrine of the prenatal existence of the human soul, only in short order decisively to reject it well before he wrote *Confessions*. That rejection notwithstanding, residual forms of that Platonic doctrine were common in the Middle Ages; one gets the impression from the accounts of most medieval theologians that somehow the soul is not fully at home in the body, is somehow captive to it, and death is a sort of emancipation from it. Thomas will have none of this, and he suspects a form of that ancient body-soul dualism to be implied in the very question, "By what means may the soul be united to the body?" For Thomas, the question addresses a false problem, akin to wondering how an instance of the color yellow could acquire a surface to be the color yellow of: an occurrence of the color yellow just is a surface with the property of reflecting that part of the spectrum. Just so for Thomas and the soul. The human soul just *is* the life of a body; it is how this body's life is human.

That much having been said, by way of Thomas's "materialism," we are, of course, left with a problem the default Augustinian-Platonist of his day did not have and sorely wished to avoid having: "how can a soul so described survive death?" The Augustinian-Platonist had no such problem because, on his account, the human soul is in any case an existent spiritual individual person in its own right—at any rate, insofar as the human soul is rational it is a naturally immortal human being, even if the animal and vegetative parts of the soul are subject to death and cease to exist with the death of the body. Thomas, on the contrary, cannot take this way out, especially because of his maintaining the view that there is only one form of the body, and that is its intellectual soul. For if on Thomas's account the human soul is in its nature the form of the body, then its survival of the body's demise would seem as impossible as the survival of a patch of yellow with no surface for it to be the color of, as impossible as the Cheshire cat's smile surviving the demise of the Cheshire cat. And it was because the natural consequence of Thomas's Aristotelian account of the human soul as the single form of the body seemed in his times to entail the denial of the doctrine of the soul's immortality that posthumous condemnations in Paris and Oxford were visited upon him. It seemed obvious to his critics that only a soul naturally endowed with an independent, complete, and wholly spiritual existence of its own could possibly guarantee the survival by persons of their bodies' deaths.

Thomas knew he was in a tight corner on this issue, with few allies and many opponents. The issue ran deep down within his theological priorities, which is the main reason why his views on the soul are so revealing of his intellectual and theological profile. It is clear that Christian theologians are going to have one problem or another about survival of death, depending on where they start from. You may buy into the immortality of the soul on the Platonist ground that thereby you can ensure the survival of the person when the body rots. But then you must pay the price, as Thomas thought, of being unable to account for the unity of personhood pre-mortem. At the very least you provoke the question of why human persons need bodies in the first place if their survival as persons in a bodiless condition post-mortem is natural to them. But Thomas's rejection of Platonism is stronger still: the bare survival of bodiless human souls would not be the survival of persons *at all*. "A human being naturally desires the survival of his or her selfhood, and the soul, being part of a human person's body, is not a whole person, for *I am not my soul*. Consequently even were the soul to survive into another life, [that surviving soul] would be neither I nor any other person."[1]

Which is not to say that Thomas's position is without difficulties. If you are as adamant as he is that I am not my soul, that my soul is my body's form, its source of life, and that if only my soul were to survive death I would not, then no doubt it is easier to give an account of the body-soul unity of my pre-mortem personhood. But to the degree that that problem is the more satisfactorily solved it is correspondingly difficult to see how anything of me could survive death—in short, how personal immortality can be defended on any grounds. There are profound, and not merely tactical difficulties here, and Thomas knows it. Knowing how difficult it is to hold together two equally compelling truths, it is clear which way Thomas inclines: were a choice between them inevitable he would rather have a problem explaining how to sustain the Christian teaching of personal survival of death than a solution that risked the dualism of the Platonist concerning pre-mortem existence.

Typical of Thomas's refusal to take the easy way out theologically at the cost of the plainly wrong way out philosophically is his reading of Paul's teaching about the resurrection in 1 Corinthians 15. In view of Paul's insistence that in Christ we are raised in our bodies it would be exceedingly odd, Thomas says, if Christians were to give doctrinal priority to the Platonic, and so pagan, belief that the pre-mortem embodied condition of the human person were to turn out to be temporary and merely provisional, and that having won salvation we should be left hanging for eternity as person-fragments, suspended forever in an unnatural condition of separation from the body. In any case, he notes, even the pagan Platonists were aware of the absurdity of this consequence, and though their solution was itself in conflict with Christian teaching, they at least acknowledged the difficulty of their position by postulating an endlessly repeated cycle of reincarnations.[2] Even the Platonists, then, agree that life without a body is not a properly human life at all. Thomas holds on to that conviction at all costs. Plainly for Thomas the core Christian belief is in the resurrection of the body. Immortality of the soul comes into it only as necessary in the explanation of that doctrine of resurrection.

Besides, Thomas clearly does not see why one has to be forced into the apparent dilemma. In his day two different doctrinal sources, one more ancient, one more recent, defined the parameters of Christian solutions to the problem of personal survival, and

Thomas saw no reason why they should be thought mutually exclusive. The first, by a thousand years the more ancient, and by the same measure more authoritative, was the doctrine taught in the Creeds of the early Church, sourced in turn in that Pauline text of 1 Corinthians 15 among others, that spoke (as does the Apostle's Creed) of the "resurrection of the body" just as Paul himself speaks of a "body of resurrection" (1 Corinthians 15:35–44). The second parameter was a belief that the human soul survives the death of the body and is immortal, that is, it cannot naturally die, a doctrine of much Greek philosophy universally defended in Thomas's time and before, though its official proclamation as Catholic teaching still awaited a decree of the Fifth Lateran Council in 1515, centuries after Thomas's death. There is no evidence at all that Thomas doubted either article of orthodox faith. What is a good deal less clear is what Thomas thought was the relation between them.

It is not in doubt that Thomas does maintain that the human soul is naturally immortal, even if, by itself, the soul's immortality is insufficient for the survival of a person. It is also clear that Thomas thought this natural immortality of the human soul could be demonstrated more convincingly out of Aristotle's *De anima* than out of any Platonist doctrine, and that, even had it been declared in his time an article of faith to be maintained dogmatically by Christians, he would not have needed to be told so in order to be convinced of its truth—he thought it perfectly capable of rational demonstration. It is sometimes suggested that Thomas's position on the immortality of the soul is for him a philosophically embarrassing concession to theological need, the need being to provide some principle of the continuing identity of individual persons across the time gap between a person's death and his or her resurrection on the last day. The suggestion, then, is that for Thomas, the surviving soul provides just such a tenuous thread of continuity between my pre-mortem and post-resurrection *persona*. In fact I am aware of no evidence that Thomas thought there was a problem of this kind that needed to be solved. Moreover, there is much to be said for the view that even had Thomas thought there to be a problem of continuity between pre-mortem and post-resurrection identities, he could not have consistently offered a solution to it by way of the immortality of the soul. After all, every argument of Thomas's to the effect that "I am not my soul" would seem to rule out the separated soul as the provider of that thread of continuity between the "I" who died yesterday and the "I" who is raised at the end of time. For if my separated soul is not an "I" at all, how can it be the same "I" as the I who died? It might be replied that if not the same "I" then at least it can be said to be the same soul that survives death. But that is not without its problems either. Peter Geach argued that my separated soul cannot indeed derive its identity as mine from the Denys Turner it was once, before death, the soul of; rather, its identity is determined by virtue of its being the soul of the Denys Turner who (Denys Turner hopes) will be raised in a glorified body on the last day.[3] But in that case, it is my separated soul's identity as mine that is in need of guarantee, and, according to Thomas, gets it from my body's resurrection from death. It cannot be my separated soul's pre-resurrection identity that guarantees the identity of the soul of the raised me. And that seems to be the way round that Thomas would have it. As we saw, he is emphatic. "It would not be easy," he says, "indeed [it would be] difficult, to sustain the immortality of the soul without the resurrection of the body." Not easy for Thomas. Easy only for Platonists.

It would seem, then, that Thomas is not to be found arguing for the immortality of the soul on theological grounds; nor is he to be seen arguing the case philosophically for theological motives. He appears to think that the human soul is naturally immortal; that is to say, though divine action could annihilate a human soul, it cannot naturally die. The human soul cannot naturally die, Thomas says, because it is "intellectual." But now we may seem to encounter a general problem of consistency between two elements of Thomas's account of human nature. The first element is all that is contained in the case for describing Thomas as a "materialist" in the sense thus far explained: there is but one human soul, and it is the individuated form of the body. The second, which seems scarcely compatible with the first, is that this one human soul is not corrupted by the body's corruption in death, and thus is capable of existing independently of the human body. Moreover, this soul is capable of disembodied immortality because its nature is "intellectual"; being intellectual, it is immaterial; and, being immaterial, it is not subject to natural corruption and decay.

THE IMMORTALITY OF THE SOUL

The argument is complex, technical, and variously presented in different texts of Thomas. However, the essential aim of all Thomas's discussions of the "immaterial" character of the human intellect is to demonstrate that human intellectual activity is not the activity of any bodily organ. Of course Thomas knew that the normal exercise by the human intellect of many of its characteristic activities is dependent on the functioning of appropriate bodily organs. And it follows that a soul separated from its body cannot gain any new experiences by means of its normal powers of knowledge acquisition, since, the person being dead, its body rots away and the intellect has available to it none of the bodily organs required for learning anything new. Nonetheless, Thomas makes an important distinction. The eye is the organ of sight, because the eye is what you see with. It is not in the same sense that the brain is the organ of thought, because, Thomas says, the brain is not, and could not be, what you think with. You cannot see unless you have at least one functioning eye. You can learn nothing new about any part of your environment if, lacking a body, you lack a brain, because all the cognitive functions that put us in contact with our world depend upon a working brain. But the human intellect's capacity for reflection upon its own already acquired mental contents is not, Thomas thinks, disabled by its separation from the body. In effect, for Thomas, the human soul separated from the body is a functioning store of memories that it can continue to tell but can no longer edit, add to, or revise; it is a life frozen into the shape it possessed at the moment of death. That is why it is exactly that condition of soul that is subject to the divine judgment—that is, because the soul's memory is at last totally exposed to view, no masking pretenses being available to it anymore. It is a whole life, as Thomas says, become like a book, the book of life, but a book now closed. It is therefore wholly at the mercy of the divine judgment. Totally exposed, there are no longer any excuses, no plea-bargains.

There is no doubt, then, that Thomas believes in the soul's survival of death, even if the soul's survival is not the survival of the person whose soul it is. It is, for Thomas, like the survival of a *life*, a person's life of course, but not the survival of the complete person whose life it is. How so?

Compare the different ways in which the five senses of the body relate to their objects, and under what conditions. The organ of hearing is the eardrum and its associated mechanisms. To register sound accurately, the hearing activity of the organs of hearing must themselves be soundless, because any sound that the act of hearing itself makes, as in the case of a person suffering tinnitus, interferes with the act of hearing itself. We may say, then, that for the organs of hearing to register differences of pitch and volume, they must themselves be indifferent with respect to sound; that is to say, the activity of hearing sound must itself be soundless. The same may be said of sight: of course the organs of sight—the eye, the retina—being physical objects, are all themselves colored. But, Thomas says, the acts of those physical organs that consist in my telling one color from another cannot themselves be physically colored, because were they to be so then the act of discriminating one color from another would be distorted by the color of the act of seeing, as rose-colored spectacles determine what the heedless optimist sees in the world. To be able to see polychromatically, the act of seeing must itself be color-neutral: to see red cannot be a red act of seeing. Along the same lines, Thomas reasons that the proper object of touch is not and cannot be variations in temperature, for the skin itself has a felt temperature that determines perception of the temperature of the objects with which it makes contact—because my hands are cold, what seems to me hot seems to you cool, because your hands are warm. Hence, what we perceive by means of the nerve endings on the surface of the body as the nervous system's "proper object" is not temperature but pressure, registering degrees of hardness and softness.

The general proposition concerning the bodily senses and their objects is that, in respect of their specific objects—sound, color, smell, taste, hardness/softness—they must themselves be neutral: you can only soundlessly hear sounds, colorlessly see colors, and, as Thomas says, when a person's organ of taste through illness itself has a taste, you cannot taste food properly, and so with smell. Hence, by whatever act we come cognitively in contact with a specific range of objects, that act must itself be indifferent with respect to those objects. And what holds for the five senses, Thomas says, holds for cognition generally. A melody remembered "in the head" is inaudible to the ear, for the acts of remembering sounds are themselves soundless; a sight reimagined in its absence is invisible to the eye; a smell you are reminded of after the event is odorless to the nose; and as a general condition of every form of cognition, it holds for what we know intellectually. The mind is filled by what it knows—that is to say, it is filled with the meaning of all that through senses and through the power of imagination it encounters in the world. Consequently, what Thomas calls the "form" of the thing understood—that which determines its nature as the kind of thing that it is—becomes meaning in the understanding. The form in the thing making it to be what it is—a tree—and the form by which we understand it— the meaning of "tree"—are one and the same form, he says, at once determining the object's nature and its concept in the mind. But the manner of existence of the form in the thing is quite different from the manner of existence of the concept in our understanding. Early in the *Summa theologiae*, Thomas explains:

> The proposition "an understanding that understands something otherwise than it is is false" is ambiguous. . . . If the "otherwise than" qualifies the object of the understanding, then the proposition means: "an understanding that understands something *to be* otherwise than it is is false" and that is true. . . . [B]ut if the "otherwise than" qualifies the [act of] understanding itself, then the proposition is false. For of one kind is the manner of existence of a thing as understood in the person doing the understanding, quite another is the

manner of that thing's existence in itself. For it is clear that our intellect understands material things beneath its level in an immaterial way, which is not to say that it understands them to be immaterial, just as it understands simple things above its level in complex ways, which is not to say that it understands them to be complex.[4]

The argument is typically compressed, but for the moment let us consider the general proposition it contains: the judgment that the computer keyboard I am writing on now is material cannot itself be a material act, just in the same way that seeing something red cannot be a red act of seeing. "Just as": except that, not being limited to the perception of color, but, on the contrary, being unlimited in every way as regards its objects, the human intellect's acts of knowing cannot in themselves possess the same manner of existence as that of any of the objects it knows. But if in their manner of existence the human intellect's acts of understanding are wholly "other than" what it understands by means of them, then, Thomas argues, the manner of existence of the human intellect itself must in its nature be wholly other than the manner of existence of the objects of its understanding. If acts of understanding cannot be material acts and so cannot be the acts of any material organ, then the intellect that understands cannot be a material agent. The human brain does not think. It is no more than what we could not think without. A tennis racquet isn't what plays tennis even if you cannot play tennis without one.

One way of rephrasing all this—though this is not exactly how Thomas thinks the issues through—is in terms of the relation between language and meaning. For someone who cannot read, the shapes on this page are just that: they *are* words indeed, and even if you cannot read you may know that they are words; but if you are illiterate they cannot bear the meanings that they bear for a reader. What is it, then, that the literate elicits from the shapes on the page, which the illiterate cannot? The shapes are objects common to the eyes of both. There are no additional shapes visible to the literate and invisible to the illiterate that constitute the meaning of the shapes they can both see. Nor do the meanings the literate elicits which the non-literate cannot elicit inhabit some place other than the shapes that are the common visual objects of both. Where, then, is the meaning of the words to be found if not in the words? Yet, since words are themselves material objects (shapes on a page, sounds registered in the ear), how could it be that some material objects can mean other material objects in the way that language can meaningfully describe something? If not in the words themselves, written or oral, do meanings then exist somewhere else, perhaps in the mind? If in the words, why cannot they be seen by anyone who can see the words? If in the mind, how can mere shapes on a page be the means of access to them?

There seem to be at least two general kinds of bad answer to these questions, as Thomas would see it: the Laputan and the Lockean. The Laputan answer, satirized as the crudely empiricist theory of meaning in Jonathan Swift's *Gulliver's Travels*, is the view that words function as labels for objects—in fact Laputans, having no time for words, instead carry stone objects around in sacks and when they want to denote some object in the world by means of them, they lay the relevant stone down on the object in question, thus somehow "naming" it. Of course, as a theory of naming, the satire aptly displays its absurdity. The idea that words get their meanings from the objects they name fails to explain anything at all, in just the same way that the theory must fail according to which words get their meanings from the objects they point to—as if the word "yellow" gets its meaning from the yellow objects the word is used to pick out. For you cannot explain how words connect up with the objects they describe by way of an action that is itself linguistic, namely the action of pointing. To understand that someone's index finger is pointing at an object is something a baby has to learn to do—dogs can never learn to do it: attempt to instruct a dog by means of pointing results only in getting your finger licked. In learning to understand pointing, a baby is already beginning to understand a bit of language—like a sentence in what Wittgenstein called a "language-game," in this case, of gestures—the meaning of which, being something learned as with any other bit of language, cannot itself explain how language succeeds in meaning the objects it names.

The second and equally unsatisfactory account of meaning and its relation to language is the Lockean, and, in explanation of Thomas's position, it is not only unsatisfactory but also particularly misleading. Locke and Thomas both employ the common term "abstraction" as the name of the act by means of which the human mind discovers "meanings." But though they call it by the same name, they could not have more different accounts of the nature of the act of understanding a meaning. In fact, when it comes to Thomas, it seems best simply to drop the word altogether, to translate his *abstrahere* and its cognate *abstractio* in some other way, and leave the term "abstraction" to find its own place within the history of empiricist philosophies.

Of course, at one level, Thomas and the empiricists have at least a starting point in common. Both maintain that, as Thomas puts it, "there is nothing in the intellect that is not first (experienced) by the senses." In short, Thomas and empiricists generally are at one in sharing that generic materialism according to which the source of all human knowledge is the human body's orientation by means of the senses to the material world. Once one moves beyond that very general agreement, however, Thomas and the empiricists could not move further apart, as, along with the empiricist mentality in general, has our contemporary culture at many levels. For more than two centuries in the Anglophone part of the Western world, our everyday perceptions of what is real have been weighed down under the pressure of a sort of empiricist presumption, which, to put it in a rather casual metaphor, would have us construe the real as what we bump into—the hard knocks, as it were, of the immediate, such that by contrast, meanings are mediated, secondary, soft *derivations* from the hard knocks of experience that stand in a more or less distanced relationship with the real. But this empiricist prioritization of experience's immediacy over the mediated character of meaning gets everything the wrong way round for the purposes of understanding Thomas. And this is especially true of that word "abstraction" that Thomas and Locke share as the name of the process by which meaning is elicited from experience.

For Locke, meanings are possessed by means of concepts, or, to use his word, "ideas." And ideas are abstract—indeed, the noun phrase "abstract idea" for Locke is pleonastic: ideas *are* abstractions. But for Locke, the abstraction that yields a concept or idea is more like an *ex*traction than anything else. If, for Locke, you want to grasp the idea, or "nominal essence," of the human, for example, you do so by identifying all and only those features common to all instances of human beings thereby to elicit the Highest Common Factor uniting all such instances into the "idea" of the human. Abstraction, on this account, sets aside the variations that differentiate one human being from another, and in effect, therefore, it thins out the concept to a degree of density that all possess: which is little enough. On Locke's account, "featherless biped" would probably meet his conditions for the "idea" of the human, because de facto all and only human beings are featherless bipeds. Ideas, for Locke, therefore, are what the mind grasps of the thin tissue connecting up descriptively the individuals that fall under them. Ideas, being abstractions, are essentially *simplifications*, paraphrases of complex experiences.

Thomas's account of abstraction reverses all this. To return to the example given earlier, if you bump into three hard objects in a darkened room, you are (in Locke's sense of the word) in possession of purely abstract impressions of them: that is to say, you have grasped of all three objects that they possess in common the property of solidity, minus any others. But if, as we saw Thomas to say, you then turn on a light, you see them all in the medium of much greater complexity and variety, you experience them no longer as abstractly tangible objects, but as furniture. You grasp their wealth of differentiation in respect of position and color and shape and size and elegance—or ugliness, as the case may be—their usefulness, their layout, you begin to understand the social purposes of the room thus furnished. In short, you see a sitting room. And as you learn more and more about what you see, you more and more successfully grasp the meaning of what you see in the room, precisely in your grasp of its complex variety, its diversity and differentiation; and so it is that you know what kind of room you are in, you know where you are, and the experience is now *intelligible*, as Thomas would say: you have the concept of a furnished room, a mental and linguistic act by which you are concretely situated within, not abstractly distanced from, your bodily experiences. And so Thomas says that the mind's forming concepts out of particular experiences is like turning on a light: it reveals the color of those experiences, it *thickens* them, reveals their depths and densities. It does not, as Locke thought, thin experience out. Lockean abstractions are pale and effete, or, as Hume said, they are faded impressions; Thomas's "abstractions" (if it is not wholly misleading to call them that) are polychrome and dense.

Now for the human mind to be able to elicit the meaning of human experience resulting from the hard knocks of the senses, it has to be, in relation to the sensible world, like a light that reveals that complexity and can, as it were, make a *picture* of it, or, to switch metaphors, make a *story* of it, or make a *musical work* out of it, or even, perhaps, make a *meal* of it—the analogies from the senses are deliberate—they are analogies *from* how the senses serve the mind *to* what the intellect makes of what it is served with. The intellect elicits the meaning from what it senses in an enormous variety of ways, the description for which we have to employ metaphors from the very senses from which, as Thomas puts it, the intellect "abstracts." As a result we can now see that, for Thomas, the Latin verb *abstrahere* has very little meaning in common with the modern English verb "to abstract," because for Thomas, the intellect draws together in acts of understanding the "abstract" experience of each of the senses, thereby grasping the concrete and dense realities wherein is found their meaning. For in truth there are no actually existent abstract sounds—it is only the ear that disengages sound from color; it is sight that disengages color from fragrance, the nose that disengages fragrance from softness to touch. For Thomas it is the senses that in Locke's meaning of the word make abstractions; it is the intellect that elicits from bodily, sensory interactions with the world the meaning of the conjunction. The deep red seen, the complex fragrance smelled, the velvet surface felt— these are the *abstract* sensory inputs that the intellect draws into the *concrete* unity of the rose, whose significance is elicited from the story of love between the man and the woman, a story that is told of a date and a gift. Thereby those abstract sensations are given a voice by the power of intellect to evince the significance of their concrete convergence. Locke's intellect is about thinning experience analytically out. Thomas's intellect is about thickening experience synthetically up, disclosing, thereby, its meaning.

And the power to do this depends, Thomas thinks, on the intellect's not possessing any of the characteristics of its own objects, just as in its own particular domain the act of seeing must be colorless if it is to have the power to distinguish colors. So the human power of intellect, whose object is completely unrestricted in range (since, as Thomas says, anything whatever that exists is a possible object of intellect), cannot possess any of the material characteristics of what it knows. That is why the acts whereby we come into the possession of the meanings of objects in the material world cannot themselves be material acts, acts *of* any material organ.[5] And by the word "intellect" Thomas refers to that power with which human beings must be credited in order to account for the common and typically human practice of eliciting meaning from matter. For that, after all, is what language itself is, spoken or written: sound and shape that utters, matter articulate, stuff that speaks. It is the intellect that has the power to elicit that speech from that stuff: it cannot itself be made of the stuff that is spoken.

MATTER AND MEANING

It was a typical mistake of judgment, still too often made by teachers and students alike in modern universities, that Thomas's extreme reluctance to join in academic chatter (in class and out) caused his fellow students in Cologne to nickname him "the dumb ox." Their teacher Albert the Great knew his student better, and is reported to have declared that this dumb ox would one day bellow so that the whole world would hear him, and promptly employed Thomas as his thirteenth-century equivalent of a teaching and research assistant. In a world filled with loud, attention-seeking clamor, sometimes the best way of drawing attention to something that matters is to lower the volume and pitch, so that if people want to hear, they must fall silent themselves. And as we saw, that, generally speaking, was Thomas's way. He spoke low, and eventually the theological world around him fell relatively silent in order to hear.

Just occasionally, however, Thomas did truly bellow. And on one occasion concerning issues about the soul he bellowed without restraint. Here is Thomas in anger:

> If there is anyone so full of himself in his knowledge of what is falsely paraded as a science who wishes to say anything in response to my words herein, let him, if he dares, reply in writing to what I have written, and refrain from speaking in corners and to young boys who are not in a position to judge of such difficult matters. He will find that it is not

I alone, who is the least of them all, but many others whose concern is for the truth, who will resist his error and counsel his ignorance.[6]

Thomas wrote these words at the end of a polemical work addressed to some philosophers in the Faculty of Arts in the University of Paris who, in his view, were systematically misreading Aristotle on the nature of the soul through the interpretative lens of the twelfth-century Arab philosopher Ibn Rushd, known in the Latin Middle Ages as Averroës. Whether the so-called "Latin Averroists" were getting Averroës right, whether Averroës was getting Aristotle right, and whether Thomas was getting either the Latin Averroists right or for that matter correctly reading Aristotle himself, are issues to the side of our purpose. What is closer to our concerns is why Thomas was so angry with his "Latin Averroist" colleagues in the Faculty of Arts at Paris.[7]

Undoubtedly one reason is that given in the first chapter. These philosophical followers of Averroës were, in Thomas's view, refusing to step foot into the public marketplace of writing and debate, instead influencing young minds by means of unchallengeable insinuation, exercising the power of the teacher over students while bypassing the standard academic checks on its abuse: public debate with one's peers. At one level, then, Thomas the teacher was outraged simply at the blatant failures of professional ethics among some of the philosophers and theologians. Plus ça change.

But there is another reason, closer to the concerns of this chapter than to those of the first. The Latin Averroists were, Thomas thought, teaching a version of Aristotle's *De anima* which, if a correct interpretation, played straight into the hands of the Augustinian-Platonist opponents of Thomas's Aristotelianism. Their conviction that Aristotle's account of the soul was theologically threatening was confirmed by the version of *De anima* promoted by the Averroist philosophers. Thus was Thomas's Aristotelian philosophy of mind doubly threatened: if the Averroists were in fact correct in their interpretation of Aristotle, then Thomas had no one on whom to rely for his alternative account of soul, no stick with which to beat the Augustinian-Platonists. What is worse, if the philosophers were to be believed in their interpretation of Aristotle, then Aristotle became a stick with which his theological colleagues could beat Thomas as a heretic. Without an alternative to the Averroist reading of Aristotle, Thomas's whole theological project was, as we will see, firmly wedged between a rock and a hard place.

There is no doubt but that the "Averroist" reading of Aristotle's *De anima* yields an account of the human person unsustainable by any Christian. As the Latins on all sides read him, Averroës claimed that in book three of *De anima*, Aristotle maintained that while human beings are individuated by their bodies, and while human bodies are alive and individuated by virtue of their vegetative and animal souls, the human intellect is not in the same way individuated, for there is but one single intellect for all human beings. What is worse is the consequence: since it is intellect alone that survives the death of the body, it follows that there can be no personal survival of death, for immortality belongs to the one and only intellect that all persons share. It matters not what sense, if any, can be made of these doctrines, still less whether there are grounds in Aristotle's text for the Averroist reading of it. It is in any case obvious from all that I have explained about Thomas's doctrine of the soul that he could not abide that interpretation of Aristotle. It is even more obvious that Thomas would make no concession to the Averroist account of the intellect, whether or not it was attributable to Aristotle: Thomas's authorities were important to him and he defended them when he could, but always *magis amicus veritas*—great and doughty friend to Thomas that Aristotle was, "the greater friend is the truth."

What matters from our point of view is the curious way in which, on one crucial issue, Thomas's two sets of opponents, the Christian Augustinian-Platonists and the Latin Averroists, actually agreed with one another, and why that curious coincidence of natural opponents should have mattered so much to Thomas. The point of agreement between his opponents is simply this: both the Averroists and the Platonist-Augustinians unbind the unity and integrity of the human person. Both locate the center of gravity of personhood in the intellect. Both in their different ways conceive of intellect as "separate" or "separable"—consisting in the one case (Averroism) in a single intellectual soul separated from the individuated human being, and in the other (Platonist-Augustinianism) in individuated intellectual souls separable from the animal and vegetative life of persons. In consequence, neither can make sense of that which Thomas believes the Christian needs in order to explain the psycho-physical unity of the human person, wholly vegetative, wholly animal, wholly rational, on which the doctrine of the resurrection of persons, body and soul, depends.

And it is here that we get to the heart of the matter, to the issue that was so important to Thomas that, just for once, it was worth his shouting. I have insisted on describing Thomas as a materialist; and, as such terms often get their sense from that with which they contrast, we can see that what unites the traditional, indeed conservative, Augustinian-Platonist theologians with the radical Averroist philosophers is that for one and the same reason, neither can make good sense of matter. Or, to put the problem in another way, they cannot make good sense of matter because they cannot account for how matter can make sense, how it can bear meaning. For if I am my soul, and my soul is my intellect, and (in the Averroist case) the numerically one and only intellect subsists independently of the identity of persons, or (in the Augustinian-Platonist case), my intellectual soul is really distinct from my animal and vegetative souls, then the proposition central to Thomas's account of the human person is denied. It was this belief of Thomas's that set his theological cat among the episcopal pigeons, French and English. What exists is a person; what makes me a person is my possessing an intellectual soul, and that one and only soul runs all the way down through my animal and vegetative life, just as my vegetative and animal lives run all the way through and up into my intellectual life. Thus it is that my vegetative and animal life (eating, having sex) can bear sense, carry meanings, become a discourse, become a language of human transaction. For what else is language but the material world replete with the human meanings that it bears, what else are human beings but matter articulate?

But it is just at this same point that an even more dramatic juncture is reached—a crossing of the paths that is, theoretically, wholly surprising *until* you see just why Thomas insists upon that form of moderate materialism I have attempted to describe in this and the previous chapter. For it is just at this point where the extreme "spiritualisms" of the Augustinian-Platonists and the radical Averroists converge (a wholly surprising result, given their mutual animosity in the thirteenth century) that, in turn, the materialisms of our times intersect with both (an even more surprising result). Thomas's position would appear to entail the rejection of all three, and all three on exactly the same ground, ground which more than anything else defines the distinctiveness of Thomas's account of human life.

For if it is true that what is distinctive about Thomas's position on the nature of life merits description as a form of materialism, yet, relative to the philosophical and commonly atheistic material-isms of our own times, his materialism stands as a critique of its dogmatic narrowness. At its simplest, for Thomas the atheistic materialism of the twenty-first century and the theological immaterialism of the thirteenth are equally wrong about the same thing and in the same way. Both are wrong about matter. Today's materialist believes that matter is all there is, and that matter is meaninglessly dumb, for all meaning is talk *about* matter, none of it matter talking. But in just the same way, the mainstream Augustinians of Thomas's own day, along with their natural opponents the philosopher Averroists, believed that because matter is meaninglessly dumb, there must be something more than matter, something more than, and separable from it, that constitutes the individual human person. And the important consideration that unites all three and differentiates them from Thomas is therefore the conviction that matter is meaninglessly dumb, while for Thomas, matter could not exist if it were not alive with meaning, or as he called it, "form."

At which point we are brought back to the first of the two propositions condemned in common by Stephen Tempier and Robert Kilwardby in 1277, the proposition namely that God could not create matter without form. For Thomas, the conception of matter actually existent but without shape, form, or meaning is nonsensical. As one might put it, for Thomas it is precisely in matter that meaning principally and in the first instance shines forth. And it was in that belief that his theological enemies across the board identified his "materialism," as if Thomas were playing their game only on the opposing team—as if, that is to say, Thomas played off matter against spirit in the same way that his opponents played off spirit against matter. Thomas, simply, is refusing to play on either side. He refuses to play the game according to his opponents' rules, be they Augustinian-Platonist Christians or Averroists, Christian or Muslim alike.

Why, then, is it so important to Thomas to say such things as that matter is inconceivable without form? Why devote so much distracting energy to battling opponents who would deny it? One clear reason, the importance of which will transpire later, is this: Thomas knows that one of the most sublime of all Christian mysteries, the mystery of the Eucharistic presence, is the mystery of how the lowest and most material of all forms of human life, the life of nutrition and feeding, the form of life humans share with cabbages, carrots, and cauliflowers, carries the weight of an utterly transcendent meaning, the meaning of the cross, resurrection, and ascension of Jesus. In that Eucharistic meal of bread and wine, so intensely and intimately present is the meaning of the raised Christ that, Thomas says, their reality *as* bread and wine is overwhelmed and transformed into the food and drink of life, the body and blood of Christ. If ever there was a case of matter making sense, of material life becoming word—indeed the very Word of God—then the Eucharist is it. When, therefore, Thomas defends Aristotle against the Averroists, and defends a non-Averroist Aristotle against the Augustinian-Platonists; when he defends his position along lines that seemed to his Christian opponents to threaten Christian teaching with pagan materialism, it is because he can see the consequences far down the theological line of failing to do so. He knows that he needs to be able to say how matter makes human sense if it is to be explained how it makes divine, or as he will say, "sacramental," sense; and to be able to do that, he must be able to explain how to make better sense of matter than anything found in the theories of his opponents, whether spiritual Augustinians, philosophical Averroists, or *ne plus ultra* materialists.

FOUR

God

CHRIST VERSUS GOD

Deus vere [est] subiectum hiuius scientiae,[1] "It is God who is the true subject of this discipline." So says Thomas at the outset of the *Summa*. By contrast, talk about God is curiously unfashionable among Christian theologians today. They seem to prefer to talk about Christ, as if you could theologize with Christological adequacy without standing on secure doctrinal ground concerning God. This seems perverse, being somewhat akin to an English person's attempting to describe to an American the conduct of a cricket match while suppressing any indications that cricket is a sport. The American, after all, might reasonably conclude that the description referred to some tediously long-winded religious ritual that devotees of most English-speaking nations[2] engage in for periods of five days whenever it is not raining during the months of summer. In the same way, Christian beliefs, Thomas says, might be about anything at all, might for all we know be make-believe fairy tales, allegories, or metaphors for goodness knows what, or, as many nineteenth-century critics of Christian beliefs maintained, have nothing to do with God and are just a roundabout and misleadingly alienating way of misdescribing human nature and the world. Thomas, therefore, insists. We know that they make sense *as theological* only insofar as they are revealed by the God they in turn reveal. And Thomas seems both to be right in thinking that you need to show this and to have judged well pedagogically in deciding to begin with the logic of talk about God.

It is thus very early on in the *Summa* that Thomas raises the question whether one should not distinguish between the specifically Christian *topics* of theology—grace, redemption, the incarnation, the Trinity—and what is the standpoint from which those truths of faith are the object of *theological* enquiry—as distinct, for example, from a historical, or an anthropological or psychological enquiry into the same topics. And his answer is that what is distinctive about theology is that it enquires into the truths of faith specifically insofar as they in some way reveal the God who is the author and source who originally revealed them to us. It is, therefore, as revealing God that theology studies what it studies. As a formal discipline of enquiry it is defined not by *what* it is about—what he calls its "material object"—but by the aspect under which it studies what it is about, its "formal object." And that formal object is God.[3]

It is for this reason that Thomas begins his theological exposition in the *Summa* with God. In fact throughout his theology Thomas talks a great deal about God. He always did. The legend has it that when Thomas had barely learned to talk he would wander around the family castle asking out loud, "What is God?" And as a mature theologian he tells us that theology is our talk about God in response to God's talk about God. God's own talk is the very life of the Godhead. That conversation within the godhead is, as Christians call it, the "Trinity": an uttering in love, a word uttered and love returned, a sort of tryst. God himself is, as it were, all talk, all love, all loving talk. And that the Trinitarian life of God took the form of a Word made flesh and became speech addressed to us, the Word that is Christ, is what Thomas calls "holy teaching." Theology, Thomas says, is neither more nor less than our human reception of and response to that Word of God that is spoken to us in Christ. Being in this way our talk about God's talk about God, the discipline of theology begins and ends in the God it is about, the Trinitarian conversation extended into the human through Jesus' prayer to his father, so that, reciprocally, our human conversation might by grace and prayer extend into the Trinitarian life of God. Thus does the Christian, through faith, participate in the conversation that *is* God.

Hence, for Thomas, you cannot dogmatically set in any essential order of priority, less still in any form of exclusion, talk about

God, talk about the Trinity, and talk about Christ. To set talk about Christ or the Trinity in opposition to talk about God, or the converse, is to disrupt the most intimate of all linkages that make up Christian teaching. For this reason, that is, because for Thomas it is so obvious that you could never engage in Christian theology otherwise than in the medium of these inner connections, he can afford to let it go without saying that when he does talk about God he does so as only Trinitarian Christians must, even if he is also prepared to talk about God as a Muslim or a Jew does when the occasion calls for it. Not forgetting that the structure of the *Summa* is governed by its pedagogical purposes, however, and given that in the construction of a learning curve curricular sequencing is all, in the *Summa* Thomas makes a choice: he prefers to talk about God first, then about the Trinity, and only in the third and final part about Christ. Why not? After all, as Elizabeth Trang has pointed out to me, Thomas's order of theological exposition corresponds to the scriptural order of exposition, insofar as one conceives of the progression of books of the Old Testament through to the New as describing a whole nation's "learning curve," an enormous arc of salvation history progressively revealing the one God of Exodus to be the one and only Trinitarian God that the Christian Church in due course comes to believe was revealed in Christ. Why should not the pedagogical *cursus* of theology map on to the historical *cursus* of the revelation which is its source?

And why is it that theologians today are so strangely dogmatic about the sequencing of theological exposition as if alternative schemes of exposition necessarily entailed alternative doctrinal, as distinct from pedagogical, priorities? The proposition that the fullness of revelation is in Christ warrants no entailment that Christology must be the one and only authentic starting point in the pedagogical order. Thinking it imperative to begin Christian theology with distinctively Christian doctrines, especially Christological ones, some contemporary theologians seem to suppose that Thomas's beginning his theological expositions with talk about God is as if he were giving some *logical* priority to an abstract "theism" shared in common by Christians, Jews, Muslims, and even pagans, over specifically and exclusively Christian teachings. For this, it is said, allows theological method to raise too many questions of theological substance in a manner that would subsume under theistic generality that which is a distinctively Christian revelation. The best you can get from "God" on this account is some thinned-out theistic lowest common denominator that can be shared in common terms by Augustine and Aristotle—or even perhaps (for some will say it) by Jesus and Mohammad. The Christian theologian has at best only marginal (perhaps ecumenical) interest in a thinned-out God. Distinctively, Christian theology is what answers not to "God" but to the thick Trinitarian description that Jesus proclaimed. Such is the view of many in recent times.

In consequence, it was a shock to an older generation of such theologians, dominant in the first half of the twentieth century, and it arouses among them some hostility to Thomas' theology in principle, to discover that on all three occasions when Thomas attempts a systematic exposition of Christian faith at length, he begins with a discussion of God without any reference to the God of Jesus' faith and prayer. For Karl Barth, on the contrary, and for more than a generation of Protestant and Catholic theologians following his lead, to start out from there guarantees getting the rest wrong. A "neutral" God inevitably neutralizes Christian faith, reducing its distinctiveness to a sub-species of "theism."

In fact, of course, for both sides, things are much worse than that. On the side of contemporary theologians, not only does Thomas begin the *Summa* with an apparently religion-neutral understanding of God—he begins with a *philosophical* understanding of God, as if he supposed that the whole edifice of faith must rest on philosophical foundations. Catholic theologian Karl Rahner took exception to the strategy no less than in his different way did the Protestant Karl Barth.[4] And on the side of Thomas, those "treatises" on God that initiate his three mature systematic works appear to seek out neutral ground not only between different faith traditions, but even, he seems to think, with God-deniers. Why else would Thomas begin all three works with philosophical arguments for the existence of God—arguments that he thinks are properly valid and sound on the rational principles of inference that atheists also accept, if it were not that he thinks, with Aristotle, that "one and the same is the knowledge of contraries"? Unless, that is, what believers and atheists respectively affirm and deny is the same for both, they cannot be said genuinely to disagree; rather they are just unlit ships passing one another in the night—a fair account, by the way, of Thomas's doctrine of God and the atheist denial of someone like Richard Dawkins, there being scarcely a proposition of Thomas's theology that Dawkins is able to formulate accurately enough to succeed in accurately denying. Hence, Thomas appears to say, if, unlike Dawkins, the atheists truly deny what the Christian affirms, then they agree at least on the meaning of the contested proposition "There is a God," just insofar as they are opposed concerning its truth. And unless their disagreement is no different from that between those who do and those who do not like sushi, then they respectively affirm and deny God's existence on grounds and for reasons, that is to say, across agreed territory of disagreement. And it is on just such ground that Thomas sets his arguments for the existence of God. In short, for Thomas, the existence of God is rationally debatable, even if he knows as a matter of faith which side ought to win. If this is the right way to read Thomas's theological strategies, it is hardly surprising that so many theologians today accuse Thomas of a form of rationalist foundationalism, according to which the edifice of faith, depending on a substratum of rational argument, is thereafter a tilted and tottering house built on the shifting sands of philosophy.

That much being supposed, it is unsurprising that after opening with a few methodological preliminaries, the first substantive question with which the *Summa theologiae* begins is: "Is there a God?" And the first step toward an answer is, no more surprisingly, to admit that the matter is arguable—that is to say, to admit that the question is a genuine one, and it possesses the character that Thomas says belongs to theology as a discipline: it is *argumentativa*. Therefore, saying that the question whether there is a God qualifies as a genuine (as distinct from spurious) question places on the theologian the responsibility of telling the difference between good and bad procedures for answering it. Specifically, in the second question of the *Summa* Thomas tells us of one very famous way of attempting by rational argument to settle the question in favor of an affirmative answer, a way that he regards as failing badly by required standards of soundness and validity, namely that offered by the great eleventh-century theologian Anselm of Canterbury. That procedure became known (in modified forms) by later centuries as the "ontological argument."

Anselm thought that a valid argument could be constructed from the very thought of God (the thought, that is, that the believer and the atheist share in their respective affirmation and denial); for that existence of God in thought, he argued, entails the existence of God in reality, mistakenly supposing, as Thomas responded, that the thought "God's existence is a necessary existence" entails the truth of the proposition "Necessarily God exists." Both, Thomas thinks, are of course true, at least in the sense that were there a God, then these propositions would be true of him: if there is a God, then God's existence is a necessary existence, unlike mine. For though I exist I might not have done so and in due course will not. But the first does not entail the second; for the first is no more than a statement of what the word "God" means, whereas the second is an existential claim declaring that there is one in fact; and logically no definition can entail the existence of what it defines, otherwise you could not know what a dodo is because there aren't any left. And that would mean "There are no dodos" cannot make any sense.

Today, most believe that Thomas is right and that Anselm's argument fails to provide a valid and sound proof. In view of which some argue that he is in any case misread as having intended to offer a formal proof of any kind and that he meant it rather as a sort of prayer of praise addressed to God, by means of which the person who prays is drawn into the certainty of God's existence (I am unpersuaded by this case[5]—but no matter). Even if Thomas's interpretation of Anselm is mistaken, the point may be made hypothetically. Were the case made in Anselm's *Proslogion* to be offered as formal proof of God's existence—and most took it that way at the time, and still do—then as such, it fails. If, as Thomas thinks, the theologian has a responsibility to sift good from bad arguments, even those that entail a true conclusion, then it matters to him that as arguments go, Anselm's is a bad one, whatever else it may be.[6]

Again, continuing to expound what Thomas seems to say, though there are bad arguments for the existence of God, there are also good, sound, valid arguments whereby "that there is a God can be proved." Moreover, he adds, he is prepared to back five ways of doing this—which is not to say there are not others:

perhaps it is that he thinks these five are the most easily defended and will do for the purpose—whatever that is.[7]

All this is what Thomas appears to say in that famous second question of the *Summa*, and it is this so-called "rationalist foundationalism" that was the butt of so much criticism in most Protestant and some Catholic theological circles in the twentieth century. However, fashions in theology change as rapidly and as outlandishly as do fashions in the clothing industry, and today's scholarly readers of Thomas are more likely to seek to persuade us that no more than was Anselm with his "ontological" argument was Thomas seriously intending his "five ways" as formal proofs of God's existence, still less that their success as proofs was foundational for his whole theology. Even if Thomas appears to say that they are so intended, the current fashion is that Thomas does not really mean that the existence of God is rationally demonstrable, for the very simple reason that a God whose existence is demonstrable by rational argument is a God enclosed within the limits of the reason that demonstrates it. To put it very simply (in effect, to put the whole of Kant's *Critique of Pure Reason* simply), if an argument succeeds by the ordinary secular standards of soundness and validity then it fails theologically, because what it succeeds in proving the existence of could not be God; and (to put the whole of Kant's *Critique of Practical Reason* simply) if at the end of some process of thought or experience you truly are led to God, then that process cannot be dependent upon the constraints of valid and sound argument of speculative reason.

More generally put, and in a manner less directly indebted to Kant's philosophical strictures, the theologians' objection to philosophical proofs of God appeals to the unbridgeable gap they claim there to be between the abstract and vacuous God that reason could at best come up with and the God of Christian worship, indeed, the true God of Jewish worship too—whether therefore one is speaking of the Yahweh hidden in a cloud on Mount Sinai whose face even Moses could not see lest he die, or the Christian God who is Father, Son, and Holy Spirit, the Father whose Son became man and, executed on a cross, thereon prayed surrendering his Spirit to his Father, and whose Trinitarian nature is therefore honored every time Christians make the sign of the Cross. This God, then, who is not very God-like at all, who in the end is counterintuitively more like the beached debris of a human shipwreck than a proper God, belongs to a world of thought and spirit immeasurably distant from any possible conclusion reached by means of limited reason's powers of sound and valid proof. So the story goes, implicitly or explicitly, of what would be wrong with the way the *Summa theologiae* sets out, that is, from a starting point in a rational proof of God's existence. It is as if the modern theologian would prefer to say, as was said to the person in Galway who asked the way to Limerick: "Well, if I were you I wouldn't start from here."

Such commentators, therefore, cannot believe that Thomas did "start from here," for they are quite certain that he could not have been so naively "pre-critical" as not to have anticipated Kant's demolition of the pretensions of theoretical reason and of the possibilities of rational proof. Therefore it is suggested, as one recent author has put it, that Thomas was indeed not seriously proposing the "five ways" as proofs of anything, but only as what are rather curiously described as "weakly probable modes of argument, and very attenuated 'showings.'"[8] Of course, this reading of Thomas's position ignores his bald statement that his five ways are five successful strategies of proving there to be a God.[9] I can see absolutely no reason why he should not be taken at his word, although in doing so we are left with a question: *Why* does Thomas "start from here"? Why as a Christian believer start with God and not with Christ? Even more to the point, if you *are* going to start with God, why start with the God who is the "one" and "simple" God of common theism, rather than with the Trinitarian God of Christian faith? Worst of all, if you are going to start with the "oneness" of God rather than with the Trinitarian God of Christian revelation, why start with the *philosophers'* God, and not even with the one God lying to hand in the revelation common to Muslims, Jews, and Christians in their shared Hebrew scriptures? And a question of another sort that I will merely raise and then leave on one side: is it not a paradox that in Thomas's age, rational proofs of God's existence were two-a-penny though hardly anyone was an atheist (and any who were would have been most unlikely to admit it), so that such proofs served little apologetic purpose; whereas in an age of widespread rationalist skepticism like ours, when you might suppose that an argument on common rational terms with an atheist could well serve a purpose, most Christian theologians have abandoned all hope of proof of God and have (in the name of the God of faith) surrendered the territory of reason to "secular" unbelief?

THEOLOGICAL METHOD

To approach anything like adequate answers to these questions we need to set Thomas's theology back into its historical context, which was, to put it only a little too bluntly, a cold war between European Christian and Middle Eastern Islamic military powers, interrupted from time to time by episodes of superheated, if inefficiently conducted, open conflict. On the Christian side the political and military situation was complicated by a bitter and deep theological and ecclesiastical schism between the Western church, more or less submissive to papal authority, and the Eastern Orthodox church, organized on the lines of a quite different and more ecumenical conception of ecclesial authority. Endlessly complex are the criss-crossings of these different conflicts. The internal Christian hostilities were from time to time patched up and thus would reinforce, sometimes they were exacerbated and thus would distract from, resistance to the common external threat of Islam. And of the paradoxical consequences for Thomas the most paradoxical was the tortuous route by which the works of Greek philosophy, especially the texts of Aristotle, found their way into the theological culture of the Christian West. As it happened, Aristotle offered nothing philosophically or theologically appealing to the theologians of the eastern Christian church, who had long had access to his Greek texts, and so it was only toward the very end of his life that Thomas, who knew no Greek, was able to obtain through his Dominican confrere, the western bishop of Athens William of Moerbeke, fresh Latin translations of Aristotle's works made directly from the Greek texts. Until then, Aristotle came to Thomas exclusively from the hands of Islamic philosophers and theologians, translated into Latin from Arabic translations of Persian versions made in Baghdad from original Greek manuscripts. Considering just how alarming the threat of Islamic military power seemed to the Western church, and considering that in Thomas's lifetime that power was secure along the whole of the North African shoreline (approximately fifty percent of the whole Mediterranean perimeter) and deep into African territory inland; and considering that, in addition, the Muslim world possessed a naval force that Venetian sea power was barely able to hold at bay—considering all this, the calm demeanor with which Thomas sifted through the mix of Aristotelian text and Arabic interpretation of it reminds the modern author, old enough to remember it, of what it was like during the days of the Cold War to appeal to the works of Marx and Engels with any sense of intellectual subtlety or discrimination between those authors themselves and what was made of them by the official ideologies of the Soviet Union. The thirteenth-century theological and philosophical world was hardly freer of its

McCarthys than the political world of the United States in the early 1950s.

There is no doubt that Thomas is deeply indebted to Muslim philosophers and theologians, and not merely to them as providers of the texts of Aristotle. Of course, as we have seen, Thomas is far from sympathetic to all the influences that Islamic thought exerted upon Western Christianity—and to be sure, Averroës occupied a position on the far left of the Muslim philosophical world and was as theologically unacceptable to the Islamic mainstream as in a different way he was to Thomas. Nonetheless, Thomas takes what he can from the hands of Ibn Sina, or Avicenna as he was known in the Latin West, and more generally did not doubt that the one God of Islam was none other than the one God to whom Thomas prayed as Father, Son, and Holy Spirit. Thomas knew, of course, that he had to be at odds with Islam, as with Judaism, over the doctrine of the Trinity. But he did not think that on account of the doctrine of the Trinity he had to be at odds with them over the oneness of God. And for that reason Thomas could happily borrow from Muslim and Jewish sources, including such arguments for the existence of God as their philosophical traditions had to offer, because if successful, such arguments would demonstrate the existence of the one God common to all three faith traditions.

As a result, three elements are at play in Thomas's doctrine of God: the possibility of philosophical proofs of the existence of God which, appealing only to reason, are in principle available to all—Christians, Muslims, Jews, even pagans; the doctrine of the divine oneness and simplicity shared in common with Islam and Judaism; and the Trinitarian faith that is distinctively Christian. How, in Thomas's theology, do these three strands of teaching about God relate to one another? Into what sequences, logical and theological, do they fit?

THE NATURE OF PROOF

Most readers of the first part of Thomas's *Summa* are at some point or other troubled by a niggling question of how those "five ways" of article three of question 2 really fit with the doctrine of the Trinitarian God that we find treated at length from questions 27 through 43. And even before that question arises, there is another puzzle: how can the supposed proofs themselves possibly do their work in the absence of an utterly basic necessary condition for any proof whatsoever, a definition of what it is that is to be proved? Yet Thomas does not provide one. He simply asks the question: *Utrum Deus sit*, "whether there is a God," without any discussion at all as to how we would know that what the arguments prove is, after all, "God."

It would of course be easy to suppose that Thomas omitted such a discussion because in an "age of faith" such as people today imagine was Thomas's (more optimistically, one may say, than the evidence fully warrants), precision of definition was unnecessary since everyone knew what God was. After all, if a proof proved the existence of "God" everyone would know whether or not the God thus proved was the God invoked when, for example, they recited the Lord's Prayer. However, even the most cursory glance at the text of those famous proofs raises some doubts as to Thomas's procedures. Within none of the Abrahamic traditions is prayer commonly addressed to the "prime mover" or the "first cause," and on the Christian side, I know of no pious Catholics who, in despair at the failure of Mary to intercede successfully with her Son on their behalf, tried an invocation to the "necessary being" as offering better prospects for intercessory prayer. It is easy to see when we look at those "five ways" why something would appear to be wrong with them if their character as proofs is to be judged by standards of demonstration with which a proof is normally expected to comply. In general, two things might seem wrong with them. First, even if they are valid as inferences go, the criticism can seem plausible that what they prove is hard to recognize as the God of Christian faith and prayer. And second, the risk of producing the sort of bizarrely technical descriptions of God that Thomas's arguments yield might have been reduced if only he had submitted his proofs to the ordinary disciplines of good argument, and had he explained what the definition of God is that a successful proof would show the existence of. Noticeably (indeed, you might almost think willfully so), Thomas fails to do this.

Perhaps even Thomas's severest critics will concede, however, that it is unlikely he had not noticed when in the third part of the *Summa* in his discussion of the nature of Jesus' prayer in the garden of Gethsemane that Jesus is not described as pleading with a "necessary being" that his suffering might be avoided. Thomas, of course, knows that there is a great deal of theological work to be done in order to show that the "necessary being" of the third of the five ways is one and the same existent as the Father to whom in the Spirit Jesus prays in Gethsemane, and Thomas certainly takes his time over it. If anything, his pace is plodding: it takes exactly 146 articles of powerfully concentrated theological argument (in word length that of an average academic monograph of our times) to get him from "necessary being" to the Trinitarian godhead. The movement from the one to the other is governed by a simple and clear distinction of which his critics are too often neglectful or else simply ignorant: "necessary being" and "Father, Son, and Holy Spirit" do not, of course, *mean* the same, and it is not to be supposed that Thomas is unaware of the need for a demonstration that the two descriptions, differing as they do, refer to one and the same existent—it is a poorer theologian than Thomas who cannot see this. But then, it is a poor mathematician who thinks that "square of x" and "square root of x" must mean the same since when $x = 1$ in either case the answer is the same: 1. Hence the plodding pace. Bit by bit, as Thomas progresses through those 146 articles, the plot thickens, the picture sharpens up, and the transition is made: "necessary being" and "Father, Son, and Holy Spirit" are in meaning undoubtedly different. But they are, Thomas shows, and must be, one and the same God.

ONE GOD?

It is here that Thomas's doctrine of God takes what might reasonably be described as a thoroughly Muslim and Jewish turn. Between question 3, in which he discusses the simplicity of God, and question 26, when he discusses God's happiness, Thomas takes not a single step that a Muslim theologian could not take. In particular, the emphasis on the divine simplicity and oneness is so strong that the reader is tempted to think that Thomas is setting himself up for theological disaster as an orthodox Trinitarian Christian. For so emphatic is Thomas that in whichever of two ways you construe the divine oneness—whether as absolute uniqueness (there being but one God, there is no "other"), or as absolute simplicity (there is no number or distinction in God)—either way, all possible hint of multiplicity is driven out. In consequence he appears to leave no room whatsoever for a doctrine of the Trinity: for according to that doctrine there would seem to be required several straightforwardly numerical determinants since Christians say there are three persons in God—not two, not four. It was this perilously "pagan" emphasis on the oneness of God that so troubled the Catholic Rahner along with the Protestant Barth about Thomas's *Summa*: it appeared to Rahner that the core doctrine for Thomas is a belief-neutral doctrine of the one God. For as they understood Thomas, the Christian doctrine of the Trinity would seem to get a look in only after the event, when terms have been settled with that generic oneness.

Rahner has a point. When it comes to his discussion of the doctrine of the Trinity, Thomas is especially careful to ensure that none of the ways that could conflict with or imply qualification of the absoluteness of God's uniqueness and simplicity is defended. But Rahner is also wrong: for Thomas can see no good reason (though he can certainly see some bad ones) why the Christian doctrine of the Trinity should be so understood as to conflict with the oneness and uniqueness of God. Hence Thomas will stand with the Muslim as to the oneness that Islam affirms. But he has no hesitation in departing from the Muslim as to the Trinity that Islam denies.

TWO WAYS OF BEING ONE GOD

What, then, does it mean to say that God is "one"? It means at least two distinguishable things, about which Thomas and Muslims undoubtedly agree. First, Christians and Muslims believe that there is one and only one God—polytheism is ruled out, there is no multiplicity *of* gods.[10] Second, they are agreed that there is no multiplicity *in* God—God is utterly simple, without composition and without distinction.[11] And in conjunction, the two propositions mean that God does not enter into any sort of relations of multiplicity at all. Christians, Muslims, and Jews all agree on ruling out at least that much. When it comes to God there is no counting to do of any kind, and Thomas is not departing from mainstream Christian theologies in any way when, Trinitarian theologian though he is, he says without quali-fication: "There is no number in God." How so?

One might construe one aspect of what Thomas meant by this "uncountability" in God thus. Suppose, in the conduct of some quite lunatic thought-experiment, you were to imagine counting the total number of things that there are, have ever been, and will ever be, and you get to the number *n*. Then I say: "Fine, that's the universe enumerated, but you have left out just one being, the being who made all that vast number of things that is the universe, namely God," and, because you are not an atheist, you agree that this is so. Do you now add God to the list? Does the total number of things that there are now amount to *n* + 1? Emphatically not for Thomas, who says that God's oneness is not such that God is one *more* in any numerable series whatever.[12] And this is because Thomas agrees with the sixth-century Syrian theologian Denys the Areopagite that "there is no kind of thing that God is."[13] Hence, not being any kind of thing, his "not possess[ing] this kind of existence and not that"[14] God cannot be counted in any list of the "everything that is." God's oneness is not the oneness of mathematics, as it would be were I to say of any creaturely oneness: "I'll have one pie for lunch, not two."

It might be objected that the oneness of God must be at least minimally mathematical, for it enters into mathematical relations of negation—"ruling out" particular enumerations must come into it somewhere on any conceivable account of God's oneness. For however transcendent you may say your understanding of God's oneness is, it must entail the denial of a plurality of gods, polytheism. It might seem that there being one and only one God is, after all, just like my one pie for lunch, at least as far as it excludes there being two of them.

The comparison is facile, though revealingly so. For that is exactly how *not* to think of the oneness of God, according to Thomas. It is true that God's being "one" rules out there being two or more Gods. But this is not for the reason that God's oneness excludes plurality in the same way as does the oneness of the just one pie excludes there being two of them. What is wrong with saying that there are two, or twenty-two, gods is not that you have added up the number of gods incorrectly. A plurality of gods is ruled out by God's oneness because God's oneness entails that *counting* is ruled out in every way. That being so, it also follows that in saying that the one and only God is numerably "one," you are no less mistaken than you would be in saying there are many gods. As so often, Thomas is trying to find a way of saying two things that seem each to rule the other out without laying himself open to the charge of attempting to eat his cake and have it. First—concerning God, our grip on ordinary senses of oneness is loosened. Second, if positively God's oneness is beyond our ken, our grip on the divine oneness is not so slack that we cannot know what it excludes.[15]

COUNTING NUMBER IN GOD

But does not Christian Trinitarian doctrine reverse any such agreement with Islam and Judaism in respect of the divine simplicity, as regards, that is, number *in* God? Granted that an agreed understanding of God's oneness rules out polytheism, does not this Trinitarian understanding of the divine oneness introduce multiplicity and counting into God's inner life by means of its differentiation of (three) persons? That Christians do not just happen to say such things, that they are impelled to say them by force of their core doctrine of the Incarnation, can only make matters worse—for the close relationship between the doctrines of the Incarnation and of the Trinity in Christian theology is exactly what a Muslim finds wrong with the doctrine of the Incarnation. The Muslim responds that you cannot consistently say "God is one" in the sense of being utterly simple, and yet maintain that Jesus is the incarnation of one of three persons. In short, Muslim oneness appears to rule out the Christian Trinity. And if, as I have argued, Thomas's oneness of God is consonant with Islam, does not his own doctrine of the divine oneness then seem also to be in conflict with his avowed Trinitarianism, as Rahner supposed?

The Muslim objection to Trinitarian theology—on this point of the logic of theological language—should not be thought justified on the grounds that the doctrine of the Trinity involves a contradiction between belief in a personal God, one and in every way undivided, who is at the same time divided three ways. Of course nothing's being just one in a certain respect can be three in just that same respect. There cannot be more than one Denys Turner, even if, for all I know, there are three people in the Connecticut telephone directory called "Denys Turner"—for of each of *them* too there cannot be more than one. In consequence, it might seem as if in speaking of the Trinity of persons in one Godhead, nothing more is claimed than to say that there are three instantiations of the divine nature in the same way that three persons called "Denys Turner" are three instantiations of (one) human nature. But Thomas is clear: Christians are not saying that just as there are three human beings called "Denys Turner" there are three divine persons, one the Father, another the Son, and the third the Holy Spirit, albeit one in that each is an individual instance of the divine nature. For that is self-evidently tri-theism and is on any account utterly indefensible. So the problem for Christian Trinitarian belief seems to be this: either their saying there are three divine persons is to say that there are three Gods, or else their saying that there is one and only one God entails the denial of the doctrine of the Trinity of persons. Christians cannot eat their cake and have it.

Augustine and Thomas alike saw that what gets in the way of Trinitarian orthodoxy is the troublesome word "person." It is clear why the word is needed theologically, for how else than in and through the vocabulary of personhood is the language of knowledge and love to get any purchase on God, which the scriptures of all three Abrahamic traditions not merely warrant but require? But it is also clear that it is not only for Christian Trinitarians that our ordinary understanding of the word "person" is going to cause theological trouble. Augustine and Thomas knew, and forewarned,[16] that tri-theistic mayhem would ensue from their Trinitarian theologies were they to try to work them through on the basis of the standard meanings of "person" available in their own times, namely the definition of Manlius Boethius of "person" as "an individual substance of a rational nature."[17]

That said, none of the monotheistic traditions can afford to rush too quickly to judgment on this Christian theological predicament. If Jews and Muslims want to speak of God as a "person," then they too must take care lest unacceptable consequences arise within their core doctrine of the divine oneness. For Thomas appears to see that just as indefensible as Christian tri-theism, according to which the Trinitarian persons are three instantiations of the one divine nature, is any account of the oneness of the divine personhood that construes it as the one and only, even as the one and only possible, instantiation of the divine nature. For that, after all, is (in one sense of the expression "the one and only possible") the condition of the last dodo. The last dodo is of course unique. And being the last one of a species that procreates sexually, it is necessarily unique: there *cannot* be any more. But otherwise than on a merely contingent and de facto circumstance such as that of the extinction of all but one dodo, there is no possible sense to the notion that *logically* there can be only one instantiation of a nature. For any nature whatsoever, it is necessarily the case that *logically* it can be replicated.

For that reason it cannot be said of the divine oneness that it is the individuated instance of *any* nature, even of the divine nature: that is what the pseudo-Denys meant when he said that God is not any kind of being, not "one of a kind," as if there were a kind of thing that is a God, and there were just one of them. Thomas is explicit: whereas Socrates's being a man and Socrates's being *this* man cannot be identical because Socrates is but one instance of humanity of which there are many others, God's being God and God's being *this* God are, and must be, identical. Hence, unlike Socrates, it is not and cannot be as just one of a kind, or even as the *only* one of a kind, that God is "one"; but then, neither can it be how the persons of the Trinity are counted as "three." As Thomas said, "there is no counting in God"—not, as we must now understand him to have meant, as thereby somehow prioritizing the oneness of God over the Trinity, but as a condition equally of non-idolatrous talk of the Trinity and of non-idolatrous talk of the divine oneness. There can be no such counting in God *either* way.

The trouble with talk of persons, whether deployed of the divine Trinity or of the divine oneness, is that by force of its natural meaning Trinitarian theology tends to generate either tri-theistic heresy or plain contradictory nonsense, depending on which way you play it, just as, alternatively in the Jewish and Muslim traditions, the divine oneness generates an idolatrous conception of God as just a special case of an individuated nature where one individual exhausts all that nature's possibilities. Christianity, Islam, and Judaism are equally vulnerable to their respective forms of idolatry. And Thomas knows that such a notion cannot be what Jews, Christians, or Muslims teach about the divine oneness. Hence, given the requirements of the respective scriptural authorities in all three traditions that we by right should speak of the "personal" character of God, we have to ask how much of that natural meaning of "person" can survive its transference upon the divine being. Or, to turn the problem around the other way (it amounts to the same problem) when it comes to the personhood of God, what can be left of our secular notions of *either* oneness *or* threeness?

Given his warnings about the theological trouble caused by a naive employment of the language of "persons," Augustine, with Thomas following close behind, resorted to the admittedly more abstract, and certainly humanly less appealing, category of divine relations; not, be it known, to relations *of* or *between* divine persons, but to persons as being *nothing but* relations. That, of course, is hard talk, and the language twists and bends under the pressure of having to say not that the Father generates the Son, but is *the generating of the Son*; not that the Son is *what* is generated by the Father, but is *the being generated by the Father*; and even more awkwardly, not that the Holy Spirit is *what* is "breathed forth" or "spirated" by the Father through the Son, but is *the being spirated by the Father through the Son*. There is nothing here but relatings, no somewhats doing the relating. The language strains. But bent and twisted as the language is, does it break?

Here is an analogy that, like all such analogies, does some good explanatory work so long as it is not thought to do all of it. There is one and only one highway known as Interstate 95. But it has two directions: one south from Maine to Florida, the other north from

Florida to Maine. The direction north is of course really distinct from the direction south, as anyone knows who has entered I-95 in the wrong direction a long way from the next exit. And yet both are really identical with the one and only I-95. In this case, we are under no temptation to say that the difference between the direction north and the direction south is just a driver's point of view, because if you are mistakenly traveling to Houlton in Maine when you want to get to Miami in Florida it is the *direction* of your car you need to change; merely changing your "point of view" on the matter will do nothing to alter your destination. As a Christian theologian might analogously say, "modalism" fails to meet the case; the distinction of persons is real, not notional, not just a fictional mode created by our limited understanding with no corresponding reality in God. But equally, in the case of I-95, we are under no temptation to say that there are three I-95s—the road north, the road south, and the road that north and south are the two directions of. For the relations of northbound and southbound directions are not only really distinct from one another, but also really identical with one and the same I-95. So we might say tritheism is not entailed on this analogy: there is one and only one highway constituted by three really distinct relations.

Of course this is at best a partial analogy, one designed to allay some initial suspicions concerning the logical consistency of Trinitarian orthodoxy with a resolute defense of the oneness of God. But that the analogy at best limps is shown by the fact that whereas the two directions, north to Maine and south to Florida, are real *relations*, and are really distinct from each other as relations, by contrast, the tarmac-covered strip is a real *entity* and is distinct from the directions north and south, not as they are distinct from one another, but only as in general any entity is distinct from any of the relations in which it stands. And if you were to press this analogy on the doctrine of the Trinity too far, you might indeed avoid modalism and tri-theism, but you would certainly get out of it some form of heterodox subordinationism—the doctrine that the Father is existentially prior to the Son and the Holy Spirit, just as I-95 as entity is existentially prior to the relations that depend on it. And for Christians, as Thomas knows, Nicaean orthodoxy plainly rules that out.

In consequence, Thomas believes that the conciliar traditions leave no option other than to say that Father, Son, and Holy Spirit are three "relatednesses," which is where, in the end, he must leave it. It is hardly the most appealing conclusion to a doctrine of God; there is something more than a little artificially strained about the language here, and one may well share Rahner's impression that in Thomas's Trinitarian theology the constraints of technical accuracy rather take over the interests of devotion and prayer. And yet, however strange such talk may seem, Thomas will put it that way because only on such terms can it be said without gross inconsistency both that the three persons are really distinct from one another, while at the same time really identical with the one, undivided Godhead. In defense of Thomas, one may legitimately say that his responsibility as a theologian is not the preacher's; his work is not to inspire devotion but to provide a framework of limits, conceptual and doctrinal, within which alone true Trinitarian piety may be practiced or preached. Thomas regards it as his specific responsibility to ensure that pious devotion lapses neither into the banality of a practical tri-theism, nor into sophisticated subjectivism that reductively plays down the Trinitarian distinctions to the level of a mere Christian *façon de parler*. For Thomas, the doctrine of the Trinity is not incoherent nonsense. Neither is it a marginal Christian add-on to a common doctrine of God. It is the central Christian mystery, just as the sign of the Cross is the central Christian practice of it in prayer, invoking the inner life of the Godhead as revealed in the pathetic death-throes of a humiliated and utterly defeated man. Later, in Part Three of the *Summa*, Thomas fills in that narrative by showing how the Cross is the supreme revelation of the Trinity. But here in Part One he is not to be reproved for having done something else— namely, to have provided the doctrinal terms of reference within which alone that narrative can be told in its revealing truth. Whatever else, then, that narrative may tell, it narrates the untellable mystery of God.

And therein lies the point. If, under the pressure of Christian belief in the doctrines of Trinity and Incarnation, the meanings of "person" and of "threeness" migrate off the semantic map of our secular vocabularies, so also does the "oneness" that Thomas shares with the Muslims and Jews. For, as we have seen, the oneness of the one personal God of questions 3 through 26 of Thomas's

Summa cannot be understood in terms of the one and only instance of the divine nature, not any more than the persons of the Trinity can be understood as three instances of it. So the point is that all the way through the *whole* doctrine of God, whether in that part of it in which the one God beyond number is emphasized, or in that part of it in which the threeness of God beyond counting is emphasized, the vocabulary available to us is put under the same intolerable pressure because the meanings required—whether of "person," of "threeness," or of "oneness"—have all migrated theologically off the same semantic map, and to the same extent.

To which conclusion one might supply this addendum, which is that it is as easy for Christians as it is for Muslims and Jews to forget that all three are plunged headlong theologically into the same utter unknowability of the one true God. After all, it was for want of understanding the point of Thomas's demonstration that whichever way you conceive of God, whether as one or three, God is unutterable mystery, that the Catholic Jesuit theologian Rahner thought that Thomas had in some way robbed the Christian doctrine of God of its mystical character through its prioritization of the divine oneness over its Trinitarian nature. That is as much as to say that, for Rahner, the mystery of the divine oneness is somehow less intense than that of the divine Trinity, as if the oneness of God were easier to get into your head than the Trinity. It is not. Christian Trinitarianism does not rock a unitarian boat that would otherwise be plain sailing for Jews and Muslims. Not for Thomas. Whether by God's oneness or God's threeness, we are in equal measures theologically benighted, or, as one might more positively put it, believers of all three faith traditions are thereby invited into a participation in love with the same unknowable, indescribable Godhead.

THE PROOFS REVISITED

If in this way the two discussions of God in the *Summa theologiae*—that on the divine oneness from questions 3 through 26, and that on the divine Trinity from question 27 through 43—fit into a sort of seamless continuity, is it possible to fit into that same stream of continuity the third element, that awkward question 2 article 3 in which, as I maintain, Thomas believes he has five times proved by reason alone the existence of God? Many are unable to see how it may be done.

The answer is that Thomas's rational proofs will fit into that sequence only if we turn away from the anachronistic dictates of Enlightenment and post-Kantian conceptions of reason, and go back to that account of reason that we tried to track down in Chapters 2 and 3. We must do this because if to understand the formal structure of Thomas's arguments requires our moving away from the Kantian confinement of reason to the world of space and time, it might seem as if we may do so only on some conception of reason that spontaneously escapes the limits of our sense knowledge, as if capable of some kind of supra-rational, perhaps intuitive, knowledge of the transcendent. This is of course exactly how Kant himself construed the options, and the theologians have generally followed him since. For given the impossibility of some conception of reason that spontaneously escapes the limits of sense, capable of supra-rational, perhaps intuitive, knowledge of the transcendent, the remaining alternative is a conception of speculative reason that not only (as in Thomas) arises from and is oriented toward, but (unlike Thomas) is constrained by and cannot break through, the bounds of sense. And so, being contained within the boundaries of spatio-temporal experience, speculative reason must be denied *all* access to the transcendent.

Not so for Thomas, as we saw in the last chapter. If we know God "rationally" it is as rational *animals* that we do so, and not as quasi-angelic hybrids. The most cursory glance at those five ways makes the point clearly enough. Each begins from basic human, earthbound experience—typically Thomas avoids illustrative examples and sticks with generalities: we observe material objects to be set in motion, we observe one thing to cause change in another, we observe things to come into existence and pass out of it again, and so on. We, however, might fairly fill out his abstractions: a rock falling down a hill in a landslide will do to launch the "proof from motion"; a stonemason chipping a corbel for Notre Dame cathedral will do to get off the ground the proof from "efficient causality"; a daffodil blooming, fading, and dying would open up the third argument from "contingency"; one corbel being better than another is material enough for the fourth way; and an apple seed's meeting one's expectations of its becoming a tree will do for the fifth. The arguments for God are rational because they make their way to God beginning from the world human beings inhabit as animals and interrogate rationally. Thomas does it in one way, as we will see. In a very different—direct, dialogical—rhetorical style, Augustine does so, too:

And what is this God? I asked the earth, and it answered, "I am not he"; and everything in the earth made the same confession. I asked the sea and the deeps and the creeping things, and they replied, "We are not your God; seek above us." I asked the fleeting winds, and the whole air with its inhabitants answered, "Anaximenes was deceived; I am not God." I asked the heavens, the sun, moon, and stars; and they answered, "Neither are we the God whom you seek." And I replied to all these things which stand around the door of my flesh: "You have told me about my God, that you are not he. Tell me something about him." And with a loud voice they all cried out, "He made us." My question had come from my observation of them, and their reply came from their beauty of order . . . all these messengers of the senses report the answers of heaven and earth and all the things therein, who said, "We are not God, but he made us." My inner man knew these things through the ministry of the outer man, and I, the inner man, knew all this—I, in the highest part of my soul,[18] through the senses of my body. I asked the whole frame of earth about my God, and it answered, "I am not he, but he made me."[19]

What for Augustine is constructed in the form of a dialogical interrogation of the world, for Thomas takes the form of the explanatory causal question. The stone rolls down the hill in an avalanche: "How come?" The stonemason carves a corbel: "What does it take to do that?" The daffodil dies: "On account of what does it come into existence and then go out of it? Could everything be like that?" Today questions like these have answers, usually provided by the relevant form of scientific knowledge, though in Thomas's time causal questions were thought to be more complex and differentiated in character than the constructively simplified mathematically quantifiable causal question of modern science. In any case, the character of the argument-form of Thomas's five ways, and the manner in which Thomas's causal interrogations of the material world differ from those of modern science, are aptly illustrated by the double question asked about the daffodil. For clearly, in the modern sense of the word, the first half of that double question is "scientific": "On account of what does the daffodil come into existence and then pass out of it?" The question is botanical, and as far as I know the answer has something to do with the nature of chlorophyll, and if you know your botany you can give a complete answer to it. But no amount of botanical knowledge can begin to answer the second half of the question, which, as to the daffodil's coming into existence and passing out of it, asks, "Could everything be like that?" It is not only that the question is not botanical. It is not even scientific, though clearly it is causal.

At this point we are reminded by how far today we are afflicted by a certain kind of provinciality of mind, a reductivist mentality that can conceive of a question's being worth asking only if we know in advance some routine procedures guaranteed to provide intelligible answers to it. It is indeed an exceedingly curious reversal of commonsense intellectual priorities that a pre-formed procedure for answering questions should be allowed to dictate the legitimacy of the questions that may be asked. Thomas is intellectually braver, even perhaps more irresponsible: there are for him questions that have to be asked, but cannot be answered. He is prepared to ask the question: Could everything's being like the daffodil—"contingent" is his word for the fragility of existence— be just a fact, a sort of brute fact, requiring no further explanation? Or must everything's being like that demand an explanation, a cause, whose hold on existence does not need to be accounted for?—his word for such a mode of existence being "necessary." Thomas's answer to that last question is in the affirmative: it has to be the case that some necessary being exists, otherwise the existence of all the contingent beings that there are is impossible to account for.

Though a concerted defense of Thomas's five ways has no place in a book written to our purposes, it is worthwhile pausing to consider a feature of the third of these arguments, this so-called argument from "contingency" and "necessity" that has puzzled many modern philosophers. As the argument is commonly read today, it seems to be so obviously invalid that it is hard to credit

Thomas, who knows his logic as few theologians before or since seem to, with so poor a standard of argument, an argument that, it is thought by his critics, goes like this. Some things—our daffodil—are contingent, that is to say, they come into existence, and go out of existence, in time, not necessarily because anything causes them to do so by violent intervention, but simply because they would anyway, for that is the way at least some things are: they have a lifespan. Now were everything to be in that way contingent, then at some time there would be nothing; and if at any time there had been nothing, then there would be nothing now. But it is false that there is nothing now. Therefore, not everything can be contingent. At least something must be a necessary being, that is, something must be such as cannot in its nature come and go, it must be such that it cannot not be. And a necessary being would either be God or else would be such as only God can cause to exist. Either way, if anything exists now, and it does, then God exists. So God exists.

This argument is routinely accused by modern logicians of committing what is called the "fallacy of the quantifier shift," the fallacy that you commit when, for example, you infer from the proposition "every husband is married to some wife" that "there is some wife (poor thing) that every husband is married to." Thomas's argument, it is said, would appear to commit this fallacy, because it seems to rely on the inference that if each thing were such as came into existence in time and passed out of it in time then the impossible conclusion follows that at some time nothing would have existed—impossible, because were that so, there would be nothing now, which there is. Now this line of argument is said to be obviously invalid, because (so it is argued) what is a property of each and every thing severally in a totality must be a property of that totality itself. There is therefore no reason why there could not be an infinitely long chain of contingent causes and effects such that at no time was there nothing at all—in which case the sum total of everything would be a contingent totality requiring nothing further for its existence than the contingent existence of its constituent causes and effects. Nor is there any reason to require a non-contingent cause of there being such a chain of contingent causes. After all, we can easily imagine the universe to be an infinitely long rope made up by the entwining of an infinite number of overlapping threads of finite length. Just because each of its threads has a beginning and an end it does not follow that the rope does. Thomas's argument, then, trips up on the simplest of logical obstacles. So it is argued, for example, by Anthony Kenny.[20]

Objections of this kind to the validity of the third way are so widespread, and agreed to be so conclusive, that it is surprising that Thomas's reputation has not suffered more than it has upon the observation that one of his most famous arguments commits a fallacy that every freshman undergraduate learns not to commit no later than by their second lecture in Logic 101. It would be even more surprising, however, if the accusation of the Quantifier Shift fallacy were justified of this third of Thomas's arguments when it is plain that in his exposition of each of the other four arguments Thomas is careful to avoid just that mistake. Nowhere does he ever construct an argument of the form: every chain of causes must stop somewhere, therefore there is somewhere where every chain of causes must stop. Thomas needs no critic to inform him that an argument for the existence of God that relies on so plainly invalid an inference must be rejected. The argument of the third way is no different in this respect.

The criticism of that argument is, of course, misplaced. The third way does not in fact rely upon demonstrating that there could not be a contingent world infinite in duration or that such a world must at some time have not existed. On the contrary, as we will see in the next chapter, Thomas was at odds with almost all of his contemporaries in believing that theoretically the created world could have been such a totality and that it could have been eternal (although for reasons of faith he believes it is in fact temporarily finite). The third way, rather, notes that there might have been a sum total of contingent things existing without beginning or end, each member of which has a finite life span, but that there should be such a world at all is possible only if not everything is thus contingent. For the existence of such a contingent totality depends upon the existence of some being not itself contingent—otherwise then there would be nothing at all.

Now when it comes to fallacies in logic, every bit as erroneous as the Quantifier Shift fallacy, of which Thomas cannot fairly be accused, is the Fallacy of Composition, of which some of the critics of the third way fall foul. For it is the fallacy of that name to suppose that the property of every member of a totality is necessarily a property of the totality itself. Every member of a crowd of rioting looters may well be in possession of two legs. But a rioting crowd of two-legged people is not the same as, and cannot entail the existence of, a rioting two-legged crowd. Thomas's argument is that even if every constituent element of the created universe is a contingent being, and so can come into existence and go out of existence in time, it could not be the case that a contingent totality is all that there is. On the contrary, it follows that something or other must be not contingent. For if there were nothing but that contingent totality, then that *totality* as such must at some time not have existed, and so could not now exist. In that case necessarily there would be nothing now. But since there is something now it follows that not everything is contingent and that something must exist that cannot just come and go, cannot itself be a contingent member of the contingent universe, a necessary being, therefore, that either is, or is caused by, God.

The difference between the one (invalid) reading of the third way and the other (valid) reading of it is aptly illustrated by the famous first "shewing" of the fourteenth-century anchoress Julian of Norwich in her *Revelation of Love*, in which she is shown a "little thing the quantity of a haselnot." In response to her request to know what it was, she is told that it is "all that is made." It is the lot, the totality. But the totality is not just there: it is "made," she says. She is struck by how small it is, how tenuous its hold is on existence, thinking that it "might sodenly have fallen to nought for litelnes." Upon which she is told that it "lasteth and ever shall, for God loveth it . . ."[21] What is noticeable is that Julian's understanding is brought not by some poet's route, as Gerard Manley Hopkins might be led, from the individuation of some particular "litel thing" to God, but, like Thomas, by the metaphysician's route, which extends from the sheer contingency of "*all* that is made," which is but a "haselnot" teetering on the edge of nothingness, to the love that alone holds it all in existence over against the "nought" into which it "might sodenly have fallen." For Thomas it is not the "thisness" of particular contingent things that leads to God, but the impossibility of the whole lot accounting for its existence when there might have been nothing at all, that draws the mind to the being who holds it in existence by an act of creating will, that is, by the power of love.

Of each and every thing, therefore, it is possible that it is contingent. And your argument does not get you to a necessary being—ultimately to God—simply by tracing through the contingency of each and every contingent being to its cause, because for each and every contingent being there can be a contingent cause just as, again, a single rope can stretch infinitely into the distance, composed of endlessly overlapping strands of finite length. But as to the rope's contingency, its existence is a possibility only if, taken as a whole, it is, as Julian puts it, "all that is *made*." For if it were not made—that is to say, if it were not the creature of a being not itself contingent—then now there would be that "nought" that, even as it exists, the "haselnot" teeters on the edge of and is held back from only by the love that made it.

Upon encountering this argument, the reader may well ask of it what could possibly be meant by a "necessary being," a being which absolutely could not not be? Suppose we grant, as Thomas believes it to be, that the existential fragility of everything has to be accounted for otherwise than in terms of a self-sustaining, self-explaining fact, in terms, therefore, of something or other whose existence is "necessary," what we know about such a being is that we could not know what it is. We are animals, what we know is the fragility of things, that is our familiar world, ours are the animal experiences of life precariously poised between birth and death. For us life is like the act of walking in Schopenhauer's description of it as the sustained condition of only just not falling flat on your face. That existential fragility runs right through everything else that exists, through each thing severally and everything in totality, especially the latter. For I suspect that for Thomas the mind begins to think theologically when the thought occurs that there might have been nothing at all, and a dormant question is aroused to active enquiry: "Why is there *anything*, why not nothing at all?" And that question is, for Thomas, characteristically rational. In fact our being rational is principally shown in our power to transcend that universal contingency, a transcendence that lies in the very fact that we *can* submit that contingency itself, as a general condition of our world, to interrogation. Indeed, there is more to it than that: for Thomas it has to do with the nature of rationality itself that the question "How come there is anything at all?" *demands* to be asked.

We can ask that question; indeed, to refuse to do so is irrational. The ability to do so is what the word "rational" names, a power to question that is also an obligation. But there is no answer to be found within the things that exist as to why there is not nothing rather than something, not nothing rather than *any*thing at all. All those things that "stand around the door" of Augustine's flesh can know that they are made. But that "out of nothing," that "rather than" in the expression "that there is something rather than nothing," utterly defeats the mind's capacity to comprehend. For as Thomas makes clear, the making that is "out of nothing" is not to be thought of as if there were some soupy kind of undifferentiated lawless stuff called "nothing" out of which what there is was made by some explanatory causal process. The "nothing," he explains, governs the "out of," so as to say: there is a making here, but it is a making with no "out of" at all, no process, no antecedent conditions, no "random fluctuations in a vacuum," no explanatory law of emergence, and, there being nothing for the "something" to be "out of," there can be no physics, not yet, for there is nothing yet for physics to get an explanatory grip on: "Big bang" is an explanation of the natural laws governing the something that exists. It is not an explanation of how come there is anything for those physical laws to be true of. The head spins, because here too, in a movement of convergence upon the doctrines of the divine oneness and of the divine Trinity, meaning has once again migrated off the semantic map, for we know that the question we must ask we cannot know the meaning of the answer to. Here in the apotheosis of reason is its chief instrument, language, finally defeated. And there, where the mind reaches the end of its tether, is, as Thomas says simply, "what all people refer to when they speak of God." Here, then, is no question-stopping, intelligible, answer. Here is an answer-stopping question, "Why anything?" At the end of its tether, the human mind, in its characteristically rational modality of interrogating the world, finally falls silent before the mystery of the unknowable Godhead, the same unknowable God who is one beyond all counting, three beyond all plurality. Nor even here is reason at some ultimate cognitive disadvantage to faith, as if reason's failure of knowledge is to be estimated by the degree to which it falls short of faith's success. Indeed, for Thomas, as the degrees of divine darkness rank, faith's is the deeper. Let us remind ourselves that, for Thomas, "in this life we do not know what God is, even by the grace of faith. Hence, by grace we are made one with God as to somewhat unknown to us." And so it is that although reason cannot know this for itself, its arguments have drawn it into the same territory of transcendent mystery that faith inhabits knowingly and as a matter of course. It is, for Thomas, by faith alone that we know that reason, at the end of its tether, has stepped across the boundary of knowledge into the land of unknowing that is God. It is by faith alone that we know that the transcendent mystery of God is a mystery of love. And as we will see in the next chapter, it is by faith alone that we know ourselves to have been invited to share in that unknowable mystery of love that is God.

FIVE

Friendship and Grace

Given the prevailing caricature of the man whose physiognomy consisted of nothing but an oversize cerebellum, the chances are exceedingly low of anyone guessing Thomas to have been the author of the following sensitively practical reflections on how to cope with sadness. First, he says, you should cry, both tears and groans, though you might also try talk therapy. Above all, no stiff upper lip:

> First of all, because anything that is causing you inner hurt afflicts you all the more for being contained, as the mind becomes fixated upon it. But when it is let out it is in a certain degree dissipated and the inner sadness to that extent diminished. For this reason when people are afflicted by

sadness and vent it with tears and groans, or even tell of it in words, the sadness decreases. A second reason is that human beings always get some pleasure out of acting appropriately, and weeping and groaning is just what the person who is sad and doleful should be doing. Being in this sort of way appropriate behavior it gives a certain kind of mitigating pleasure that reduces the sadness.[1]

Next, if sad, count on your friends.[2] That is the natural thing to do. One reason, the weaker of two, he says, is that if a friend shares your sadness it will seem as if the burden of it is lightened by virtue of her carrying part of it for you. But the better reason is that being prepared to share a friend's sadness and console him is a way of showing love for him, and the perception of the love thus shown to him by a friend gives the sort of pleasure that alleviates the sadness. You could also, of course, try contemplative prayer, if, like Thomas, you find contemplation to be the most intense of all pleasures,[3] the point being that it is always some kind of pleasure that drives sadness away. If, however, weeping, groaning, therapeutic talk, prayer, and friends all fail to cheer you up, take a hot bath and get a good night's sleep.[4] Thus all-brain Thomas.

Thomas clearly values friendship, personally. You can tell from this sort of practical advice that he has had good experience of friendship, and his experience flows into the way in which he talks about it theologically. Almost uniquely among theologians of his time⁵ his core model of Christian love, *caritas*, is not that of the erotic, *amor*, but that of friendship, *amicitia*. Given the popularity within the monastic traditions, and especially among Cistercians, of that most erotic of all biblical texts, the *Song of Songs*, and given that Thomas's last illness was spent in the Cistercian monastery of Fossanova where he died, it is not altogether surprising that the story gained some credence of Thomas's having dictated a commentary on the *Song* on his deathbed in gratitude for the monks' hospitality. Nonetheless, the legend is implausible, and no textual evidence of such a commentary has ever come to light.

For the *Song* is not Thomas's style.⁶ In fact, on one of the few occasions when he is presented with having to make the choice between erotic love and the love of friendship as a model for the divine love, Thomas makes his preference plain. In chapter 4 of his *Divine Names* the pseudo-Denys apologizes for his use of the vulgar and pagan language of *eros* in order to speak both of God's love of creation and of creation's return of love to God. In his defense, however, he comments that though historically *eros* has indeed had a principally pagan meaning (he is thinking, no doubt, of Plato's *Symposium* and of his *Phaedrus*, but also of erotic pagan priestly rites), nonetheless, he claims (most implausibly) that within the biblical traditions the more distinctively Christian understanding of love as *agape* or charity has coincided with *eros*, and the pagan overtones of the latter elided. Thomas in his commentary on this text takes note, nods in apparent approval, at the same time subtly reversing the emphasis: insofar as *amor* translates the Greek *eros*, he says, it is reducible to *dilectio*, translating the Greek *agape*.[7] It is clear that in terms of emphasis both literary and theological, it is the language of friendship that figures the more prominently for Thomas. Correspondingly, he appears not to share the otherwise almost universal medieval preference for the *Song of Songs* as a biblical source for his doctrine of Christian love.

As far as his model of Christian love is concerned, it is, then, friendship that wins the day for Thomas. Here again, it is the influence of Aristotle that is nearer to the surface than either Plato or the *Song*. Remarkably, there is a theological topic in the *Summa*, but also in his lectures on John's gospel, which maps closely on to an ethical topic in Aristotle. Noting in his *Nicomachean Ethics* that the love of friends is possible only on the basis of a fundamental equality of status between them, Aristotle concludes that there cannot properly speaking be friendship between a Greek master and a barbarian slave, at any rate as such—though he adds that insofar as master and slave are able to relate to each other simply as human, friendship is possible.[8] This latter qualification of what otherwise would be a piece of unqualified xenophobic snobbery plays straight into Thomas's theological hands, immediately calling to mind its reversal in Jesus' last discourse, as reported in the gospel of John. There Jesus tells his disciples: "I do not call you servants any more, because a servant does not know his master's business; I call you friends, because I have made known to you everything I have learned from my father" (John 15:15).

In his lecture on this passage Thomas seizes the opportunity to agree with Aristotle just as he turns him on his head. Of course, as between God and human beings there can be no natural relations of friendship, because the inequality between God and creatures is as radical as any can be. It is infinite, that is, incalculable. And it is worth noting that, for Thomas, this inequality is not in the first place the result of the Fall. The inequality between creature and Creator is even more "original" than any caused by original sin, and is such that God and human creatures cannot naturally share anything, above all they cannot share a common life. For slaves may serve the life of their masters in the role of "instrumental cause," like a living tool, slaves being the hammers and saws and lifting gear of the Greek economy and polity. But even living tools cannot share the life of their masters as friends do, who "know [one another's] business," its *ratio*. Thus far, then, Aristotle is right: friendship is possible only insofar as there is basic equality of status. Therefore, if Jesus proclaims that now his disciples are to be called his "friends," this can be only because in some way the radical inequality of Creator and creature has been overcome, because there is, as it were, a *new* creation, establishing a new order of relationship between God and human beings. Since, however, there is no possibility of that inequality being leveled by action on the part of the creature, it must be that the initiative has been taken on the part of God, entirely gratuitously, to make human creatures thus equal to the divine, so that friendship becomes a possibility between them. Or, as Thomas puts it in the

Summa, solus Deus deificat, "only God can make us godlike."⁹ Thus, from a comment typical of Aristotle's chauvinistic Greek *hauteur*, Thomas provides the foundations of his doctrine of grace, the entirely free gift of friendship with God, the life of God shared in friendship with human beings.¹⁰

It is this model, moreover, that provides some of the crucial distinctions in Thomas's doctrine of grace. There is of course the grace that comes with and within the friendship that obtains between God and creatures, the grace that flows from and sustains that friendship over time in growing intimacy, "sanctifying grace," as Thomas calls it, the grace that actually transforms our lives, as all friendships do.¹¹ But prior to that there is the grace of justification itself, that is to say, the instantaneous, one-off foundational act of grace that is the originating gift of friendship, within the "economy" of which alone the work of grace that sanctifies us can operate. That originating gift of friendship, of course, is the Incarnation, God's becoming a human being so that, in Christ, human beings may become God. This is the primordial work of Christ, the source of all grace. And for us it is absolutely necessary work. For only action that is already the work of grace can enable us to merit the grace that makes us holy: ungraced free human agency is powerless to merit the grace of justification; and only the grace of justification can merit the grace of sanctification. Nonetheless, human freedom and grace mutually interact, and Thomas explains how this gift of initial justification works in dialogical partnership with the free consent of the human will, and only so. For, it is as obvious to him as it is to anyone, friends *choose* one another, freely on the part of both:

> Since God acts upon each thing in accordance with its own manner of acting . . . so therefore [God] causes justification in human beings in harmony with the human condition. It belongs to human beings, then, that they possess by nature freedom of choice. Hence, in a person who has its use there is no action of God productive of justification without the movement of that free choice: rather God infuses the gift of the grace of justification in such a way that at the same time he moves free choice to accept that gift of grace, at any rate in those who are capable of [such free agency].[12]

"Now I call you friends," says Jesus, and it is from this offer of friendship that the whole doctrine of grace evolves, as also the complexity and precision with which Thomas interlaces the elements of irresistibility on the side of grace and freedom of choice on the side of the human. At one point Thomas says that grace does its work "infallibly" but not "coercively,"[13] and he seems to mean that the work of grace cannot fail, because grace does *all* the work and its efficacy depends on only such conditions obtaining as it effects for itself: for "no pre-condition of God's infusing the soul with grace is required other than such as God himself brings about."[14] While it is true, then, that the grace, whether of justification or of sanctification, cannot do its work without the free consent of the human will, that free consent is itself the work of grace. Therefore, because there are no conditions not of grace's making to impede its work, the action of grace is "infallible." And yet because the free consent of the human will is precisely what grace does bring about, its action is not "coercive." As in another context Dante had Piccarda in Paradise say: "en la sua volontade e nostra pace."[15] It is in the divine will that is our peace, because it is in the divine will that is grace that our free consent to it is itself grounded. The very freedom of our consent to grace is itself the work of the grace it consents to.

It is here that we encounter the center of gravity of Thomas's mind, in the paradox that the divine will for human beings is infallible, being dependent only on a free consent to it that that divine will itself creates. It is clear that Thomas is constrained to speak thus paradoxically, because his central model for the work of grace is that of friendship. On one side that friendship between God and creatures can only be pure gift. Since it cannot be deserved, its being undeserved is no impediment to its being received any more than it is an impediment to its being offered. On the other side, it can be friendship that is offered only if the free choice of it comes with the offer. Hence, so that that offer of friendship is unimpeded by any conditions on the human side, God has no alternative but to build freedom on the human side into the gift itself as the condition of its reception. Therefore if it is true that *all* the work is the work of grace, including the freedom of consent to it that is its condition, it is just as true that *all* the work is done by human free choice, for that is precisely what grace creates in us. Not otherwise than if both of these propositions are true would it be possible to speak of friendship between God and human beings. For friendship is inconceivable without that equality and reciprocity.

"Infallibly" but not "coercively" God effects the work of our salvation through the offer of the shared life of friends: that is all that grace is, utterly irresistible, utterly free, a friendship infallibly brought about by means of human free choice enabled to share in the divine life itself. For whom is that a paradox? Today's theologians are caused much anxious frenzy of mind by such words. By contrast Thomas is calm. Why is he so unfazed? And why are we so disturbed? The answer to the first is that Thomas understands love. The answer to the second is that we do not.

GRACE AND FREEDOM

Walking up Wall Street in New Haven toward Yale University's Hall of Graduate Studies, I told my friend Philip McCosker of a former colleague in Cambridge University who had explained how Catholic and Protestant theologies may be distinguished. "Protestant theologies are 'either/or,'" he had said. "Catholic theologies are 'both/and.'" "That can't be right," replied Philip (like me, a Catholic). "Because if 'either/or' and 'both/and' are mutually exclusive alternatives that means that you have to choose one or the other and that in turn means that Protestant 'either/or' wins. Take your pick: either both/and or either/or." And so between us we agreed that true Catholic theology must be both "either/or" and "both/and," so that Catholic "both/and" wins the day over Protestant "either/or."[16] At any rate, true or not of Catholic and Protestant theological styles, it seemed to us at the time to be true enough of the theology of Thomas, though, as we will see, this still does not get Thomas quite right. What we can say at this stage is that Thomas's theology is inclusive of "either/or." Opposed are those theologies which are exclusive of "both/and."

The assumption prevailing in our times that grace as infallibly effective must in the nature of its infallibility rule out the freedom of the will—or vice-versa—does not occur to Thomas, or to Augustine, though it did occur to Calvin who, like Thomas, borrowed from Augustine the teaching that the grace of predestination is irresistible. We saw Thomas to say—in view of later theological developments it might seem somewhat artlessly—that grace succeeds without fail but not by force, and that what in God is the unimpeded action of grace is in the human will the freedom that grace elicits: they are one and the same reality, seen, as it were, from opposite ends. As we have seen, it is grace that causes the free consent that is the condition of its own effectiveness. And this account seems to some to be so naively innocent of the contradiction it might seem to fall into that they propose an alternative account, known in our times (in its connection with the problem of evil) as the "free will defense," the mirror-image reversal of Calvinist determinism.

The problem to which the free-will defense is proposed as a solution is this, simply put: the God of Christian faith and belief, who is said to be all good, and cannot will evil, who is said to be all-powerful and can do anything that it is possible to describe, cannot consistently be so characterized, given the existence of evil, in particular of sin, in the world that is God's creature. For if God is all good, then he cannot will evil; and if he is all powerful then he can will a world without it. Therefore, either God could prevent evil and does not will to do so and is not all good; or God is all good and would prevent evil if he could, but cannot, and so is not all powerful; or else evil is not something real, not something of which there needs to be a cause either on the divine or human sides of the equation. Since the third possibility is manifestly false—for who can deny that the evil of sinful deeds is real?—it follows that God is either evil and fails to prevent sin though he could; or else God is good and fails to prevent sin because he cannot.

The most common form of rebuttal of this argument by dilemma is to concede that a world without sin is certainly describable—for human beings, being free agents, it is not impossible, however low the probability of it, that even extended over a very long period of time no human agent should have freely chosen to perform even a single sinful act. That said (the argument goes on) it is nonetheless impossible that God should have *created* such a world. For were God to bring about a sinless world, its not being sinful would be, *could* be, the consequence only of God's agency

ruling out human free choice. Such a world would be sinless therefore only because inhabited not by humans but by automata,
puppets on strings manipulated by God. For the human actions
that God causes to be done cannot, by virtue of God's causing
them, be free human actions, that human action of mine being
free of which I alone am the cause, and not God. Therefore, for
the free-will defender, Thomas's affirmation of the infallibility of
grace and his denial of its being a form of coercion collapse into
contradiction: insofar as God infallibly causes it, an action cannot
be free, it *is* coerced. Insofar as it is free, God cannot be the
cause of it. Unfailingly efficacious grace and human freedom are
mutually exclusive, either the one or the other.

Thomas clearly thinks otherwise. Nor does he simply assume
otherwise. In fact, in the course of understanding why Thomas
firmly rejects the equivalents in his time of the free-will defense
we are brought back to one of the reasons why Thomas began his
principal systematic works with the doctrine of God itself. For
what to Thomas seems so deeply wrong, and perhaps even shockingly so, with all such argument strategies as that of the free-will
defense is the ill-considered nature of its conception of God, most
especially in its construction of God's relationship to human
agency. One can begin to see why, for Thomas, the theological
learning curve needs to start where it does in the *Summa*, given the
sort of erroneous consequences that, in his view, ensue from the
failure to get things right from the outset in the doctrines of God
and of creation.

The proposition that God's agency *could* stand in a disjunctively exclusive "either/or" relationship with human freedom is, for Thomas, inconceivable, and is the principal error underlying the misconceptions of the free-will defense. Note the force of the word "could." It is not that God's agency might have been of such a kind that its exercise in the work of creation or of grace would obstruct the freedom of human agency, but, mercifully it does not, because mercifully God withholds from acting in any way to the exclusion of human freedom. For Thomas the divine action of grace *could not* "interfere" with human freedom even as it infallibly brings about our justification by means of it. It is too easily taken for granted that to speak of God causing my free actions is necessarily a contradiction. For Thomas far from it: worse, to say that my actions are free only insofar as God does not cause them presupposes a plainly idolatrous conception of the divine causality.

For Thomas's is what philosophers today call a "libertarian" account of free will: my action is free insofar as I, and only I, am its created cause. Here there is a genuine completely disjunctive "either/or," it is one or the other and nothing in between. To the extent that an action of mine can be accounted for in terms of any created cause other than my own will, to that extent it fails of freedom. It is quite possible that as you jog my elbow causing the tea to spill I was at that exact moment in the course of spilling the tea intentionally, so that the action was over-determined by two simultaneous but entirely different kinds of cause, each of which is sufficient to explain the tea's being spilt. But it cannot be the case that insofar as the action of spilling the tea was caused by your jogging my elbow to just that extent it was free. To just that extent it was determined by your action. It was free to the extent that I was anyway in the course of spilling the tea, so that had you not jogged my elbow I still would have freely done it.

Now according to Thomas, of any free human action the cause can only be God and the unconstrained will of the agent. It follows that you will construe God's being the cause of the whole action as standing to that action's freedom in the same way as your jogging my elbow stands to it—namely as excluding it—only on a quasi-idolatrous reduction of God's causality to the standing of a created cause. God's action in the world is not a sort of cosmic elbow-jogging, so that where space is occupied by the divine action freedom is evacuated from it, and vice-versa. That is a theology that misplaces the "either/or" for one and only one possible reason, namely that in effect, if not in intention, God's causality, whether as Creator or giver of grace, is construed as if it were just an infinitely scaled-up creaturely agency. And this is what seems in the free will defense to be so out of line with Thomas's conception of the relationship between the freedom of God's action and the freedom of human agency.

For as to any natural causation, it is true that no natural cause can cause an effect unless God sustains the whole action in existence through his creative power. It is true of anything at all that exists, as the creed of Nicaea puts it, "visible and invisible," that unless God causes it to, it does not exist; unless God causes it to, it does not act. But when God is said to cause a natural cause to effect what it does, this is not as if to say that God suspends the natural law governing that cause's efficacy—on the contrary, God's action in virtue of which heavy objects fall is effective because of God's sustaining the laws of gravity that are alone sufficient to explain why they do so. So, Thomas concludes, you could say that God brings about natural effects by means of natural agents effecting what it is in their nature to do, as if those natural causes were instruments of his will, unfreely acting as "servants" of their master's will—natural causes are God's tool kit. But as to our free actions, the relation of divine to human causality is quite otherwise. God cannot cause my acts of free choice by means of any natural cause as his instrument, because, as we have seen, if any natural cause other than my own will brings about my action then it follows that that action is not free. Hence God's creative power exerts itself upon my free actions *only directly*, that is, as unmediated by any natural cause: or, as one might put it in the more appealing language of Augustine, God's action is too intimate to me, too within me, too close to my deepest freedom, to stand in any kind of coercive relationship to it. For God is more within me even than I am to myself[17]—which is, after all, but another way of saying what Thomas himself says, namely that God is the cause of the freedom with which I consent to his infallible agency. Therefore, of my free actions *only* God and I can be the cause, and in every case *both* God *and* I are the cause of them.

Hence, the relationship between my freely being the agent of my actions and God's infallibly causing them is not at all on a par with the relationship between my freely causing the tea to spill and your jogging my elbow so that I do so. For the reduplicative ". . . insofar as . . ." in the one case applies, in the other not: insofar as it was the elbow-jogging that did it I did not. But you cannot say that insofar as God caused my free action I did not: for God is the cause not only of the action itself, so that the action is his. God is the cause of the free choice that makes the action also mine. And it is here that we can see just why for Thomas friendship is so important a model for his doctrine of grace. Our human wills, as Thomas says, are not the *instruments* of the divine agency, as the wills of servants are the instruments of their master's will, their agency entirely at the disposal of their master's. Our free actions are the direct creation of the divine will so that grace and our free consent to it are but one action that proceeds from the shared life, knowledge, and consent of friends who, loving one another, "know one another's business."[18]

FRIENDSHIP WITH GOD

That shared life of friends is made possible by the grace of justification given in Jesus' act declaring us henceforth to be his friends. But the shared life of friends is made actual by the grace that makes us holy; not only do friends "know one another's business," they love one another and all else that they love with a shared love, loving with a single will; and they place their trust in one another in the pursuit of the objects of their love. Human friends in that way share a common human life; God's friends share with God the divine life itself. They share in the divine self-knowledge, thus knowing God's "business" by means of faith; and they love, whether God or their fellow human beings, by means of the divine love itself, a new creation, which is the gift of the Holy Spirit, and that is charity; and though an imperfect love of God might result from the hope of being "rewarded for loving God and keeping his commandments," true charity generates the sort of hope that causes one friend to count on another, for it is on those who through charity are our friends that we can most perfectly rely.[19] These three, faith, charity and hope, are, Thomas says, the "theological" virtues, because they not only conform our will to the divine will so that they are but two wills in parallel; more than that by far, they are the means by which human beings actually live the divine life itself, sharing, as friends do, a single life and a *single* will. Theirs is a sort of "interinanimation," as John Donne calls it, a mingling of souls. For

> When love, with one another so
> Interinanimates two soules,
> That abler soule, which thence doth flow
> Defects of loneliness controules.
> Wee, then, who are this new soule, know,
> Of what we are compos'd, and made.
> For th'Atomies of which we grow,
> Are soules, whom no change can invade.[20]

It is appropriate to cite Donne's poem, *The Extasie*, here, because although Donne's encomium to erotic love is hot, and Thomas's account of friendship is stylistically cooler, "interinanimation" is the perfect name for both. That said, there were theological tendencies in his own times, but more particularly in the previous century, that Thomas thought promoted unacceptably hyperbolic accounts of this "interinanimation" between the soul and God, in effect obliterating the distinction of personal identities between God and the soul in an erotic frenzy of "union." So as to avoid the excesses into which too literal a reliance on the model of love as *eros* can lead, Thomas prefers the calmer mood of friendship's sharing. The issue was raised for him immediately, however, by Peter Lombard's discussion of the status of the charity with which the soul loves God.[21] For Peter, in this following the twelfth-century Cistercian William of St. Thierry before him,[22] took the view that since God, and more specifically, the Holy Spirit, is charity, the love by means of which the Christian soul loves God *is* the Holy Spirit itself[23]—there is between charity in the human soul and the Holy Spirit but "a single spirit" as William puts it.[24] Thomas will not accept that the Holy Spirit's presence in the soul as charity achieves any such "oneness of spirit" as would displace the free agency of the human will itself. In the *Summa* as also elsewhere, he notes that it is Augustine's authority, no less, which is commonly appealed to in defense of this erroneous view. Indeed, in *On the Trinity* Augustine says that "God is said to be charity in the same sense in which he is said to be spirit."[25]

Therefore, Peter's argument goes, "charity in the soul, being the work of the Spirit, is nothing created, but is God himself."[26] To which Thomas replies that of course it is true that the divine essence is charity, just as it is wisdom and goodness. For this reason we do say that the good are good by virtue of the divine goodness and that the wise are wise by virtue of the divine wisdom, but this is because the goodness by which we are constituted as good is a kind of created participation in the divine goodness, just as the wisdom which makes us wise is a created participation in the divine wisdom. It is in the same sense that the charity by which we love our neighbour is a *created* participation in the *uncreated* divine love which is the Holy Spirit.[27] But, he adds, creaturely participation in the uncreated life of God is one thing, and it is not at all the same thing as existential identity between creature and Creator. Peter Lombard's position has the consequence that the distinct will of the creature—which for Thomas belongs to the creature "formally and in its own right"[28]— somehow disappears without created trace into the uncreated reality of God. Of course, it might just be, as Thomas charitably comments, a misleadingly hyperbolic use of language on Peter's part rather than substantive error. For "[Peter's] way of putting it is customary among the Platonists, by whose teachings Augustine was much influenced." There are, however, those who "are unaware of this and derive cause of error from his words."[29]

One way or the other, Thomas has little taste for these neo-Platonic erotic exaggerations. The charity by means of which we share in the divine life is our created participation in the uncreated life of God. The distinction between creature and Creator is ineradicable; love may unite creature and Creator, they may be fairly said to share a common life, but their "oneness" cannot obliterate the creature/Creator distinction itself. One might even say that as between the soul which perfectly loves God and the God who is love there is no distinction at all, except one, namely that what in God is uncreated love as cause is in such a soul the same love as created effect. However, the logic of that most radical of all distinctions was as frequently misunderstood in Thomas's own time as it continues to be in ours. The issue of the misplaced "either/or," of the falsifying disjunction, recurs here in acute form, showing up in the same error as we noted before, namely, the very notion that the work of grace in the soul *could* be of such a kind as to displace the work of human freedom.

For Thomas not every distinction between this and that is an exclusive *either* this *or* that. More particularly, the distinction between creature and creator, though the greatest of all possible distinctions, cannot be one of exclusiveness. For the relation of the mutually exclusive "either/or" is logically possible only between terms on a par. A surface's being red excludes that surface's being green because both are colors: what is red is not green, what is green is not red. On the other hand, unless against some specially constructed background, because a surface's having a color does not occupy the same continuum of meaning as the surface's having an area, a surface's being red can neither entail nor exclude its being four feet square: as Thomas says, you cannot make any sort of comparison between things that do not belong to the same genus. But, as between God and creatures there is no possible semantic space to which they both belong; creature and Creator are too different to stand in relations of mutual exclusion, there being nothing they differ *as*. Or, as Thomas puts it, "In the case of God, you must deny that he belongs to the same genus as *any* other good thing, not [merely] that he belongs to a different genus. This is because he is outside any genus and is the origin of every genus. And so he is compared to other things only as transcending them (*per excessum*)."[30] "Either/or" simply cannot come into it, because to allow mutual exclusion a role in the relationship *just is* to bring God down to the level of a creature, to place God and the creature in a common generic class of comparison. Or, even more simply put, to do that is idolatrously to assign God to the standing of just another, perhaps exceedingly powerful, creature, in fact to the standing of a creature so exceeding all others in power as crushingly to overwhelm their freedom to the point of its extinction. What is wrong with the free-will defense, then, is that it rules out all alternatives as if reduced to two: a God who is a hands-on interfering busybody crushing out human freedom, or else a hands-off Deist God whose relationship to the world is evacuated of presence and power just where what human beings do has any meaning and value, that is, where they are most free. God as the "author of our freedom," as the Anglican General Confession has it, has no place in such a scheme of conceivable possibilities otherwise than merely to kick-start a process of freedom over which he retains no power of subsequent providential causality.

And this in turn brings us back to the doctrine of God and to the reason why it was so important for Thomas to set out on the theological learning curve from there. An inch out on this side of the river and the bridge is a mile out on the other. In the end, we can see that neither our "Catholic" nor our "Protestant" gets it quite right. Just as "either/or" gets no grip on the relation of God to creatures, neither does "both/and," for there is no list—as Thomas puts it, no "genus"—to which God and creatures belong in common. If the logic of exclusion fails as of God, so must the logic of inclusion. One can only say, "neither 'both/and' nor 'either/or'"—or, as the Pseudo-Denys had put it more succinctly, God is "beyond both similarity and difference"[31]—if the logic of the divine transcendence is to do its work on the doctrine of grace. As we will see later, the same logical principles governing theological language in general will have like consequences for Thomas's Christology, and, further down, for his teaching on sacramental, especially Eucharistic, presence. For it is character- istic of the logic of these core doctrines that theirs is a vocabulary, a way of speaking about God that, in the end, witnesses to its own depletion. Theological language arises from the most sensual of contexts—our human experienced freedom, the presence of God in the person of Jesus, the risen body of Christ saturating the meaning of bread and wine—and yet that very language constrains its sensuous origin to yield place to the unsayable truth of the Godhead.

The logical force that drives language toward God thus takes its impetus from the world on which it retains its grip, as it were, until the last moment. But at that last moment, the moment when language reaches into God, that grip on its object that the secure logic of affirmation and negation retains for it, is lost. In consequence, our language in its theological modality, in being propelled, as the Pseudo-Denys said, "beyond similarity and difference," is propelled also "beyond affirmation and negation." This negative theology is, however, the exact inverse of atheist denial. Whereas, for Nietzsche, language, and its apparatus of truth and falsity, affirmation and negation, is ultimately without foundation in any truth-bearing bedrock, for Thomas the ladder of language that ascends to God rests securely on its foundations in our human worldly experience; but the ladder being climbed, God is reached only when it is ultimately cast away: and that is the "mystical," as Wittgenstein somewhat opaquely puts it.[32]

For Thomas, of course, the doctrine of God, together with its corresponding meta-doctrine of theological language thus sketched in its bare logical outlines, is but conceptual ground-clearing for a positive theology. Unless the ground is in this way cleared conceptually everything will be amiss theologically. But when once the logical ground is cleared and the space is opened up, the theology of grace is no longer entangled in the logician's dilemma that would entail the affirmation of the infallible work of

God's grace only at the expense of the freedom of our human consent to it. More positively, the space is thereby cleared for an understanding of the relation between creature and Creator in terms of the mutuality of friendship that requires neither the erotic's erasure of identity nor the oppositions that would set the work of justification and sanctification in competition with human choice and free consent. Grace is all: it is friendship, reciprocity, freedom, life shared, equality mutually sustained, Creator and creature "interinanimated" in love.

SIX

Grace, Desire, and Prayer

It would be impossible to overestimate the importance of friendship in Thomas's moral theology, and the role that friendship plays in his theology of grace. The central paradox of grace, for Thomas—it is perhaps one of the most distinctive and best known features of his theology—is that we do not know our own natures except through the knowledge that comes with what on the hierarchy of existence ontologically exceeds nature, namely grace. For, on account of the Fall, nature has become insufficient to achieve that which is the goal of its own, natural, being. Well known is Thomas's having said that "grace perfects nature." It is, however, possible to be misled by this formula, and there are those who have been misled by it, supposing Thomas to mean that human beings can know of nature's insufficiency to its own ends independently of grace, and, since they can know of what they are missing, they can desire it: hence, in that sense human beings can naturally desire the grace that supplies the missing "perfection."

This cannot be what Thomas means. Thomas is clear: anything we could naturally know that we need in order for nature to achieve its own ends would have to be naturally available to us too: it could not be the case that grace answers to known natural need, because what is by nature required must itself be of the natural order that requires it, and therefore not grace. For grace is the free gift of divine friendship that exceeds not only any actual human power to achieve; it exceeds any power of human imagination to conceive, attainable or unattainable. In short, grace cannot answer to natural need as naturally known; for if it did it would not be grace.

Nor will it do to say that while grace does not answer to natural need, it does answer to the needs of a fallen human nature, as if it were that because of sin, and because we are creatures fallen, grace is demanded because our natures demand to be restored to their innocent condition. At any rate, Thomas does not believe this: in fact, the objection is obvious, grace being, in name and nature, "gratuitous," it cannot be *demanded* by anything, except in a purely hypothetical sense: *if* we are to be saved then only grace can save us. As we will see in Chapter 7, for Thomas the fall is a human predicament which imposes absolutely no obligation on God to do anything about. Fallen as we are, without grace we have no right to anything but to stew in our own juice—in fact, fallen as we are, we hardly even know how far we are fallen; at best we can know that ours *is* a predicament, our ignorance of its nature being itself an aspect of that self-same fallen condition. For ours is like the condition of the person who is self-deceived: not only is he self-ignorant, he has somehow managed to hide from himself how it is that he is himself the cause of that ignorance and that he has a reason for remaining in it undisturbed. Therefore, for Thomas it takes grace to know that we are in need of grace; and it takes grace for us to know that there is a possible condition to which nature is restored, a condition far beyond the powers of nature even as they were before the Fall. It is in that sense that, for Thomas, nature is "perfected" by grace—not as if, knowing what we want, human beings are by grace given the gift of it, but rather, not knowing what we want, the gift of grace reveals to us the depth and nature of our need, a need that, as heretofore we were, was unknown to us.

Grace, therefore, does not exactly answer to our desire, as if we knew what our desire is. Grace answers to desires that only it can arouse in us, showing us what it is that we really want: grace is *pure* gift, the gift we could not have known that we wanted until we were given it. For grace does not merely solve the problem of the gap opened up by the Fall, restoring us to where we were before Adam's sin. It goes far beyond and above that, calling us into a friendship which is surplus by an infinite degree to the solution required. We need to come to know this, and to live by the knowledge that everything transacted between ourselves and God—that is, everything to do with the friendship that Jesus offered his followers—is the work of grace, a work that is of its nature supererogatory, being a solution that far exceeds what is needed by the problem it solves.

By grace, then, we are not only given what we want. By grace we come to want the grace that we are given, and for Thomas it was not only his judgment as a theologian, it was his practice as a Dominican, that prayer is the route down which grace traces us back to that place where what we really want lies dormant and all too often unrecognized. And prayer answers to the very desire that prayer itself discovers; prayer uncovers the hidden desire precisely *by* answering to it. We know from contemporary witnesses that when Thomas wants something he prays for it. That is what you should always do, he says, and it is a pity that what Thomas has to say about prayer is so sorely neglected in the secondary literature, if only because his own practice of prayer was so essential a part of his practice as a theologian. William of Tocco, one of his earliest biographers, made no such mistake.

> Every time that he wished to study, to undertake a disputation, to teach, to write, or dictate, [Thomas] first withdrew into prayer on his own and prayed pouring out tears, in order to obtain understanding of the divine mysteries.[1]

Among contemporary witnesses the stories abound of Thomas having credited prayer above any intellectual ability of his own as accounting for such theological insights as his work might have provided. No doubt some of those stories are apocryphal in detail, pious conjectures of a stereotypically hagiographical kind. It is equally doubtless that they genuinely reflect the wider reality: Thomas wanted to know, and what Thomas wants he prays for. And if he put his theological insights down as much to the outcome of his pleading in prayer for understanding as to anything else, I can see no reason why we should be skeptical. It is not that Thomas thereby claims any divine warrant for his theological arguments, as if their coming to mind in the course of or as a result of prayer in itself authenticated them, as some writers in his times, and especially in the next century, were wont to claim for their work. Thomas never claims warrant for any of his theological conclusions on the grounds (as a son of mine when three years old once did) that "God told him," otherwise than by way of appeal to what the Church claims God had told everyone. Thomas hid his prayer as he hid his bulk, and specifically insisted to any of his brethren who witnessed anything out of the ordinary by way of prayer experiences that under no circumstances should they report them to anyone else. What Thomas does know is that some kinds of understanding will come to the theologian only within a life of faith and prayer, as gift given to those who ask for it.

If his own prayer played a crucial role in the personal life of Thomas the theologian, prayer as a general Christian practice plays a far more important role than is usually admitted also within that network of connections that forms the structure of his theology itself. The general form of the interconnections that we explored in the last chapter between grace and the freedom of the will are all to be found as it were replicated in small in that interplay between the initiations of grace and the free response of desire that is, for Thomas, the nature of prayer, the conversation of friends. If any Christian practice is an "interinanimation," it is prayer, as Thomas describes it. Specifically in this connection we should note that for Thomas the word *oratio* that we translate by the amorphously generic term "prayer" meant petitionary prayer, asking God to make things happen that one wants to happen. Prayer, Thomas says, is an act of the intellect, for it is speech, but speech arising from desire, it is speech expressive of want and need. That is one direction of flow: from our free desire to the God who answers to it. But then Thomas adds, pointing to the opposite direction of flow that completes prayer's reciprocity, that is, to its character as a two-way *conversatio*: "prayer is a certain kind of hermeneutic of the human will."[2] Then again, employing a similar metaphor, he says, "prayer is a kind of unfolding of one's will before God, so that he might fulfil it."[3] Prayer, then, both arises from human desire and interpretatively "reads" the desire it arises from, so as to discover "one's will before God." What does he mean?

DISCOVERING "WHAT YOU REALLY WANT"

Thomas on "will" is a problem for modern readers. Bluntly, Thomas's *voluntas* is not best translated by the English "will" at all. It is more accurately, if more cumbersomely, translated as one translates Aristotle, as "rational" or "reasoned desire," that is, desire rationally deliberated as distinct from instinctive or nonrational forms of desire such as is caused in a hungry person by the smell of food. Typically, instinctive desire is of the immediate, it works to no strategically considered plan or procedure, it is desire as unmediated in its reaction to an object or stimulus. The power to commit to long-term strategies of desire, by contrast, involving complex interactions between long strings of ends and means desired—such as those required to intelligently engage in a degree program of academic study, and so choosing these courses rather than those as better meeting the requirements of a particular career trajectory, combining those requirements with others for potential admission to an appropriate Ph.D. program in the meantime, and much else— that power to thread a continuity of desire through often complex overlapping strands of rationally connected wants is what Thomas means by *voluntas*, the "reasoned" desires of a rational agent. If we must use the modern English word "will" in the explanation of Thomas, and there is little alternative, then, in brief, we must needs understand his meaning in some such terms. What is quite certain is that *voluntas* is not to be understood in any such manner as would distinguish in principle "will" from "desire," still less in any that pit "will" *against* "desire," as is the conventional meaning today.

What Thomas sets in contrast is will, that is, desire as pursued through a rational course of means and ends, with desire that is simply a response to a stimulus, the first being the cause of what it pursues, the second the effect of its object, the first being will, the second being instinct—but in either case they are forms of one and the same phenomenon of desire. The position for Thomas, as regards the relation of desire to will, is analogous to that as regards the sense of danger as instinct and a response to danger as strategy: what is simply a stimulus to undeliberated defensive fight or flight in panic is, for a rational animal, a terrorist threat to which one can set up a CIA team in response. For humans possess the language of threat, as we saw in Chapter 3, which enables us to place the danger within a complex narrative context in a way that merely reactive flight cannot. So too of desire: human beings can react in response to the immediacy of attraction to a particular object, so that their actions are caused by the immediacy of their desires. Or their action can fall within a pattern of ordered desire, a pattern of reasons, of which there is, as it were, a grammar. And human desire obedient to a grammar, desire that is the cause of its object, is roughly what Thomas means by *voluntas*.

Another way of putting all this would be that a person's "will" consists in what he or she can be said "really" to want—except that the meaning of the word "really" is too ambiguous to be clear. In one sense of the word "real" a person's "real" wants are shown most convincingly by what they do, commonly less convincing being what they say they really want. For self-deception is all too present a possibility. I might deny that I am in love with Mary-Jane, and I might do so almost, but not quite, sincerely. For my awkward speech in her presence, the goofy expression of face, the feeling of loss in her absence, the blushes upon mention of her name, the sweats upon thoughts of rejection, the absentminded daydreaming, the excessive energy of the denials, all tell a different story than that which I tell even myself. There is, in such a case, something I "really" want, only I do not know it, because I am hiding it from myself. At any rate I do and I do not know it, in the way that I do and do not know where my cigarettes are that I have hidden from myself in an attempt to give them up. Hence, the force of the word "real" is in this case that of what in truth I want by contrast with my desires as I like to believe them to be. It is not in this sense of the expression that for Thomas my will consists in what I really want. For what the self-deceived person "really" wants may very well be, in another sense that for Thomas is more fundamental, false and unreal—as my self-deceived desires for Mary-Jane would be were I someone else's husband and Mary-Jane some other man's wife. Adultery might be the strongest temptation I have. But in the sense of the word "real" that Thomas has in mind, it is not what I really want. The desire for adultery is for him like the child's desire for six ice creams in a row. Perhaps the child can think of nothing better; but it takes little subtlety to know that she does not *really* want all six of them in the sense that had she taken thought for what eating them all would be like she would continue to want all six.

The sense in which what Thomas means by "will" is to be identified with my real wants is this: whatever else I may want, in wanting it what I really want is happiness. Unfailingly that is so. I may be wrong in thinking that adultery with Mary-Jane will make me happy. Indeed, most people are wrong some of the time about what will make them happy, some are wrong much of the time. But if I can be wrong in what I think will make me happy, I cannot be wrong that it is happiness that I desire when I contemplate adultery's (false) attractions. For while I may pertinently ask of any other characteristic of a course of action or way of life that is for me a reason for engaging in it, "why does that make it desirable?" Thomas says it cannot make any sense to ask what makes happiness desirable. "It makes me happy" puts an end to *any* chain of questions concerning why you want this or that. Nor does it put an end to a chain of such questions in the way "Well, I just do" puts an end to the question, "Why do you like caviar?" For though it is true that if I like caviar it is for the taste of the stuff that I like it and for no further reason, when I say "I *just* do" this is to admit that my liking it is a contingent fact that might be otherwise for me, as no doubt it is in fact for you, since you dislike it. Whereas for Thomas, "It's connected with my being happy" is to give a reason that is decisive not just for a person with my particular desires or yours, but as arising from the nature of desire itself, for anyone at all. Though there need not be, there can be a reason why I like caviar. There cannot be a further reason why I want happiness; the word "reason" loses all meaning and any power of motivation when the question is asked of happiness itself: "Why would you want that?"[4]

Thus far Thomas in the first five questions of the *Prima Secundae* is following closely Aristotle's argument in book 1 of the *Nicomachean Ethics*. He continues to do so when he goes on to say that since of course anyone can be mistaken as to what will make them happy, human beings have to learn how to be happy both in the sense that they have to learn what kind of life will in fact make them happy, and in the sense that they have to acquire the stable dispositions that make it their common practice to live a life conducive to happiness in the event. And what today we are likely to call the "moral" life, for Thomas is more simply described as the "happy" life, or at least the life lived in the pursuit of true happiness. Moreover, we can say that for Thomas a person succeeds in living the happy life when she gets to do, regularly and routinely, what she "really wants."

But here the force of the word "really" is not, as before, that in which it contrasts with the false perceptions of desire that characterize the self-deceived. There is a very profound sense in which even the most perfectly honest person may not know what she wants: not, that is, the case where, of two things both of which she wants, she does not know which to choose, like whether to marry John or James. More problematic is the case where there is something that we want but we do not know what it is, except that it is somehow importantly connected with our happiness. Such is the case when we are morally befogged, because our deepest desires are hidden from us by veil upon obscuring veil, of upbringing, of socialization, of personal insecurities and fears, of relationships abusive and abused, of desire habitually unfulfilled and frustrated; and in this sense of "want" in which we want something but for all these reasons do not know what it is, we do not know our own "wills." For what we will is happiness; and what we *really* will, whether or not we know it, is whatever it is that will make us happy, but we may not—and all too often do not—know what it is. It is for this reason that the moral life consists in the first place in those practices that enable the discovery of what it is that we really want, the happy life, and the power of insight that leads to that discovery is what Thomas calls *prudentia*, skill in seeing the moral point of human situations, what true desires are to be met within them. It is then, and only secondarily that the moral life consists in virtuous forms of living, the practices of desire that *prudentia* has interpretatively uncovered within the maelstrom of desires as actually experienced.

And it is here within his conception of moral practice as desire-discovery—or as he calls it, "practical wisdom"—that for Thomas a principal means of tracing the way back to what we really want, is prayer, *oratio*. And our only available starting point for that practice of self-discovery is our wants and desires as we actually experience them. Therefore, Thomas says, we ought to pray for what we think we want regardless. For prayer is "in a certain manner a hermeneutic of the human will," so that by way of placing our desires as we experience them before God we are asking also that those desires be "unfolded," "explicated," thereby to release their real significance, the *real* want that is wrapped up in, "implicated" in all their opacity in their form as experienced. Therefore, says Thomas, we ought to pray, as Jesus did in the garden of Gethsemane, "in response to our animal desire" (*secundum sensualitatem*). For when we pray as Jesus did then, out of animal need and desire—for Jesus was scared of death, as naturally any animal is—we are placing that animal need and desire within the interpretative power of the divine will itself, wherein alone we will discover our own real will. Therefore, Thomas concludes, we ought always to pray for what we think we want; for Jesus prayed as he did in Gethsemane so as to teach us just that lesson, namely that it is "permitted for human beings naturally to desire even what [they know] is not God's will";[5] and, as if in reinforcement of what for many is a startling thought, he cites the authority of Augustine to the same effect, commenting on the same prayer of Jesus: "It is as if [Jesus] were saying: 'See yourself in me: for you [too] can wish something for yourself even though God wishes something else.'"[6] Only thus, in the prayer of *honest* desire, is there any chance of our discovering what are our *true* desires, our real will.

"REAL WANTS" AND THE MORAL LAW

Our real wants are for us, Thomas adds, a kind of law, in that they are normative for us somewhat as a law obliges, but—and now we have to reintroduce the word—"naturally," meaning here principally that our real wants are normative not as imposed by decree externally, but arising from their being constitutive of what it is to be human. For when it comes to the moral life we are in truth talking about a form of *self*-discovery, about an understanding of what it is to be human, for the desires that grace evokes in us, and through prayer reveals to us, are not those of some other nature than our own, but are in some sort a revelation to us of what we humans were created to be, that is, human. Though Thomas speaks of this self-discovery as a *lex naturalis*, it is probably unhelpful to think of what he has in mind as being like a "law" in our modern sense otherwise than in its being in that general way normative. For Thomas places little emphasis on natural law's being experienced in the way the law of political communities is experienced, as commands issued by a legislating authority backed by sovereign power, even a divine one. It is interesting to note, moreover, that in Thomas's moral vocabulary there scarcely ever occur any Latin words for obligation of the kind usually found in legal contexts, or any of their cognates—not *obligare*, not *debere*, not *oportet*. The device of grammar that Thomas uses to express how our deepest natural desires make demands on our behavior is commonly that of the gerundive: "such and such is the thing to be done," or perhaps the gerund, "is the thing to do," and "the thing to do" is what you can see to be demanded in a given situation by the needs and desires that are best served in it.[7]

Thomas tells us that the awareness of real human desire as having a normative character is as fundamental to the practical life as the principle of contradiction is to the theoretical or speculative. You cannot think or speak coherently, you cannot reason cogently, except in obedience to the principle that to affirm p is to deny not-p; likewise, you cannot judge or act with any degree of moral discrimination (in short, in a diagnosis unknown in such terms to Thomas, you are a psychopath) if your practice of living fails to be obedient to the principle that "the good is to be done and evil avoided," if, that is, you are so lacking in the power of moral perception as to be unable to see how a thing's being good makes a claim on your action. It is true, Thomas knows, that we have become dehumanized, and therefore demoralized, by sin, but not so radically that, short of psychopathic illness, we cannot tell the difference, in point of their bearing on how to act, between aimlessly kicking a paper bag down the street, and aimlessly kicking a baby down the street, the one being generally harmless, the other always vicious, the one a bit of fun, the other indicating a total loss of humanity. There is *moral* point, and not merely anthropological, in knowing what it is to be human, and so in knowing which are the "real" desires to live the life of meeting which is intrinsic to being truly good, truly human, truly happy.

For some desires are so basic to human living that an awareness of the normative character of meeting them is, Thomas thinks, analogous to a "law" universally promulgated and ineradicable from human consciousness. Just in as much as we are each alive, wanting to stay alive (or at least not refusing to stay alive) is normative, and so a variety of courses of action required for survival—the provision of food, warmth, clothing, organized forms of defense against danger and threat—become the "thing to do," imperative, they are goods "to be sought." Likewise, species survival is not just an evolutionary fact, it is an instinctive impulse for all animals, and a normative one for human beings. Hence, Thomas says, it is a good for the species, the desire for which is one of the ways in which animals are characteristically alive, that a certain level of reproduction is maintained, entailing that enough of its members engage in enough sex open to procreation, and that they commit enough to the nurture and education of their young as will ensure a future for the human species. And living together in community, and seeking to live in accordance with discoverable truths, especially truths about God, are in their own ways impera-tives that come with the "fact" of our being rational animals. For it is by means alone of such forms of human association that the other human goods can be secured; therefore it is "the thing to do" that human beings devise forms of social organization required for the survival of the present generation, the reproduction of future generations, and the means of acquiring every kind of truth. These elementary forms of living are normatively human, they are "what is to be done" and thus far, in their extreme generality, are discov-erable, Thomas thinks, without reference in any form explicitly to the divine law that in fact they embody.

As Thomas sees it, then, what we discover when we discover for ourselves these things that are to be done, is like a law built into our creaturely existence, it is the divine will written into our natures, more specifically written into our truest, most real, desires. But Thomas does seem to think that at least at a very general level our natures are not so far deformed by sin that we cannot know these needs and wants simply as those of our desires that are truly human. It is *thus* that are they normative, for it is as nature's demands that they are the commands of the God who made us so. Consequently, at this highly general level, to know what to do, and to know that it is to be done, it is enough, Thomas thinks, to know that answering to such desires *just is* to answer to the call of our natures as made by God. Hence our natural desires are in themselves divine summons to action and response. To be truly human is, then, in a loose manner of speaking, to know a "natural law." And so in calling natural desires a "law" Thomas is primarily indicating that they have an imperatival character, and not a merely factual anthropological one: the truest facts discoverable by us about being human are also demands made on us to become human. For that, being truly human, is what will make us happy, because that is what we really want.

SIN

And that would be all well and good were it not for sin. Because of sin, however, human desire is an opaque palimpsest, layer upon layer of obscuring experience masking what it is that we truly want. If prayer is the hermeneutical tool that can thread its way back to what we really want, to the normatively desirable, it is because it is grace that has first caused in us the desire from which that prayer arises. Knowledge of our human nature is for us the work of grace, it is knowledge of a *new* creation that is made possible *only* by grace. Raw nature does not any longer exist; for like John Henry Newman's haunted man who, having once seen a ghost, can never again be as one who has not seen it, so it is with us: redeemed as we are, we are haunted by sin and by innocence lost, and we can never again be as once we were, naturally whole, innocent, unfallen. Thomas's moral theology, therefore, could not in the end be grounded in anything beyond some abstract generalities—and certainly not in any of the necessary detail of a moral life to be lived—if all we had available to us by way of means of moral discovery were some conception of human nature hypothetically constructed on a model of how matters would have stood with us had Adam not sinned. Such a hypothesis is too diluted a moral brew to serve at the moral party.

For "human nature" as an abstract, theoretically constructed, counterfactual conditional has no independent moral power except as a prelapsarian standard of natural wholeness by which we might at best measure the degree of our fall. But otherwise than as a onetime real condition, now only as an ungrounded abstraction, raw "human nature" in its original state no longer figures as morally normative, for it is, as it were, no longer sufficiently morally visible. Our human condition is no longer that of innocence; nor yet is it the condition of the fallen but not yet redeemed; it is the condition of those who, having fallen, are now redeemed by grace, of those who having collapsed beneath the level of the human are restored immeasurably above it. Raw human nature is lost as anything more than normative generality. Within the dramatic maelstrom of fall and redemption we can never again be as not three ways haunted: by our original innocence, by its loss through sin, and by our salvation through grace.

Which is why, for Thomas, if the normatively human is to become once again visible to us, it is not by means of some image of "natural man" recovered by a theoretical reconstruction of what the good person looks like from within the debris of our fallen condition. As Aristotle thought, the only option is by looking to how the "good person" actually lives, if you can find one—which of course, Aristotle cannot. But Thomas can. And this is why that massive second part of the *Summa theologiae*, containing perhaps the most comprehensive account ever written of the virtues that constitute the good life, and so of the habits and practices of the happy person, makes sense in terms of theological and pedagogical structure only insofar as it is read in relation to the Christology, but more particularly the sketch of the life of Christ, of the *Summa*'s third part. For in Christ alone is the visibility of the normatively human restored. In what Christ preached, in what Christ did, in the friends that Christ made, in how Christ ate and prayed and cried with them, in what Christ suffered, in how Christ died, is seen what it is truly to be human, no longer as a thin and abstract moral outline, but in polychrome and densely colored portrait, and, more than that, as an actual life narrated. Nor is it incidental that in that life is seen the price exacted by a sinful world from anyone who strives to imitate that humanity.

That is the Christ who, just before he died, extrajudicially executed on the majority recommendation of a corrupt committee of very religious people, declared to his followers that henceforth they would be his "friends." For Thomas, in that moment in Jesus' last discourse, when he calls his disciples into friendship with him, he was inviting them to share in his own divine life so as to be restored in their own, human, life. Thus would they learn to become, like him, truly human in the only way now possible, by the grace which is our share in the divine life itself. For Thomas, the only way back for human beings to their true humanity is by means of a grace that is also a new law of free desire. Human beings can become human again only insofar as by grace, by way of an unmerited pure gift of friendship with God, they become *more* than human.

SEVEN

Christ

THE DISPUTE OVER THE ETERNITY OF THE WORLD

Thomas was plagued by hostile colleagues throughout both tenures of his mastership of theology at Paris. In or around 1270, during his second stint as master, Thomas became embroiled in more than one open conflict with them, one of which concerned the much vexed question of the eternity of the world. In summary, two positions occupied the center stage in Paris: that of Aristotle and of some of his followers, mainly philosophers, according to whom the world was demonstrably eternal, that is to say, had always existed; and that of the conservative theological majority, according to whom not only was the temporal finitude of the universe a matter of revealed faith, it was also demonstrable by reason that the universe had been created in time. Thomas himself wished a pox to be visited upon both their houses.

Back in the days of his first mastership in Paris in 1256 and before, when he was composing his commentary on the *Sentences*, Thomas had even then maintained his rejection of the majority opinion of the theologians, including Bonaventure. Now, in 1270, he faced the openly declared opposition of John Pecham (the future archbishop of Canterbury), who avowed in his inaugural lecture as theological master in Paris (which Thomas attended) not only that revelation taught, but that the proposition is "easily proved" by reason, that the world had a finite beginning in time.[1] On the day, and perhaps not wishing to spoil Pecham's party, Thomas kept his disagreement to himself. But persuaded by his students who were furious at what they took to be a personal attack on their Master, Thomas soon enough responded, arguing in a polemical *opusculum*, "On the Eternity of the World," that there could be no incoherence in the proposition that God created out of nothing a world that had always existed, just so long as one did not make the mistake of identifying the endless duration of a finite and changeable world with the immutable eternity of God. The distinction was all important to Thomas: a continuous succession of events without either beginning or end, cumulatively adding up to a cosmic history of one thing after another is, for Thomas, perfectly conceivable. But such "eternity" is not to be confused with God's eternity, which is a wholly actual timeless now, without any constituent elements of before and after. Earlier in the *Summa*, and immediately following his discussion of the Trinity, Thomas had already made his position concerning creation plain: "That the world has not always existed can be maintained by faith alone, and it cannot be conclusively proved, just as was said above about the mystery of the Trinity."[2] The parallel with his discussion of the Trinity tells us much about Thomas's theological method. In that case it was his principal concern when discussing the simplicity and oneness of God to ensure neither that the possibility of the Christian doctrine of the Trinity is closed off thereby, nor that the necessity of Trinitarian faith is entailed by that simplicity and oneness. In short, if reason can know God to be one and simple it can also show the question to be open whether or not the godhead is personally triune, for reason can show that such Christian teaching is not ruled out *a priori*. Just so with creation. Although Thomas claims to know by faith that the world is not eternal, he is at pains to insist that the eternity or non-eternity of the world is demonstrably undecidable by reason alone.

Naturally, then, Thomas agreed with Pecham that on the authority of Genesis we can be certain that the world had a beginning in time—though he notes that "beginning in time" is a curious way of putting it, and a misleading one, since if the universe has a beginning then its beginning *is* the beginning of time—and that much Thomas readily concedes to Aristotle. What Thomas will not accept, however, is the inference Aristotle appeared to draw from it, namely that necessarily the world is eternal.

Aristotle and Thomas are therefore agreed on one point at least: time itself is intrinsically bound up with the existence of a changeable world; if time begins to exist only with the beginning of the universe, then "before" being a chronological term, there can have been no "before" the universe's existence. But where Thomas departs from Aristotle is when Aristotle goes on to say that if there is a stretch of time with no time "before" it, then that stretch of time had no beginning. And if time has no beginning, then, Aristotle concludes, time always was. Hence, the world is eternal. Thomas's response concedes what in Aristotle's argument is clearly right: because there is no universe-independent clock, and because time is universe-bound just as much as the universe is time-bound, there can have been no point in time when every-thing whatever was created, as if God made up his mind to create the world at 3:00 p.m. on Saturday, 28 October 4004 B.C., and at 2:59 p.m. that day there was one minute to go before God pulled off creation on schedule. Of course, then, Aristotle is right, there cannot have been a time when time was created, and Thomas says as much: for the first "now" of creation is not itself *a* time of the day, but is the beginning of time such that there can thereafter be calculations as to the durations of temporal sequences.[3] But the proposition that a finite and calculable amount of time has elapsed since the world was created is not for Thomas incoherent, and the strength of his position is that in showing the age of the universe to be rationally undecidable, the option is left open to the evidence, whether dogmatically theological or empirically cosmological.

Thomas's position ought therefore to mean peace in *our* time between the theologian and the cosmologist. By contrast, the bitterness of the hostilities that this issue provoked in his *own* time needs some explanation, for more is at stake than meets the eye. What meets the eye is contention over Aristotle, who, Thomas says, is not necessarily wrong in holding the world to be eternal; it could have been, but we know it isn't. Bonaventure and Pecham are not necessarily right in holding the world to have existed for a finite time, just right as we happen to have been told—by God.

Much more, however, was at stake for Thomas than the issue concerning the interpretation of Aristotle. General, long-term principles of theological method lie at the heart of the immediate issue about the finite or infinite duration of the universe. Thomas was unlikely to have been provoked to write this polemic on the eternity of the world simply with a view to setting the record straight on Aristotle, important as doing so would have been to him. As usual, Thomas saw the implications of this apparently purely philosophical disagreement much further down the theological line than could most of his contemporary theologians. For him, something of intrinsic importance was at stake about the logic of Christian belief, and in consequence of theology as a coherent discourse.

THEOLOGY, *SCIENTIA*, AND THE RATIONALLY UNDECIDABLE

Theology, Thomas maintained, is a *scientia*. As we have seen, this means that it is a true *disciplina*, and among the conditions required of theology in that regard is that the strings of propositions that make up its content are linked systematically with one another by means of connectives in sound logical order. As I explained in the first chapter, the roughly 4,500 theological propositions of the *Summa* form an enormously long, but single, chain, the sequencing of links being governed principally (I argued) by pedagogical considerations. But if the order of that sequence is pedagogically determined, the theological propositions themselves are connected up so as to be formed into a chain by rule-governed inferences—by the rules, that is to say, that govern logical, and not just pedagogical, sequences: "if . . . then," "either . . . or," "both . . . and," "*p* because *q*," and the formal procedures of affirmation and negation. Insofar as theology may be understood as a *scientia* (at any rate in that minimal sense that Thomas had in mind when he described theology as *argumentativa)*, then, such will be the rules governing the way its subject matter is formally structured.

On such an understanding of *scientia*, inherited principally from Aristotle, however, theology was never going adequately to meet the full requirements for scientificity, and Thomas's polemic on the subject of the eternity of the world shows exactly why. What a *scientia* achieves, for Thomas as for Aristotle, is the demonstration of necessary connections out of what otherwise might seem to be merely random facts or states of affairs that just happen to occur in conjunction or succession. For even when states of affairs occur in succession with almost exceptionless regularity the mere observation of those sequences can of itself demonstrate no necessity. It may be obvious that the light's nearly always going on in my office when I flip the switch is not mere happenstance. But however accustomed we may have become to the conjunction, the constant recurrence of conjunctions of this sort is not itself an explanation of anything at all. Regularities of such a kind are what *call* for explanation, and you have responded in a scientific manner to my puzzlement as to how my flicking the switch on the wall occurs so frequently in conjunction with a light appearing in a globe of glass on the ceiling when you have provided the laws and initial conditions from which it follows of necessity that this is what will happen. We would know, though Thomas of course did not, that, other things being equal, the one *has* to follow the other, because we know about electrical conduction down metal wires and a current's conversion into light, and so forth. It is thus that the connections between my action of switch-flicking and the light's coming on are now seen to be not an "accidental" conjunction of events, but a necessary one, as following from what Thomas calls the *naturae* of the phenomena in question. For Thomas, as for Aristotle, *scientia* is the conversion of the contingent observation of what just so happens into that happening's being seen to be just so, into exactly what you would expect, given one's knowledge of the natures of things.

Aristotle, then, thought that the eternity of the world was "scientifically" demonstrable as a necessary truth. Thomas maintains that there is no reason why Aristotle could not have been in fact right as to the world's eternity, it is just that Christians know that he is not; that is to say, Thomas thinks that the eternity of the world is a possible truth but a de facto falsehood, and so not a necessary truth. And from this it follows not only that Aristotle is wrong in thinking the eternity of the world is a scientific, because a necessary, truth, but also that Thomas's own theological case for saying that the world was created a finite time ago is not a scientific claim either. For Thomas, neither his own position nor Aristotle's is a necessary truth.

And this is not just a special case. As we saw, the demonstrable undecidability of the eternity of the world is on a par with that of the doctrine of the Trinity—you can prove that whether or not the oneness of God is also a trinity of persons is undecidable by anything short of the revelation that it is or is not so. Jews and Muslims could have been in possession of all there is to be known about God, knowing as they do God to be one and undivided. It is therefore just a fact that we might not have known, and not a necessary or unavoidably knowable truth, that the one and undivided God is also the one and undivided Trinity of persons. For knowing that God is a trinity of persons is not deducible from the divine oneness. Hence, short of the revelation that it is so, we could not have known it.

And thus it is in general: the world of theology is replete with rationally undecidable truths, that is to say, with truths that are incapable of rational demonstration one way or the other, because those truths are not derivable by necessity from any rationally self-evident truths prior to them but only from the free decision of the Creator to tell us. There is no necessity, Thomas believes, that there should be anything at all other than God, but there is something other than God—the world as we have it.[4] There is no necessity that the world as we have it should be the sinful world that it is, but that sin abounds is a fact.[5] The world being replete with evil, there is no necessity that God should provide any remedy for it, but God does.[6] For there to be a completely satisfactory remedy for sin there is no necessity that the second person of the Trinity should become human flesh in the person of Jesus Christ, yet just that is the remedy.[7] There is no necessity that the incarnate word of God should die on a cross executed at the instigation of his own people, but die on a cross he does.[8] There is no necessity that, being dead and buried, the incarnate word of God should be raised from the dead—body, soul, and divinity—on the third day, yet raise his Son from the dead is what the Father does.[9] There is hardly any proposition at all central to Christian faith that is a demonstrably necessary truth; there is nothing at all distinctive to Christian belief that could not have been otherwise than it is. Christians believe to be true a great number of revealed facts. But as Christians, they can appeal to very few natural necessities and to none of a logical kind. How then, on terms that require of *scientia* the demonstration of necessities, can Thomas maintain theology to be *scientia* when nearly all the beliefs of Christians recited in their creedal formulae are, on Thomas's own terms, contingent—true only because willed by the free will of God and out of no necessity of any kind? That *in fact* the world was created in time is, therefore, by no means the only belief of Christian faith that might have been otherwise; on the contrary, that they might have been otherwise is a general characteristic of the propositions Christians hold to be true *being* a "matter of faith."

In Thomas's time the question of the logic of Christian doctrinal belief arose most significantly in the form of a question about the incarnation, stimulating a debate initiated by the work known as *Cur Deus homo?* composed by Anselm, the eleventh-century prior of the Benedictine abbey of Bec in Normandy, later to become archbishop of Canterbury. The question "Why did God become man?" is tricky, because single in form as it appears to be, it is in fact a double question. For, prior to any possible answer given in terms of divine reasons for the incarnation, there is a question concerning the nature of the explanation-seeking word "Why?" What sort of answer is possible to that question?

Medieval theologians, Thomas included, ruled out any answer to the question "Why?" in terms of strict necessity. The world that God has created, the world exactly as it has turned out, did not have to be just so; much that turned out this way could have turned out another way. It is not even as if sin were necessary and unavoidable. A world of free human beings that is not only as a matter of fact without sin, but is one willed by God to be sinless for all eternity, was for all medieval theologians not only, as we saw, a logical possibility. It was an actuality. Medieval believers knew such a world existed and hoped one day to inhabit it themselves—they called it "heaven." So if the world's being sinful is the result of no necessity, does that mean that its being a sinful world is just a fact, that its so happening to be that way is just the way things went, events lacking *rationale*, happening willy-nilly and therefore not conceivably a matter of systematic enquiry, no object for scientia?

And does that contingency of historical events as they have turned out entail that it is impossible even for God to have foreseen that things would turn out as badly as they did because sins are free actions, and that which can be foreseen must be determined by antecedent causes and so not free? But if that is so, are we not then forced back into the position we have already seen Thomas to reject, according to which the incarnation is a divine response provoked by what freely, and therefore contingently, happens—a sort of Plan B, since Plan A failed so miserably almost from the starting gate?

WHY THE INCARNATION?

One of the most delightful works of late medieval English theology is Nicholas Love's *The Mirrour of the Blessed Lyf of Jesu Christ*.[10] Written around 1410, approximately 140 years after the death of Thomas, it is a Middle English life of Christ much indebted to a thirteenth-century Latin text which Thomas would not have known. It reports a fanciful celestial debate conducted before angelic hosts made anxious by the unresolved condition of the human race, which having fallen and remaining yet unredeemed, was fully in the devil's hands. The debate consists of a dispute between the unforgiving arguments of Truth and Justice and the more compassionate responses of Mercy, with Peace acting as referee. Truth and Justice argue that the human condition is no worse than the human race deserves given its sin, and that justice, which ought to be done and ought to be seen to be done, can be served only by leaving human beings to the fate that, after all, they chose for themselves. Mercy disagrees, arguing that because she reigns in heaven, she should by right also reign over the human race on earth, which longs for her regime of forgiveness. Peace, however, steps aside from the disagreement between Truth and Justice on the one hand and Mercy on the other, and demands an end to the contention between them, for in heaven there should be no such disharmony. Peace therefore appeals to the adjudication of Sovereign Wisdom, who, acknowledging the claims of both parties, decrees the only possible way "to accorde all thise to gidre [to get agreement between all parties together] and for a final dome [judgment] in this matire" is if "be made a gode deth of man; so that [that is, so long as] one be founden with outen synne that may and wole innocently and for charitee suffer deth for man." The problem is, of course, that no such wholly innocent man is to be found, and, upon being consulted, Reason concludes that the way to handle the situation that best fits the case ("is most conuenient," "skilful") is for the second person of the Trinity to become incarnate and redeem the human race, not, as it were, by a general decree of pardon from above, but by initiating a movement of human beings back to God from *within* their catastrophic condition. Thus the best solution is in the hands of the Son, who by offering his own life destroys the power of death. "And whanne resoun had saide this verdyt the fader seide it was his wille that it schulde be so; and the sone gaf [gave] gladly his assent therto: and the holy gost seide he wolde worche [work] therto also."

Though far from being his style, on one score Thomas would have approved of the theological thrust of this narrative, which is that if any such metaphorical representation could do justice to the rationale of the incarnation, it is that of a conclusion arrived at as the result of deliberation concerning what is the most appropriate or "fitting" (or in Love's words, "skilful" or "conuenient") thing to do. The character of genuine debate between equally compelling divine attributes—Justice and Truth, Mercy and Peace—as to the most appropriate action concerning the human race aptly represents the fact that the Anselmian "Why?" demands no necessary and constraining reasons to be found anywhere down the line of events that make up salvation history: the decision has the contingency of narrative rather than the necessity of logic. The options are all open. There is no necessity in that the world was created, none in Adam's sin, none in the choosing of the chosen people, none in the incarnation—but only, linking them all, the free choice of the will of a God who is, Thomas says, *maxime liberalis*, absolutely "free-handed," doing everything simply as the expression of the divine goodness, and, as it were, out of the sheer joy of doing it. Nothing God does is done *propter suam utilitatem*, as if in response to a private interest of God's own, but only because God is just plain good.[11]

In his typically succinct fashion, Thomas conducts exactly the same debate as the wordier Nicholas Love when he asks in the *Summa* which properties take priority in the transactions between God and the human race—justice, or mercy. Thomas replies that logically mercy precedes: for though God's dealings with human beings are indeed just, relations of justice obtain between God and human beings only due to the work of a prior act of mercy,[12] which draws human beings into an equality that, just as it made friendship between them possible, so does it make justice possible: "Even in respect of those things which are owed to creatures, God delivers more generously out of the excess of his goodness than the degree of the thing requires. For less would suffice for the preservation of due justice than what the divine goodness delivers, and it exceeds every creaturely proportion."[13] In either case, Thomas's or Nicholas's, the point is the same: "Mercy and truth have lovingly met, justice and peace have kissed."[14]

But if the elements of this sequence strung along the temporal course of salvation history cannot be linked through relations of necessity, neither are they linked merely contingently. In one sense Nicholas Love's sequentially temporal narrative presenting the incarnation as if it were a divine afterthought or reaction to a crisis of unexpectedly bad events as they happened to unfold, importantly misrepresents what for Thomas is the logic of the incarnation. On Love's conception of the divine governance and plan of salvation, there is nothing in the nature of *scientia* left to it at all. The unfortunately misleading picture presented in the *Mirrour* is that of a God attempting to catch up with events that have got out of hand, not that of a supreme governor of the universe acting out of overwhelming and all-foreseeing knowledge, *scientia*. For Thomas, on the contrary, the whole sequence was foreknown and foreordained in a single act of knowledge and will from all eternity. Of course, what in God is a single, indivisible, eternal act of providential willing, a willing that is *maxime liberalis*, the entirely free expression of the divine goodness and so an act of sheer generosity, is for us experienced as history, as a contingent narrative sequence, as one event following the other—creation succeeded by the fall, the fall succeeded by a prophecy to Abraham of a savior to come, the choosing of a prophetical people to whose prophecies Christ comes as fulfillment, who is then sacrificially killed, raised by his Father from the dead, and sends the Spirit of them both to his followers of whom Thomas numbers but one. Thomas the theologian knows the story to which he belongs is that which makes sense of him; but it is also a story that, as theologian, he has to attempt to make sense of for himself and for the church. It is his task as theologian to work out the logic of the historical sequence as in some way revealing, piecemeal, that which in God is but a single, undivided, and eternal act of love. But if it is a sequence, if it is history, indeed if it is what later comes to be called "salvation history," then well it may be that it is no sequence generated out of any necessity of nature, for it is the free love of God that generates it; but neither is it just history as "one damn thing after another," having no rationale, for it is the work of an all-knowing wisdom.

Therefore it is neither what *had* to happen, nor is it simply a whimsical post factum response to an unanticipated turn of events. Cur Deus homo, then? Why? Because it was *conveniens*, says Thomas in the first question of the third part of the *Summa*[15]—or "conuenient" and "skilful," as Nicholas Love says. Or "behovely," as Love's contemporary, Julian of Norwich, has it.[16]

EXCESS AS THE DIVINE NORM: THE "LOGIC" OF THE INCARNATION

Philosophers debate the logic of what is called "supererogation," that is to say, they debate the problematic nature of the call to act above and beyond what duty requires. What kind of "call" does the supererogatory make upon you? A kind of paradox is easily generated concerning, for example, the nature of courage. Soldiers are awarded medals for exceptional bravery—they are rewarded for acting in a way in which they are not obliged to act, and are not faulted for not so acting if they refrain from doing so. You cannot be obliged to fling yourself upon the unexploded grenade so as to shield your fellow soldiers from death, knowing you certainly will be killed when it detonates in two seconds time. But even if you cannot be court-martialed for not having so acted, you can, not irrationally, experience remorse, even a sense of failure because you did not, just as, also not irrationally, you can be rewarded posthumously with military honors if you do. What do you say, then, of the person who acts with courage above and beyond the call of duty which does not say of the person who refrains from doing so that he has in some way failed? What is the vocabulary that truly expresses the courage of the first that does not entail a false implication of cowardice in the second?

Thomas opens his discussion of the incarnation in the third part of the *Summa* with the statement that, granted God willed our salvation, his Son did not have to become incarnate; one imperious click of the divine finger and thumb would have done the job. Still, it was *conveniens*, "fitting," that he should stoop so low as to become man.[17] He goes on to explain that what counts as fitting is relative to the thing so described, for what fits a certain kind of thing is what belongs to it as a matter of its nature. Reasoning, for example, is a fitting way for human beings to employ their minds since they are of a "rational" sort. But God's nature is to be good. Hence, anything is fittingly done by God that belongs to the nature of the good. The next step is to quote the pseudo-Denys to the effect that it is the nature of the good to communicate itself,[18] and from that it follows that it is in the highest degree fitting (*pertinet*) that the highest good should communicate with creatures, and most especially (as Augustine says) that the highest good should be "so joined with created nature as to be one person, three ways uniting Word with soul and with flesh."[19] Thus Thomas.

As it stands, however, the case may seem ill made. To say the least, the comparison between the way in which it is fitting that rational beings should reason and the way in which a perfect goodness would fittingly become personally united with human nature is misleading, even if it is not (as it might well seem) plainly wrong-headed. For the sense in which it is "fitting" that rational beings engage in acts of reasoning is simply that, although human beings do not always and necessarily have actually to be reasoning just because they can, their doing so when they do is not above and beyond the normal expectations of a rational agent. There is nothing surprising, therefore, about a human being thinking through a problem of what to do about this or that, whereas when Thomas says that it is fitting that God should become man, he clearly does not mean that the Incarnation meets our ordinary expectations of what is a God-like thing to do. Yet that is the conclusion that his comparison appears to invite, namely that the incarnation was not indeed so much surprising as just what you would expect of a God who is infinitely good. And since clearly Thomas never says that the incarnation is predictable in the way that necessary truths are predictable, and everywhere denies it, he cannot mean as much here. He believes, as he says repeatedly, that the incarnation is a free expression of the divine will and, if antici-pated (as he believes the Psalmist and some of the prophets appeared to him to do), it is so only by virtue of a special divine revelation.[20]

However, the misleading impression of this argument is rein-forced by the appeal Thomas makes to the pseudo-Denys's *Divine Names*, for the text in question would seem only to exacerbate the problem. For in chapter 4 of that work the pseudo-Denys asks us to compare the diffusion of the divine goodness with the sun's diffusion of light—it does so, he says (in the Latin text that Thomas was using) *non ratiocinans aut preeligens*, "without deliberation or prior choice," just as a light source cannot but shed light: again, implying that the incarnation was not to be thought of as merely the sort of thing you might expect of the divine goodness, but was rather the *necessary* expression of it. The statement in the *Summa* referring to this passage is, however, if taken in isolation, just too compressed to be otherwise than misleading. As is often necessary when encountering Thomas's shorthand references to other texts and authorities, cross-referencing is essential because taken for granted, and so with this case—he clearly expects the reader of this citation in the *Summa* to refer to his commentary on the same passage in the *Divine Names*. There Thomas clarifies, remarking that the pseudo-Denys's comparison between the necessity of the sun's shedding light and the "necessity" of the incarnation has value only up to a point, and then only when one makes an all-important distinction. It is true that the sun simply cannot help shedding light because that is its nature. Hence, even were the sun to have the power of deliberation and choice in other matters, its shedding light or not shedding it would not be subject to that power. Whereas in the case of God, it is true that it is in the nature of the divine goodness, simply because it is in the nature of goodness as such, that it radiates. Yet not only does God *possess* the powers of intellect and will, unlike the sun— more than that, the divine intellect and will are, unlike those of any rational creature, *identical* with God's nature: so you cannot construe anything that belongs to the divine nature as in any way distinct from the free, intelligent, act of God.[21] To repeat: *et ille est maxime liberalis.*

Therefore, the obviously consistent way of interpreting what Thomas says in that first article of the *Tertia Pars* (consistent, that is, with his known views) is as the paradox that the goodness of the divine *nature* is supererogatory, superlative, excessive, "above and beyond." That, after all, is the meaning of *maxime liberalis.* One gets some idea of how this might be so if one were to imagine an army in which every soldier acts exactly as military duty requires, no one doing less, but also no one ever doing more than is expected of them: it is an army in which there are no cowards, but also no heroes. This is an army, then, from which supererogatory service is entirely absent, though standard expectations of courage are universally met. It is, as any commanding officer knows, a situation more nearly impossible than merely unlikely. For an army in which there is no past tradition of heroic courage, nor any future likelihood that there will be those who will respond *beyond* expectation to extraordinary circumstances with extreme and supererogatory bravery, is one in which morale is likely to be so low as to diminish the chances of ordinarily required levels of courage being achieved by the average foot soldier. In a certain way, then, the paradox is that the heroic action of some, of a degree that cannot be expected of anyone because it is supererogatory, is the necessary condition of the default level of courage being achieved by the many.

The logic of this is admittedly topsy-turvy but in fact is perfectly familiar in other contexts. It is comparable to the sudden change of key in a piece of music which, though it could not have been anticipated by the music that precedes it, instantly reveals those preceding bars in a new light, as being *exactly right, perfectly judged*, in how they lead to the change of key. In retrospect that shift in tonality becomes seen to have been anticipated, as it were, just as Christians came in retrospect to see the words of Isaiah to have anticipated the coming of Christ. And something like this seems to be the logic underlying the paradoxes of many patristic and medieval accounts of the divine goodness. Eight hundred years before Thomas, the pseudo-Denys described God's goodness as *ordinarily* "ecstatic," as an *excessus*, hyperbolic by default.[22] A few decades after Thomas, Meister Eckhart, his fellow Dominican, described the divine goodness as a "seething and a boiling," a *bullitio*, and, continuing with the culinary metaphor, called creation a "boiling over," an *ebullitio*.[23] And when Thomas describes God's nature as *maxime liberalis*, his rhetoric might be less colorful but the meaning is the same: just as it is in the nature of a rational creature to reason, so that reasoning is *conveniens* as human beings go, so with God—his goodness expressing itself in the incarnation is *conveniens*, that is, it is just as you would expect of a being whose default disposition is that of *excessive* generosity, *liberalitas*. The incarnation is *conveniens*, therefore, because while not exactly necessary (for what is done out of necessity cannot be done out of generosity) it is not arbitrary, either. For what is done out of generosity is done out of the full weight of an infinite goodness, not on the whim of an omnipotent being merely flexing superior muscle for the heck of it. The incarnation, therefore, shows you something about God that you could not otherwise have known, that he is *maxime libe-ralis*, just as the heroic soldier shows you something about armies that you could not have known from the handbook of expected military conduct. Armies are as good as they are only because some of their soldiers are better than could be expected of all of them: the averagely good cannot be the universally highest standard achieved. In short, acting "over the top" is, as Thomas understands the matter, *normal* for God. It is in that sense, then, that the incarnation is *conveniens*.

CHRIST, POVERTY, AND THE DOMINICANS

Unsurprisingly, the topsy-turvy logic of the incarnation—the logic, that is to say, whereby its excessiveness is exactly what is "fitting"—extends across the whole of Thomas's theology, as of his life; chapter by chapter, we have in fact been doing little but reviewing ways in which supererogation was for Thomas the norm theologically, but also personally. Expected in his family circle was a sensible career as a senior ecclesiastic in the monastery of Monte Cassino. So Thomas goes embarrassingly mad and becomes a poor friar instead. Expected as a theological master in Paris was his close adherence to Augustine's teaching as a criterion of theological rectitude. And so Thomas does, but so also will he read the pagan Greek Aristotle and any Muslim or Jewish heretics who serve his purposes, which seemed to the unreconstructed Augustinians of his day to yield an anthropology treading a line dangerously close to materialism. Expected of a theologian is a doctrine of God. So Thomas teaches a *docta ignorantia* instead, and, as a bonus, teaches the Jewish and the Muslim theologians on whom he so heavily draws that their one God is no more "knowable" than his one God who is three. Expected of Thomas the Dominican preacher is sound teaching about the good life for a human being. So Thomas says that the only way to live the good human life is by consorting in friendship with God and living by the divine life instead. Once again, the logic of excess as normal is plain—to be *at least* human you have to be *more than* human, you have to live by that pure excess that is grace. For Thomas, the Christian life itself is as such *gratis*. At every level then, the expected is the surprising, for you know Christian truth to have been told only when an eyebrow is raised.

And nothing raised more scandalized eyebrows in his time than the image of Christ that the poverty of Thomas's Dominican vocation claimed to reproduce. Thomas's formal Christology—as it were the metaphysics of the God made man—shocked no one: it was but the ancient Council of Chalcedon spelled out, the Christological lingua franca of his times. But the narrative of how Christ lived and died that emerged in the third part of the *Summa* was vintage Dominican, the image of Christ as poor friar, or, conversely, the poor friar embodying the *vita apostolica*, what Thomas calls the *sequela Christi*, the way to follow Christ for the thirteenth-century church.

Thomas untranslatably describes the life of Christ as God's *conversatio* with the human race.[24] Rightly conveying the meaning of a two-way conversation, the Latin word also carries with it stronger meanings of solidarity, a sharing of conditions—good, bad, and indifferent—and therefore by his use of this word, Thomas invites the theologian back into the vocabulary of friendship. Presented with the argument that Jesus' life ought rather to have been that of the solitary than that of friends engaged in a conversation—because the contemplative life of the solitary is the most perfect—he replies:

> Taken just in the abstract, the contemplative life is better than [that form of] the active life that is organized in concern for bodily activities: but the active life in accordance with which a person passes on to others the fruits of contemplation by means of preaching and teaching is more perfect than the life merely of contemplation, because such a life derives from an overflow of contemplation. And that is the reason why Christ chose a life of that kind.[25]

Next, Thomas asks whether Christ ought to have led an austere life of fasting and abstinence, since John the Baptist did, and Jesus ought at least to have matched his forerunner in austerity (if not to have outdone him). To which Thomas replies that Jesus came to live among human beings in solidarity with them as they are, and to have disengaged from one of the central forms of human interaction, which is eating and drinking together, would have detracted from the purpose of the incarnation itself. Hence, it was fully appropriate that he should take food and drink in common with others, and do so as they do, by enjoying meals together.[26] That he began his preaching mission with a forty-day fast is not inconsistent with this general way of life—in fact, returning to the theme of the relationship between the contemplative and active lives, Thomas adds that it is perfectly appropriate that those in the business of translating truths attained in contemplation into the word preached to others should first engage in the contemplation, and then return back to the life shared in common with those others.[27]

Thus far, it is clear that Thomas has a not too well disguised agenda of defending the Dominican way of life against the monks' taunt at his inception as a master at Paris that the friars were unintelligible extra-canonical hybrids and ought to make up their minds one way or the other which they wanted to be. They could be vowed monks, devoted to a life of prayer, manual labor, strict silence, and rigorous fasting in accordance with the ancient monastic traditions; or else they should give up the pretense of being anything other than easygoing preachers, usurping the preaching and teaching office of bishops and their secular clergy while claiming the rights of a vowed community without paying the ascetical price. Thomas's reply is not that Jesus was a closet

Dominican *avant la lettre*; it is rather that a Dominican friar can claim to be a true follower of Christ in his way as the Cistercian monk may in his, that the Dominican way of preaching is a genuine *imitatio Christi*. The Dominicans, in fact, closely follow the pattern of Jesus' life insofar as their preaching of the word is rooted in the contemplative life and practiced as a *conversatio* within the community to which they preach. Of course, then, Dominicans pray; of course Dominicans fast when common Christians fast, as, from time to time, Jesus did; but otherwise, like Christ himself, their mission is to preach the word, and they can do that only if they live a life in solidarity with, not in separation from, the common Christians whom they served.

All of which brings to a head the issue that recurrently plagued Thomas in Paris: why the friars' extreme commitment to poverty? There is little doubt that the hostility forthcoming from the secular masters to the presence of the friars in the university was provoked by the feeling that they had been ascetically outflanked by these imitators of the "poor Christ," who flaunted their rootless poverty as if in criticism of the complacent security of the property-owning ecclesiastical establishment. The conservative reaction is, after all, understandable. You can reliably count on the ways and means of religious communities and individuals whose lives are personally locked into the ownership of fixed capital. But you never know where you are with beggars who, owning nothing personally but what they can acquire of food and clothing by begging day to day and hand to mouth, are thereby locked into no fixed and enduring social commitments. If you refuse to depend on the security of fixed capital, you disengage from the stable communities organized on the basis of such securities.

Over and over again Dominican poverty got Thomas into trouble as a theological master at Paris. Dominicans—and even more, perhaps, the Franciscans—seemed to be no more than social and economic parasites who excepted themselves from the common obligation to work for a living and, in the name of Christ, seemed to think the wider community owed them a living on account of a "poverty" that was not the true need of the involuntarily indigent, but a *chosen* way of life. So they felt entitled to question the consistency in the friars' defense of their unmonastic practices, a defense made out on the grounds that their mission of preaching entailed a more open solidarity with the common community, when their refusal to work for their living and reliance on begging meant that they systematically exploited the community with which they claimed that solidarity. Thus William of St. Amour in 1256; thus, much to the same effect, Gerard of Abbeville in 1268–69, each in turn leading a revolt of the established masters against the disruptive novelties of the teaching, preaching friars.

Thomas himself noted the objection to mendicant poverty and took it seriously both in his 1256 response to William and in his 1269 response to later attacks. In the 1256 polemic *Contra impugnantes Dei cultum et religionem* Thomas makes it clear why the friars have the right to preach and hear confessions, but above all why, that being so, it is a necessary means but certainly not the point of the friars' vocation that they live lives of absolute poverty.[28] In fact, Thomas says, it is a confused and thoroughly wrongheaded reading of the preaching of Jesus to suppose that voluntary poverty, which Jesus certainly commended, should take precedence over the fundamental commandments of the Law, which are the love of God and love of neighbor. The poverty of the poor friars, he adds, has no merit whatsoever except insofar as it serves the interests of charity, which it does precisely insofar as it frees the friars from impediments to their preaching. It is in that preaching that consists the particular charism of love and solidarity with their fellow creatures, the solidarity, the *conversatio*, that is distinctively theirs. But in that service Thomas robustly defends voluntary poverty as a lifestyle directly serving the distinctive mission of preaching and teaching.

Likewise in the *Summa*, now responding to later attacks on mendicant poverty in 1268–69, Thomas argues that Jesus' life shows us how a mission of preaching requires freedom from the responsibilities of property ownership:

> It was appropriate that when in the world Christ should lead a life of poverty. Above all because this was all of a piece with the task of preaching which, he said, was the reason he had come—see Mark 1:38: 'let us go into the neighboring villages and cities there to preach, it was for this that I came.' Preachers of the word of God, if they are to give themselves

wholly to the task of preaching, ought to be entirely free of responsibility for worldly things, which is not possible if they possess wealth.[29]

Besides, as Paul says (2 Corinthians 8:9), it is in the nature of the incarnation itself that Christ came into the world himself materially "needy" precisely in order to more effectively dispense spiritual riches. And then there is the practical matter that if acquisition of personal wealth is allowed into the preacher's way of life at any point, there is danger of the preaching being seen as a form of fundraising—for the modern reader thoughts of Chaucer's Pardoner come to mind, the burden of whose preaching "ever was / *radix malorum est cupiditas*," while duping rich and poor alike into paying stiff charges for his fraudulent pardons. For the Dominican Thomas, however, it is likely to have been his founder's own experience of preaching in Languedoc that provoked this comment. Poverty and preaching go together, Thomas says, because effective preaching is impossible if there is anything in it for the preacher. That is what the life of Christ teaches—as it were, his poverty was Jesus' preaching about preaching—and that is the Christ of which the Dominican way of life is the *imitatio*. You do not have to be a Dominican to be a follower of Christ. But you do have to be a follower of Christ to be a Dominican, and over and over again Thomas's account of the life of Christ reflects the author's Dominican spiritual priorities. Not all forms of religious life in community require so radical a form of poverty to serve their spiritual purposes. The military orders need resources aplenty, Thomas says—weapons, castles, the impedimenta of war;[30] likewise the hospitallers, the nursing orders, need material stores if they are to carry out their mission effectively.[31] Poverty is less integral even to the vocation of monks living the contemplative life than it is for the friars; it is enough for monks that they collectively possess the material resources sufficient to provide for the stability of their lives of prayer, and so they too need materials to the extent that the monastery be as far as possible an economically self-sufficient community.[32] But if the friars are to be effective preachers, Thomas says, they need to be as free as possible of care for material resources, a condition that they can achieve if they are provided by the community they serve with the moderate level of resources required to sustain their mission. Hence, they have to *ask* for a living from those they serve, serving them while counting on nothing in return beyond what is sufficient to the day.

Therefore, it is not poverty but preaching that is the point of the Dominican calling—and the thing to be said for the special place of poverty in the Dominican way of life is that they above all need their poverty in order to be effective preachers.[33] Thomas is highly sensitive to the question of the standards of practice that are required of the preacher who stands absolutely exposed before the judgment of the word he preaches, for preaching is how the commandment of love is lived by Dominicans. But preaching is in principle ineffective if there is any possibility of its being bought, and wage earning by any other means can only distract from the core mission. Only total poverty and dependence on alms freely given can guarantee the freedom of spirit on the back of which alone the poor Christ can be convincingly preached.[34]

THE POOR CHRIST AND SIN

The poor Christ, therefore, is at the center of Thomas's theology, and in two distinct, but closely related, ways—first of all as Jesus' human practice of living of which the Dominican practice is the imitation, and second as a key to understanding the theology of the incarnation itself, that self-pauperization that is the abasement of the Son of God who becomes the son of Mary, a human being who is, as the Letter to the Hebrews has it (4:15), a High Priest who is "one with us in everything except sin."

A great deal of theological writing about Christ, especially in liberal Protestant circles since the nineteenth century, gets itself into conceptual tangles over traditional Christological formulas, especially with the key conciliar doctrine that Thomas's Christology attempts to expound—namely, that the person of Christ is completely divine and completely human. In fact theological skepticism in such circles seems to affect either side of the equation, whether the full divinity or the full humanity of Christ, but mostly the simultaneous assertion, as in the decree of the Council of Chalcedon in 451, of both.

As to Christ's full humanity, for some it is as hard today as it was in the first centuries of Christian history to believe that one and the same person could be fully and truly human if at the same time that person was truly and fully divine, and this for one reason above all: it would seem that the affirmation of the divine person-hood of Christ would have to exclude his being human in any sense of the word "human" that actual human beings are able to recognize if that divine personhood of Christ must exclude the very possibility of Christ's sinning. For sin, or the proneness to it, seems to be one of the most universal of all human phenomena, something you can count on in human beings if you can count on anything at all "human." In fact, some deeply embedded instinct seems to get in the way of taking seriously the Letter to the Hebrews, for we are inclined to think that we could not recognize ourselves in anything but a nature prone to sinfulness; we think that sinning simply comes with being human, that human beings tend to sin in the same sort of way that parents as a matter of course tend to love their children. That instinct causes us not to be surprised that people sin, hence an explanation of the fact that human beings sin seems otiose, and anyway, an explanation of so general a fact would itself seem to have too general a character to be an explanation of anything in particular. You might need, and you might be able to offer, a reason for the particular sin of a particular person, because that might be surprising. But it can seem too much a matter of course that people sin to require special explanations of the general tendency. And yet though there are Christian theologies that seem to work from the assumption that human sinfulness is "natural," even they must face the fact that deeply embedded in the Christian traditions is a doctrine of original sin that seems to offer just that—an explanation. Why? Why should it be thought that any such explanation is required?

We understand Thomas's theology only when we understand why he thinks that an explanation is indeed required. For Thomas, it *ought* to be surprising that human beings sin. We *ought* to need an explanation of why they do so. Even if humans were statistically just as likely to sin as they are to love their children, it cannot, for Thomas, be right in the same sense of the word "natural" to say that human beings naturally sin as that they naturally love their children. To find oneself puzzled by the words of the Letter to the Hebrews because the exception of his sinlessness seems a very drastic limitation upon Christ's solidarity with us; to find oneself wondering whether Christ could really have known what it is like to be us if he does not experience sin, as it were, from the *inside*; to imagine that one of the solidarities in which human beings share is solidarity in sin because we all do it and so understand one another in our sinning; to conclude, therefore, that it is a restriction on Christ's solidarity with us that he is absolutely sinless, for a Christ who could not sin would seem not to share our human nature in its concrete actuality—all this is, for Thomas, getting things upside down.

In fact it is just such thoughts that the doctrine of original sin is good for tearing us away from. The human predicament that is sin may be pervasive, but it is *not* natural. It is an unnatural catastrophe disruptive of, not undergirding, our solidarities. Because of sin we do *not* know what it is like to be human, which is why in the end an ethic based upon our own unaided knowledge of human nature is ultimately unsatisfactory, ultimately incapable of discerning what our nature demands of us beyond a few formal generalities. Unlike Christ, it is *we* who are incompletely human. Docetism is the heresy that Jesus is not truly a human being, but only apparently so, because he is too good to be true. Thomas's position is that it is we who, on account of our sinfulness, are not good enough to be true. We do *not* know for ourselves and from ourselves what it is like to be truly human. From ourselves and from others at best we get partial glimpses of what a true human being looks like. But we have no full picture of what it is to be truly human except from the human nature of Christ. The point about the exception made in the Letter to the Hebrews is that "solidarity in sin" is in fact an oxymoron. There is indeed, as Plato points out in a similar connection, little honor among thieves, and if it is to be supposed that gangs of Mexican drug barons represent the sort of base level of human psychology upon the foundations of which alone it is safe to construct an account of human nature, then, like Hobbes, the best that can be hoped for is a self-interested truce between robber barons as the attainable maximum achievement of human social relationships. Such is the cynical realism of the sophistical Thrasymachus in Plato's *Republic*,[35] whose Hobbesian politics is a regime of universal egoism held unstably in place by the will of the most powerful egoists, a proto-Dantean *Inferno*. Such, Thrasymachus argues, is the only politics which answers to the grim facts of human nature as it really is. To which Plato's response is that what Thrasymachus describes is far from the politics of the real. On the contrary, his is the political realization precisely of a twilit world of illusion, a politics powerfully imagined in *Republic* as the political routinization of flickering shadows projected on the back wall of an ill-lit cave.[36]

Likewise, the casual theological identification of fallen human nature with human nature as such ignores what is manifestly intended by the author of Hebrews, for whom Christ alone can perfectly communicate with us because he is perfectly, indefectibly, *human*; it is precisely because he is free of sin that the intimacy of Christ's solidarity with our sinful selves is unhindered, and in him the view of what we truly are is uncluttered by the obstructing impedimenta of sin; and so it is precisely because we are *de*humanized by our sinfulness that our solidarities with Christ and with one another are so tragically awry, and in consequence, our relationships, personal and political, beset by fantasy and illusion. For Thomas, Christ is more intimately human than we are, not less; closer to our true selfhood than we are; in closer solidarity with us *because* he is without sin, not distanced from us on account of his innocence, as we are distanced from ourselves by sin, from one another, and from God. Once again, then, voluntary poverty finds its way back into the picture. For the truly human is perfectly visible in Christ precisely because his is a humanity that has no need for the cluttering baggage of possessions, and so his humanity can come into plain view—*ecce homo*, says Pilate with unwittingly accurate truth of a *naked* Christ. By contrast, our humanity is obscured by the apparatus of neediness, hence of acquisitiveness, with which we seek to disguise our human inadequacies from ourselves. Voluntary poverty is the friar's way back into the full humanity that is visible in Christ, a humanity whose unobstructed visibility in their lives is an essential condition of the effectiveness of their mission to preach, as it was of Christ's. The poverty of Christ, therefore, is what allows us to see that he was indeed *verus homo*, truly human—indeed, the *only* truly human. Thus the Dominican Thomas and his Dominican Christ.

THE DIVINITY OF CHRIST

The complete humanity of Jesus would be a cause of doubt that he was also *verus Deus* only for those who fall into the error of supposing that the terms "truly human" and "truly divine" must stand in relations of opposition to each other, as zero to sum. And it is not as if there were none today who so suppose. John Hick did with startling directness. It is "as devoid of meaning," he declared, to say "that the historical Jesus of Nazareth was also God" as it would be to say of one and the same shape that it is both a square and a circle.[37] If nothing else would convince us of it, Hick's assimilation of the relationship between the divine and the human as formulated in the Chalcedonian doctrine of the incarnation to that of the exclusion of one geometrical shape by another would be reason enough to see the point of Thomas's strategy of first working through a doctrine of God before engaging with issues of Christology. For, as we saw in Chapter 3, it is not that somehow God *condescends* so as not to exclude human nature and agency, but rather that mutual exclusion between the divine being and agency and the human is impossible. It is true that in the logical territory of shapes, the space staked out by the square does in that way exclude the circle from it: they simply cannot be the same shape, so it *must be* a contradiction to say of one and the same shape that it is both. But the space marked out by the square in the territory of shapes neither excludes nor includes the space occupied by yellow in the territory of colors: "a somewhat that is both square and yellow" *cannot be* a contradictory description. Shapes and colors do not share enough in common such that, the one being true of an object, the other must be false of it.[38]

If that is true of colors and shapes—which, after all, share much in common in that both are properties of material objects and therefore differ in one of the ways that material objects can—then all the more will it be true that being yellow and its being 4:00 p.m. on Friday, 26 October 2011, cannot so differ as to exclude each other. The point in elementary logic that Hick evidently could not see is that in general, mutual exclusion between *a* and *b* is possible only when *a* and *b* belong to the same class of comparison. To see this one has only to ask: what is the logical space that *a*'s being of a certain color and *b*'s occurring at a certain time of the day must necessarily exclude each other from?

Now as to the divinity and the humanity of Christ, these differ in whatever way it is that Creator and creature differ and only thus, as Thomas says. For they cannot differ as kinds of being differ. Humans are beings of a certain kind, but, as we have seen, there is no kind of being that God is. To understand their difference to entail their mutual exclusion would require the description of what it is that they differ *as*, and that would require the description of some logical space occupied by God such that the human is excluded from it, for otherwise that exclusion can make no sense. But it was precisely the point of Thomas's doctrine of God that there is not, and there could not be, any such common territory. God and creature—therefore, God and the *human* creature—cannot stand in relations of mutual exclusion because Creator and creature cannot so stand one to the other. Or, to put it in another way, for Thomas the transcendence of God is so absolute that as between God and any creature all possibility of exclusion between them is excluded. It is precisely *because of*, not *in spite of*, the absoluteness of the difference between Creator and creature that the possibility of that immanence which is the incarnation, an indwelling of the divine and the human in the one person of Christ, is conceivable.

In fact, it is in Christ and in Christ alone that Donne's "interinanimation" between God and the human is fully and literally possible. Two created souls in love with each other remain two identities, for all the power of Donne's metaphor of the "new" and "abler soule" that lovers become. And for all that we understand

Catherine Earnshaw when she protests to Nelly in the kitchen of Wuthering Heights, "Nelly, I *am* Heathcliff," we know that she is not Heathcliff, and that their creaturely oneness in love is imperfect, and the rhetoric of it hyperbolic. Why? Because two creatures of the same nature necessarily exclude each other as individuals—they are always *two*. Whereas God and I? Here there can be no exclusion, just because God is distinct from me as Creator is from creature, and no relationship can be more intimate than that between my being and the Creator who thus authors and sustains it. Nor can any distinction be more radical than that between Creator and creature—between, that is, my creaturehood that stands wholly vulnerable to the nothingness out of which it is created, and the Creator who holds me secure in existence, secure in that existence *only* as thus held. Between my existence and my nothingness there is nothing but the divine love. Once again, we are back to the beginning: Donne's poem is hyperbole as of the human erotic; but hyperbole, as we saw, is the default voice of the erotic divine, which is nimiety as normal. For in Christ the human and the divine are but one person; the two natures are, as the theologians say, "hypostatically" united, one in the person they are the natures of, distinct as *only* creature and Creator can be. But on only a thoroughly idolatrous notion of God, one that reduces God to the standing of a creature, *could* it be true that, as Hick maintains, there is contradiction in saying of one and the same person that he is truly human, truly divine. That one and the same person can be both truly human and truly divine is, of course, a surpassing mystery. True as it is for Thomas the faithful Christian, false it might have been—it is not a necessary truth. Credible as it is for Thomas, implausible it certainly is. If it is true it is amazingly true. That belief in the incarnation is unamazingly self-contradictory, however, is the one thing that for Thomas it *could not* be.

ONE PERSON, TWO NATURES: EXCLUDING EXCLUSION

So much for Thomas on the logic of the incarnation. There is of course no purpose in logic other than to allow language to speak, and there is none in Thomas's logic of the incarnation other than to allow the language of intimacy between God and the human to speak with a clear voice. Within Thomas's Christology, excluding exclusion is only the first stage, though an all-important one. For virtually all the ways of lapsing into garbled or garbling talk about Christ involve either affirming the divinity of Christ in some form of exclusion of the humanity, or affirming the humanity of Christ in some form of diminution of his divinity. It makes perfectly good sense to say of the historical person, Jesus, that he was truly God, though as to his humanity he was but an apparition, as the Docetist heretics did: but it makes no sense to say so and then to prescribe for us an *imitatio Christi*. It makes perfectly good sense to say of Jesus Christ that though not the incarnate Word of God he was a good man, full of grace, as the Nestorian heretics did—but none to say that such a man's death and resurrection defeats sin and death for all time and history. Thomas wants to be able to say, along with the Council of Chalcedon, that the one person who was and is Jesus Christ was and is both fully human and fully divine, and, just as at the personal level Thomas's Dominican poverty was a practice of ditching the clutter of possessive impedimenta that would have obscured his vision of Christ, so as theologian he needs to clear away the logical clutter that will muffle the clear doctrinal voice of the conciliar decree. In the clear, uncluttered vision of Christ he can see humanity made whole, and in that humanity made whole is seen the *imago Dei.* Christ's humanity is how his nature as *verus Deus* is revealed. And Christ's poverty is the revelation of Christ's humanity as *verus homo*, an entirely unencumbered human being. It is in the imitation of that poverty of Christ alone that that vision and that life, the *claritas* of the theologian and the *sanctitas* of the Dominican, become one in the person of Thomas Aquinas. And the chief visible clue as to the nature of his holiness consists in his being, like Christ himself, a completely uncluttered man.

EIGHT

The Eucharist and Eschatology

WHERE THE SUMMA STOPS

We end with the Eucharist. This, significantly, is the last
completed topic of Thomas's *Summa theologiae*. It follows his
treatment of baptism and confirmation—though the text of the
Summa in fact continues thereafter, breaking off midway through
the discussion of the sacrament of penance. In Chapter 1 of this
outline of Thomas's theology I commented on the theological
significance of Thomas's not having brought the work to its final
state of completion: it tells us a lot about Thomas the theologian,
I said, that he is content that his life should come to an end having
freely chosen to leave his work as a theologian unfinished.
Theology, for Thomas, would not be worth writing at all if there
were nothing more important than it. Theology matters only

because—and when—there is more to life than theology, and when that "more" shows its presence *within* the theology that is done. So Thomas fails to finish, thereby exhibiting the presence of this "more" in the most dramatic way possible—by leaving space for it. His final silence is not an empty and disappointing failure to finish. It is an apotheosis. By his silence Thomas does not stop teaching theology. He does not stop thereby doing theology. On the contrary, by his silence he teaches something about doing theology that he could not have taught by any other means.

Of course, there have always been those for whom the question will not go away concerning how Thomas might have completed the *Summa* had he done so, as if it were a decidable question, and as if deciding it mattered more than all the significance that Josef Pieper discovered in the work's very incompleteness. Of course Thomas had intended to finish his treatment of penance and then to write up the remaining three sacraments of the seven that, by his time, the Church believed Christ had inaugurated, namely holy orders, matrimony, and what today is commonly known as the sacrament of the sick (in Thomas's time until nearly our own it was called "extreme unction," the ugly Latinism meaning nothing more than the anointing of the gravely ill, of those *in extremis*). Can we know, and should we care, what otherwise Thomas would have written about by way of rounding off his curriculum of theological training for preachers?

Disciples of Thomas did in fact finish the text in a way, by filling out the unfinished agenda of the *Summa* with material from his much earlier *Scriptum* on the Sentences of Peter the Lombard. But this has much the same effect as Süssmayr's completing Mozart's Requiem: it's a good guess. You know that Mozart would have completed the last few bars of the Dies irae, that he would have composed a Sanctus, a Benedictus, an Agnus Dei, and the other standard texts of the Catholic requiem mass, had he lived to do so. But what they would have been like, how they would have sounded, we can never know, the point about Mozart being that he rarely does next what even intelligent guesswork would predict he is going to do. The result: Süssmayr is predictably Mozartian just where Mozart typically wouldn't have been.

So it is with Thomas's *Summa*. We know that he would have completed his study of the remaining sacraments, we know that he would have given some account of the four "last things," death, judgment, heaven, and hell, and his disciples complete the work according to an uncontroversial plan. But the point about the *Summa*, as we have seen, is precisely that it is *not* the *Scriptum* on the Sentences. And if, to repeat, the incompleteness of the *Summa* itself says something theological that completeness wouldn't, then Thomas's intentions should *not* be gainsaid by "completing" it. He did not want the work to be completed, so it should never have been done. What is more, if one had to say that there was any significance in where exactly Thomas's work does peter out unfinished, then that it is in the midflow of his sacramental theology is strikingly appropriate. For Thomas's theology of the sacraments, and especially his theology of the Eucharist, is just where the lineaments of that theological persona that I have stressed in this little book are so distinctively his and are most distinctly to be observed. Pretty much everything that matters to Thomas theologically can be found in and extruded from his theology of the Eucharist.

CORPUS CHRISTI

In 1264 Pope Urban IV issued the bull *Transiturus de hoc mundo* ordering the eucharistic feast of *Corpus Christi* to be celebrated throughout the entire Latin Rite. Pope Urban asked Thomas to compile the texts of the office of the feast and to select the scriptural readings for the Mass of the day. This Thomas did, putting together for the office a selection of psalms and other scriptural readings and adding some hymns and antiphons of his own composition. For the *Magnificat*, recited at the end of the evening office of Vespers, he wrote the following antiphon:

> O sacred feast, in which Christ is our food,
> the memory of his passion recalled.
> The soul is filled with thanksgiving, a pledge of
> future glory is given to us.[1]

Being of Thomas's own composition, unsurprisingly this short prayer contains a précis of his eucharistic theology as a whole, it highlights his own doctrinal and devotional priorities and shows them to be rooted firmly in the soil of the scriptural texts, especially the gospels of John 6 and Luke 22. The eucharist is a "sacred feast," a celebration of food, indeed it is a celebration of Christ as "our food," based on Jesus' own declaration that he is "the living bread that has come down from heaven" (John 6:51). Jesus calls on his followers to eat this food, which is the "flesh of the Son of Man" (John 6:53) and does so on the eve of his passion, asking his disciples to do so "as a memorial of me" (Luke 22:19). Therefore, anyone who eats this food will have a pledge of "eternal life, and I shall raise him up on the last day" to "future glory" (John 6:54). Thus do Christians have reason to give thanks (Luke 22:17) as all in general do for food, but as they especially do for what Jesus calls "real food," namely himself (John 6:55).

THE EUCHARIST AS THE MEANING OF FOOD

If the antiphon, *O sacrum convivium*, is a précis of Thomas's eucharistic theology, equally we may say that his eucharistic theology is a précis of his theology as a whole. And in the spirit of summary, let us return to the topic that preoccupied us earlier in this essay, that of Thomas's philosophy of mind, and how by abstraction it forms or grasps meanings or, as we would nowadays say, "concepts." Thomas's is far from the Lockean account of abstraction, according to which by its means we pick out the minimum thread of continuous features possessed in common by a range of objects. For Thomas, to grasp the concept of a thing is to have learned a vocabulary and a set of judgments, a network of connections concretely linking that object into a world of meanings, into a language. In short, whereas Lockean abstractions "thin out" the meaning of the objects of which it forms the concepts, Thomas's abstractions thicken those meanings up; Lockean abstractions, I said, are "pale and effete," Thomas's abstractions "polychrome and dense."

But I also said that it is utterly characteristic of Thomas's theological temperament and for him no surprise, being rather exactly what you would expect of him, that the most sublime and unutterable mysteries of the divine are to be found contained in the lowest and most material forms of human life, of which, as we saw in Chapter 5, nutrition, eating and drinking, the supply of the most basic needs of *any* form of life, are the lowest, most primitive. Human eating and drinking is on a biological par with the cabbage deriving nutrition from the soil, with the sparrow pecking at my garden feeder, with the cat devouring the sparrow, with the horse at the trough; but while the sparrow, as I do, eats, the sparrow does not, as I do, eat meals, for meals are episodes of eating that are drawn into a language, a language perhaps of thanksgiving or of friendship, perhaps of hospitality to a stranger, perhaps of birthday celebration or of remembering a friend lost, but mainly of family and neighborhood sociality; so that it is fair to say that my eating a meal with my family and friends is *real* eating, eating that is more real, because more replete with density of meaning, than a sparrow's pecking at my garden feeder. Our eating is of thicker semantic texture than is the sparrow's, and in that sense is a more real eating and drinking, the food more "really" food.

Understanding the Eucharist begins with an understanding of the ordinary, secular meaning of food—giving life, sharing the gift, celebrating the giving, gratitude in receiving—the body is filled with food, and "the soul with thanksgiving," *mens impletur gratia.* The Eucharist is how Christians eat together, and their doing so gets its meaning in the first instance from the human engagement in those social transactions which we call meals—as Thomas notes, the reason why it was the custom in his time (and until recently in the Roman tradition) to fast from the night before in anticipation of taking communion is that it makes no sense to eat just before you are about to join others in a meal.[2]

But just as the Eucharist has to have some human meaning as food—it is a *convivium,* a "feast"—so food is shown by the Eucharist to have a meaning that transcends the human, and as it transcends so it deepens that human meaning—it is a "sacred feast." The Eucharist, to do its work as a sacred sign must first do its work as a sign; therefore, it must seem like what it is, namely a meal. But it is also important that it should not seem like breakfast, which it is not. If no theology of the Eucharist can get going except on the basis of humanly meaningful practices of eating and drinking, the Eucharist shows those practices to be a *sacrament* in that it reveals, and makes real, something divine about the meaning of eating and drinking of which otherwise we could not know. Just as the sparrow's pecking at the feeder is only abstractly, that is, in respect of very general biological features, connected with the eating of a human family's meals—for the family's eating together is eating drawn into a far wider, more complex, deeper set of semantic relationships—so in the Eucharist those humanly meaningful practices of eating and drinking are drawn into the eschatological mystery of the Trinitarian life itself, our share in which is pledged to us—*futurae gloriae nobis pignus datur*. The Eucharist therefore depends upon the human meaning of food, but it deepens what it depends upon.

Herein is the reason why the Eucharist appeals so directly to Thomas. It connects with such immediacy and force to the driving energy of his theology, to what I have called his "materialism." For Thomas, if you are looking for meaning you will find it in matter, and no more strikingly could this methodological principle be embodied than in the theology of the Eucharist. The Eucharist reveals something unexpected there in the meanings we achieve by eating and drinking together which, without the Eucharist, we could not know at all. And so what Thomas says about the relation of the Eucharist to food is this: you do not fully understand the *human* meaning of food until you understand its eucharistic depth: lurking within the quotidian business of meals is a mysterious dimension, waiting to be disclosed. The Eucharist discloses it.

Now in affirming that the Eucharist deepens the human meaning of eating and drinking Thomas has something in mind to deny, namely that the Eucharist simply *adds* as it were superveniently to the human meaning of food a further theological meaning, such that you might, if you have faith, prefer to *see* food that way as you please—rather as one might happen to see (as synesthetically I do) Tuesday as a blue day of the week, and Thursday as yellow. The Eucharist is not an optional add-on "sacred" meaning of the secular and human business of eating and drinking together, an option available to people of faith: it *is* the meaning of eating and drinking together: "my flesh is real food, and my blood is real drink," Jesus says (John 6:55). It's just that you need faith to see that real meaning.

There is an issue of philosophical importance going on here, and not for the first time in this essay, it is an issue about meaning. The Eucharist tells us something about *real* food, about what food is *really* like—obviously as opposed to its fantastical and trivializing "fast" forms, but also as transcending the meaning of the most meaningful human celebration. Therefore, to say that the Eucharist reveals a depth within the human transactions of eating and drinking is simply to extend to this central Christian celebration what Thomas meant when he said in more general terms that understanding the concept of something is like throwing a light on it, revealing it in its full, concrete variety and differentiation. Just so: the Eucharist shows us something in the meaning of eating that otherwise we could not see. It does not supervene upon that meaning with an optional semantic extra. The Eucharist is about how things are, even if it takes faith—the Church's faith—to see it. It is not about how things can seem, however they are, just because you choose, personally or as a community, so to see them.

EUCHARISTIC CHANGE

To put it in another way, Thomas thinks that in the Eucharist something real happens, there is a real change. It may take belief, the belief of the Church, for the change to occur—the Church says, "This is my body, this is my blood," and so it is that they are. But just because it takes the Church's belief to make that change it does not follow that the change is mere make-believe. Thomas says of the Eucharist what he says of all the sacraments, that it is a "sign that effects what it signifies,"[3] that is to say, there is an utterance, but it is an utterance of such a kind that what it says it does, indeed the doing is done *in* the saying—the Eucharist is the concrete realization of faith itself, being the "realization of what is to come and evidence of things unseen," as the Letter to the Hebrews puts it (11:1).[4] There is nothing particularly mysterious, least of all is there anything of the magical mumbo-jumbo, about such performative kinds of communication, in which the utterance of words makes a real change in what there is. Sayings that are doings are an ordinary enough piece of human communicative apparatus. When I say to you "I love you" I do not merely issue a factual report on my mental state. I *make* love to you. I *get* married when, in all the appropriate circumstances, I say to you "I do," I am not merely recording a fact that is brought about otherwise than by my saying those words: in *saying* "I do," I *do* it.

You can see how Thomas gets to this performative character of sacramental action when he raises the question as to how the words of consecration of the bread and wine can be "true." The priest, referring to the unconsecrated bread, says "this is the body of Christ," and thereby the sacramental effect is completed. The problem that Thomas takes up with this account is that it is not until the whole sentence, "this is the body of Christ," is uttered that the change of the bread into the body of Christ is effected. It cannot be, he says, that the pronoun "this" refers to the body of Christ, because then the whole sentence would turn out to be the meaningless tautology, "This [i.e., my body] is my body." But if that cannot be right it would seem then to follow that the demonstrative pronoun "this" uttered at the beginning of the sentence must refer to the bread as not yet changed into the body of Christ. But that is no better, because then the words of consecration would turn out to mean: "This [bread] is the body of Christ," which, as Thomas says, is false. For the Church's teaching affirms clearly that in becoming the body of Christ the element ceases to be bread, though Luther, seeing the difficulty, but wishing to retain the Church's teaching on the real presence of Christ in the Eucharist, suggested that (in some way) the element remains the bread it began as, though now, alongside its nature as bread, it is also the true body of Christ. Thomas, however, has ruled out this option, already known to him three centuries before Luther.[5] For Thomas, the only defensible account of eucharistic change is that the whole substance of the bread is changed into the whole substance of the body of Christ: what was bread has now become the body of Christ, even though what remains the same in either case is that both are *food*, the one sustaining life for a time, the other sustaining life eternal.

Hence, as Thomas says, you have to regard the words of consecration not as grammatically descriptive, otherwise you find yourself in conceptual tangles of this sort. Again, Thomas is relying on a standard grammatical distinction, and on nothing especially theological. When one morning the president of Yale University, feeling particularly cheerful at the state of the university's investments, emails the university community with the message "Today is a university holiday," he *makes* a holiday of today. He does not first, truthfully, refer to what at the time of uttering the word "today" is a workday and then redescribe the workday as a holiday, as if university presidents had the power by fiat to change propositional truth-values at whim. If that were the grammar of Richard Levin's utterance the utterance would, as Thomas says, be false (and the Yale president's power more like that exercised by a Goebbels, that of tricking people by means of propagandistically redescriptive goebbeldegook, into believing what is false). Richard Levin is clear: in declaring today to be a university holiday he *makes* this day a holiday, only thus making the description "holiday" true of today. Presidents of Yale University have that power.

Thomas is just as clear: if what is changed is the meaning of the food—and it is, for what once was bread is now the body of Christ—this is because from the character of the bread and wine as food is elicited its real meaning as the body of Christ. The utterance, *Hoc est ... corpus meum*, is not only *significativum sed etiam factivum*, it not only says something, it does it.[6] Through the divine agency the bread and wine made "of human hands" are drawn into the world of Christ's kingdom, and thereby, though everything that you can see, touch, taste, and smell remain characteristic of bread and wine, and so they retain their power to signify food and drink, now their reality is changed into the food of the Kingdom, which is the body of Christ: and that cannot be seen. For *Visus, tactus, gustus, in te fallitur / Sed auditu solo tuto creditur* (Sight, touch, and taste are in thee deceived / What says trusty hearing? That may be believed," as Gerard Manley Hopkins rather eccentrically translates Thomas's hymn *Adoro te devote*, composed for the office of *Corpus Christi*). Truly, then, what is eaten is food. Truly, then it is bread. But now for the faith that comes from hearing, as Paul says, it is the *true* bread, the bread of heaven, the body of Christ. That is what it *really* is. And Jesus commanded his disciples to eat it (John 6:53).

REAL PRESENCE

The eucharistic sign, Thomas says, "effects what it signifies," it makes present, really present, what it refers to. Now one of the chief obstacles to an understanding of Thomas's theology of the "real presence" of Christ in the Eucharist is the false contrast that is assumed between a thing's presence by means of a sign and its real presence. It would seem to be only the theologians with axes to grind who make these false contrasts, for ordinary speech and experience, and virtually all modern philosophy, would have us

not make them—it is a source of constant surprise how readily the
clamor of chattering theologians is allowed to shout down the
quiet voice of common sense. My lover does not cease to be really
present to me because she signifies her love for me with a kiss. On
the contrary, it is through that sign that she is most really present
to me. And it is no use responding that it is the physical contact
of the lips that constitute the reality of that presence, the sign-
value being something added on. On the contrary, when it comes
to kisses it is the thought that counts for presence, every bit as
much as the physical contact of the lips, for otherwise absentminded and merely routine kisses would count for more than the
most sincerely meant words. Yet powerful as it was in sixteenth-
century Switzerland, the theological pressure to resist what
he took to be Catholic teaching had the Protestant reformer
Ulrich Zwingli insist that "the sacrament of the Lord's body"
refers but to the bread which is the sign of the Lord's body, and
since "the sign and the thing signified cannot be one and the same
. . . the sacrament of the body of Christ cannot be the body
itself."[7] That, of course, is a proposition neither more nor less
obviously confused than some of the cruder Catholic theological
statements of Zwingli's times that seemed to take the same view
as the theologian of Zurich about the relationship between sign
and signified. Since Christ's presence in the Eucharist is "real" it
cannot be a presence in and by means of the sign—so argued
some of the bishops at the Council of Trent.[8] Luckily (or, if you
prefer, it was a gift of the Spirit to the Church) the attempt at

Trent to get some such formula passed as the Church's dogmatic proclamation massively failed to win the episcopal vote.

For Zwingli, then, you might just as well say the words and leave it at that, the kisses don't count. For bad Catholic theology, so long as the lips meet, it doesn't seem to matter whether you have any idea what kissing means. Meaningless Catholic hugs, however, are neither better nor worse than hugless Zwinglian meanings. Thomas, at any rate, will have nothing of either polarization. Had he been able to anticipate the eucharistic controversies of the sixteenth century he would no doubt have commented that of course Zwingli was right to insist that Christ's presence in the Eucharist is just as the meaning of a sign is present in the sign, but that he had no reason on that account to conclude that that presence is *not* the real presence of Christ's body. But then neither would Thomas have imagined a Catholic to have good reason to conclude that Christ's presence in the Eucharist is not that of a sign just because it *is* the real presence of Christ's body. Since, for Thomas, eucharistic presence is sacramental presence, everything concerning the mode and manner of Christ's presence in the Eucharist depends on the meaning of "sacrament." Put it at its simplest, Thomas's position concerning the presence of Christ in the Eucharist is this: if you ask, "How is Christ present in the Eucharist?" the answer must be: "Really, that is, in his body." And if you ask, "How is Christ's body present in the Eucharist?" the answer must be: "Sacramentally, that is to say, in the manner of a sign. For *sacramentum est in genere signi*" (a sacrament is a sign of one kind or another).[9] Consequently, any force you may attribute to the word "really," as in "Christ is really present in the Eucharist," must, in Thomas's view, submit to that double condition: it is a bodily presence that is sacramental.

On the one hand, then, the presence of Christ in the Eucharist is "real" in a very particularly human sense: he is present in the Eucharist in his body. This, again, is a plain and non-technical meaning of the expression "really present." No doubt I am in a way present to my friends in Princeton and Tampa by email; but any philosopher who balked at the suggestion that we would be more "really" present to one another by phone, and even more if our bodies were in visual contact with one another, and maximally so if we could shake hands, or embrace or kiss one another, should be given short shrift (as academics ought more often to be given when they theorize in the manner of a cog wheel disengaged from the mechanism—that is, at high speed but to no good purpose). But how is our being really present to one another in such ways supposed to entail that I and my friends are not present to one another as in signs: in words, gestures, smiles, silences, touching, withholdings, all of which are conveyances of meanings, signs, *constituting* the reality of our presence to one another, not obstructing it? Why make the distinction between real presence and presence in a sign into a polarized opposition unless, on some epistemic grounds derived otherwise than from a decent Eucharistic theology, the lines of connection between "presence," "reality," and "sign" have been fractured, the joints dislocated, such that presence as sign and real presence must needs be opposed to each other? We will, however, get nowhere with Thomas on the Eucharist unless we can bracket out what, for him, would have been an entirely misleading way of construing "the real" and "the sign" as terms of contrast standing in such mutual exclusion.

EUCHARISTIC PRESENCE AND THE PRESENCE OF THE RESURRECTION

For Thomas, then, the presence of Christ in the Eucharist is real because it is the presence of his body. But, and here Thomas and Zwingli agree, what is present in the Eucharist, *however* so, is the risen body of Christ, now ascended into heaven, and is not here in the Eucharist as if in a place, to be carried about from here to there.[10] For Thomas, then, Eucharistic presence is nothing but the presence of the resurrection itself, more concretely, the presence of the risen Christ himself, within time and history. If, therefore, we are to understand how for Thomas Christ is present in the Eucharist we need to understand how, for Thomas, Christ is represented as present to his disciples in the gospel accounts that tell of the post-resurrection appearances of Jesus to his disciples. And as to those appearances we might as well start where Jesus himself starts: he is present to the disciples in his body, he says, and even if later Paul describes that body of resurrection as "spiritual" (1 Corinthians 15:44), Jesus' own words serve as a corrective to the skeptical opinion that the Pauline qualifier in effect means:

"not *really* a body at all, rather a sort of hybrid, a weightless, thinned-out, not very material thing, rather like a ghost." Not so, says Jesus to doubting Thomas: "a ghost has no flesh and bones as you see I have" (Luke 24:39). In any case, Paul is just as unequivocal: "and if the Spirit of him who raised Jesus from the dead is living in you, then he who raised Jesus from the dead will give life to your own mortal bodies through his Spirit living in you" (Romans 8:11).[11] Thomas Aquinas is therefore on good scriptural grounds in so robustly affirming the reality of Christ's raised body, as we should expect, given his account of the relationship between bodies and persons that we encountered in Chapter 2. For Thomas, the man Jesus is not raised at all if his body is not raised. And bodies, for Thomas, involve matter, that is to say, measurable quantities.

For this reason, Thomas rejects the view taken by some theologians of his time that Jesus' being able to walk through the closed door of the upper room where the disciples are meeting (John 20:19) is a natural consequence of his body's being raised—a raised body can do just that sort of thing as a matter of course, such theologians supposed. Not so, says Thomas. If in effect you strip the raised body of Jesus of all those properties that belong to bodies as such, then your theology of resurrection in consequence entails the denial of the resurrection of the human person who is Jesus. Human bodies are material objects, and no two material objects can naturally occupy the same place at the same time as one another. It follows that a raised body is not a material body if it can of its nature walk through closed doors, and Jesus' body is not a human body if it is not material—indeed, if it is not material it is simply not a body at all, just a ghost. Therefore, Thomas says, it cannot be on account of his body's being raised that Jesus can walk through a closed door, but only by way of the sort of miracle that, as he maintains, has been wrought in the case of some of the saints pre-mortem. In short, as an indicator of the nature of Jesus' body of resurrection, there is nothing relevant in Jesus' being able to walk through closed doors.[12] The key point is that, raised or not, the essential properties of human bodies remain continuously the same between their pre-and post-resurrection conditions. For otherwise, how could it be said that the raised body of Jesus is the *same* body as that of the Jesus dead on the Cross if, in the relevant sense, the raised person of Jesus lacks the essential properties of a *body* in the first place?

Rather than confusing us about the nature of the human body by the introduction of a very odd, conceptually indefensible, special case of it, the resurrection ought, on the contrary, to clarify what we mean by the human body by revealing to us something deeper, something we might otherwise not have understood, about the body's true nature, about its reality. For our bodies are how we are present to one another. Our bodies are how we speak to one another. We might say, the human body is the human person's extension into language. Herein is a further consequence of Thomas's materialism, now about language, his position being plausible enough. For what else but human beings are capable of conveying meanings through their bodies? How else than by their bodies can human beings convey meanings? What are words spoken but noises emitted which bear meanings? What are words written, but marks scored on a surface which can be read? What else are gestures, but bodily movements which say something, as waving the hand says "hello" or "goodbye" as the case may be? We are, of course, apt to think of bodies as bits of matter, and of meanings as bits of mind. And that, as we saw, is for Thomas all right so long as we do not find ourselves denying that how we human beings are meaningfully present to one another is through our material bodies: we know one another's minds in bodily meanings, as Jesus after the resurrection, revealed himself to his disciples: by eating fish with them (John 21:9–14).

Hence, if we ask, how did Jesus communicate with his disciples, when after the resurrection he appeared to them in the room or on the shore of Lake Tiberias, we are asking how does the resurrection itself—"the kingdom" as we otherwise call it—speak to us. That is the same question as how does Jesus' raised body speak to us, because Jesus' body now belongs to the kingdom itself. Hence, either way we are asking how is that kingdom present to us, here, now, in our temporality, in our carnality and mortality, in our equivalently mortal condition, as it were, of being, like the disciples, housewives, and fishermen. For Jesus' body is raised, but ours are not, our bodies do not yet belong to the kingdom except through our communication with a presence that is at once bodily, but also, because Jesus is raised and we are not, is of necessity sacramental, present in the sign. But to say that Jesus' eucharistic presence is a presence "in the sign" cannot be meant as if to entail that the kingdom is present to us in some other way than as bodies speak to bodies, as eating fish together communicates something. It is in eating and drinking together, in that sharing with one another the gift of life, that there is present among us the gift of new life, our mortal bodies sharing in, or as we say, communicating in, the immortal body, the eternal Word, the resurrection, spoken to us in the form of food.

In short, we can get a grip on what Thomas is saying about the real presence of Christ in the Eucharist only if we accept that the resurrection of Jesus does not diminish his bodiliness. On the contrary, it fulfils that embodiment. We might even say that it radicalizes it. In his natural life, Jesus' presence was limited by time and space and contingency, for his body was thus limited. For Thomas, we should not say: Jesus' presence, his availability, his power to communicate, was limited by his body. We should say rather: his power to communicate was limited by his body's mortality, by its being a "body of death." Therefore, by overcoming death, Jesus' body was released from its limitations; and so, raised by his Father to immortality, he was more present to his disciples in the room when he showed them his hands and his side than he had been when, on the hillside, he multiplied loaves and fishes— not less. He is more present to us now in the Eucharist than he could have been to us had we walked with him on the shores of Lake Tiberias—not less. And so he is more bodily now, as raised, not less, than before his death: again, he insists, "this presence of mine is not that of a ghost."

Now to say all this is to cast some doubt on a contemporary assumption—one which, I should say, can look more like a prejudice—concerning the authority of immediate personal experience. If we are to understand Thomas's theology of the Eucharist, it is important to set this prejudice aside. We are inclined think of personal experience as possessing an authority insofar as it is unmediated by anything so impersonal and distanced, and therefore vulnerable to challenge, as are doctrine or ritual. This is the sort of wishful thinking which has some imagine that to have met the person of the historical Jesus would have been ultimately decisive, immediately convincing, at any rate by comparison with the historically distanced figure we find in the scriptures, or in the doctrinally and theologically mediated reality of the Eucharist or service of prayer. It is that same wishful thinking that leads others to be more excited by the witness of the Shroud of Turin, or the experience of the Holy Places, or to place above all priorities the "quest for the historical Jesus," than by their own, often uninspiring, experience of Christian worship. It is there, in more theological form, in the thought that such is the priority of the personal and immediate experience, that faith itself has to be reconfigured as being a kind of immediate and personal experience.

In which case we should remind ourselves that all four witness accounts of Jesus' life make it plain that in his pre-mortem immediacy Jesus was not all that convincing. More perceptive people than most Christians are had serious doubts about his credentials, thinking some of his claims for himself pretty outrageous, and most honest people could not see in him that revelation of his Father's will that he declared himself to be fulfilling. In fact, in the end, hardly anyone but his mother and a few other women could see anything in him but discouragement and disappointment. So we should not count on our having been any better impressed by Jesus, had we been there to meet him in person before his death, than we are by meeting him in person in the Eucharist after his resurrection. After all, Thomas's apostolic namesake was not especially commended for being persuaded by the visible evidence that Jesus was raised; on the contrary, to his face he was compared unfavorably with those whose encounter with Jesus was, if indeed personal, all the same mediated by faith, as necessarily it must be while he is raised to his Father's kingdom, and we, as yet, are not.

For Thomas Aquinas, unlike Thomas the apostle, to prefer the experience of Jesus as he was before his death to the Jesus of faith, or to prefer the unrecognized figure who explains the scriptures to the disciples on the way to Emmaus to the Jesus who upon being recognized in the breaking of the bread promptly disappears from sight, is to have misunderstood the meaning of the resurrection itself; it is to prefer the world of human experience to the kingdom of faith. And in his *Reportatio* on John's gospel, Thomas notes that this is the significance of Jesus' words to Mary Magdalene, who, finally recognizing Jesus in the garden after the resurrection, reaches out to touch him. Whereupon Jesus somewhat peremptorily commands her not to do so: *Noli me tangere*, Jesus says, pictured in the Middle Ages as swaying away from Mary's outstretched hand,[13] *quia nondum ascendi ad patrem meum* (Do not touch me, for I have not yet ascended to my Father; John 20:17). Thomas comments:

[Mary Magdalene] seeing that Christ had risen, believed him to be in the same condition in which he had been formerly, that is, to have returned to a mortal existence, and so she also wanted to be with him as he had been before his passion, and out of sheer joy gave little thought to anything, although by means of [his] resurrection Christ's body had been made far superior. And so, wishing to draw her away from this manner of understanding, he says "Do not touch me"; which is as if to say: "Do not think of me still as having a mortal life, and of my being with you as before" . . . For this reason he adds, "I have not yet ascended to my father." And this was less an admonition, more an answer to an implied question, so to say, "although you may see me as you did before, that is not for the reason that my body has not been glorified. Rather, it is because I have not yet ascended to my father." For before his ascension he desired to strengthen in the hearts of the apostles their faith in the resurrection, and in his divinity.[14]

The test for Thomas the theologian is nothing other than the test that, later in the post-resurrection narrative, Thomas the apostle failed: which would you rather have, Thomas the theologian in effect asks, the Jesus who is known equally to Thomas the apostle who doubts and Judas the apostate who betrays, although both could "see" him, or the Jesus sacramentally present in the Eucharist, in whom "sight, touch and taste … fall short" but (clearly intending to reflect what Paul says in Romans 10:17) through hearing may be believed? Which of them is the more truly *present*, more *really* present, in either case as one human being is present to other human beings? For in either case Christ is present to us through the meeting of body with body, in the one case, that is, before his death, as in his mortal body he meets his disciples in their mortal bodies in limited time and place; and in the other as in his body of resurrection, his body being no longer limited in its power of communication by death, he meets our bodies across history and time, even though, because we have not as yet died, we are not as he is raised to immortality. For us, now, our meeting with Christ is sacramental, not seeing, a holy, but hidden encounter with the *latens veritas*.[15] Then, when we too are raised in bodies immortal, we shall see, and sacraments will then cease.

TRANSUBSTANTIATION

If, then, the answer to the question, what does the Eucharist signify, is the risen body of Christ, the question remains: in what sense does the Eucharist *effect* what it signifies? For words spoken make a new reality out of an old reality, the words of consecration at Mass do what they say, the outcome of the words' being uttered is that what were formerly bread and wine are now the true body and blood of the risen Christ, ascended into heaven. But what *happens* that brings this outcome about? The answer for Thomas cannot, as we have seen, be the Zwinglian "nothing happens" to the bread and wine. For, on Zwingli's account, what happens happens not only for, but only to the baptized Christians who in faith receive the bread and wine as a sign of a reality, though those elements cannot be said themselves to possess the reality of which they are the signs. For Thomas, unlike Zwingli, something happens to the bread and wine themselves, *they* are changed into the body and blood of Christ. But what sort of change can this be?

Thomas, for whom it is a rule that whenever at all possible the theologian should use plain vernacular Latin rather than technical jargon, is here lost for a word in any language to describe what happens. He is forced to borrow an invented term of art, "transub-stantiation," that gets its sense uniquely from within the constraints of eucharistic theology itself, a word that has no sense in any other context and is therefore a purely technical term. As such technical terms go, "transubstantiation" is more like the physicist's "quark," a term invented for an explanatory purpose and having no meaning otherwise than in that purpose's service; it is less like a term that has a meaning in ordinary usage and then is adapted to a technical purpose in physics, like "force." It is of importance to understand that, for Thomas, "transubstantiation" is *merely* a term of art, doing a limited though necessary theological job. This is important if we are not to load onto Thomas much subsequent Catholic theologizing that is not to be found in his own work. Moreover, there is no doubt that some Christians were right, particularly in the later centuries of Protestant theology, in criticizing Catholic theologians for having tried to get this word to do far too much work, spuriously representing it as if it provided a quasi-scientific account of "eucharistic change," a sort of theory of the processes whereby the bread and wine become the body and blood of Christ. That would be bad enough in itself, were matters not made worse by the archaically "Aristotelian" character of the science appealed to in the course of such theorizing. Thus goes a standard Protestant critique, alas well enough deserved by some standard Catholic expositions of the Tridentine doctrine of "transubstantiation."

But this is not Thomas. For all the fuss made over it, the sixteenth-century Council of Trent barely glossed its use of the word "transubstantiation" to describe Eucharistic change, declaring only that the change of bread and wine into the body and blood of Christ is a real change that is rightly so-called and simply left it at that. It is just as clear that for Thomas the word *has* very little meaning anyway, so that Trent would not for him be exceptionally or surprisingly reticent on the matter. Moreover, though Thomas, like Trent, thought the word is certainly needed theologically, he also believed that it *ought* to be allowed only such meaning as is absolutely needed in the service of theological and doctrinal purposes, that is, such as is required to explain all the eucharistic data of Catholic faith, and no more than that. Otherwise than to that end, for Thomas, the less meaning the word "transubstantiation" is allowed to have the better—enough, but just enough, to do the theological job. The following partial comparison comes to mind.

In 1844, Ignaz Semmelweis, assistant lecturer in the First Obstetric Division of the Vienna General Hospital, noted the significantly differing rates of puerperal fever among mothers immediately post partum in the hospital's two maternity wards, and was able to connect this difference in infection rates with differences in practices of hygiene among medical staff in the two wards. On the basis, that is to say, simply of observing two sets of facts and postulating their causal connection, Semmelweis was able to introduce practices of hygiene that drastically reduced the infection rates in the second ward to the same level as those in the first. In practice, then, Semmelweis was in the position I am in when I count on the light being shed from a bulb in my office upon the instant that I flick the switch on the wall to the up position. I know that the one causes the other, though I am entirely ignorant of the physical laws that govern the process whereby flicking the switch turns the light on. The positions are similar, because although I am certain on empirical grounds that, certain necessary conditions obtaining (such as the bulb not being broken), flicking the switch up will turn on the light, and Semmelweis was certain on empirical grounds of the causal connection between poor hygiene and the transmission of puerperal fever, he was in possession of no better account of *how* the disease was transmitted than I am of how a switch turns a light on, except that in Semmelweis's case the observed facts ruled out bacteria as the infection-carrying agent. Hence, Semmelweis's position in 1844 was that some agent or other of which he had no independent evidence was the cause of the transmission of puerperal fever, and he gave a name "virus" to this "whatever-it-is" that was the agent of this particular form of disease transmission. It was not until forty years later that microscopes were developed of sufficient power of magnification that viruses could actually be seen to exist and their properties observed directly. In the meantime the name "virus" denoted whatever it was that possessed all and only those properties required to explain the particular facts of disease transmission that Semmelweis had observed in 1844. In other words "virus" was just the name of an explanation, an explanation that worked even though the mechanism of its effectiveness was at that stage still beyond the scientist's power of observation.

To that extent the parallel with the doctrine of transubstantiation holds. There is not, and cannot be, a *general* theory of the sort of occurrences described by that name. You cannot get transubstantiation to do any work, theological or otherwise, except as the name for whatever it is that happens such that, upon the utterance of the words *Hoc est enim corpus meum*, what were formerly bread and wine are now the body and blood of the risen Christ. It is therefore not unfair to describe the term as a "makeshift," even though it be now embedded in official Catholic teaching—and has been since the Council of Trent in the sixteenth century. For in the sense that the term exists solely for the purposes of explaining the singular case of eucharistic change, and otherwise serves no explanatory purposes, theological or secular, it is clearly a term of art, a *device* of explanation of a purely technical kind—the word "transubstantiation" has no meaning whatsoever outside of the explanatory context for which it was devised.

It does not follow that the word is meaningless mumbo-jumbo, as some were inclined to say in later centuries (for example Hobbes), even if the very fact that the term of art has to be invented does indeed show language to be under exceptionally severe pressure. The word "virus" was not meaningless just because for forty years or so nothing answering to that name was observable: the term did its explanatory work even in 1844 just because it stood for the precisely definable conditions that would have to be met by whatever it was that explained the transmission of puerperal fever. Just so, Thomas maintains, is the case with the word "transubstantiation."

For these reasons I think there is little prospect of making clear what Thomas has in mind by way of answer to the question "what kind of change is effected by the Eucharistic action?" so long as we confine the terms of any explanation to the makeshift language of transubstantiation. I am inclined to the view that, measured against the standard of positive contributions to our understanding of the sacrament, Thomas would have been indifferent to the matter of whether the term "transubstantiation" is used or not, and we, as readers of Thomas in the twenty-first century, could no doubt heave a sigh of heartfelt relief not to be so heavily loaded with the incubus of this word could we avoid it. For the intellectual heavy lifting that is required to get close to what Thomas means by a "substantial change," never mind close to what he means by a change that has to be described as "transubstantial," is unlikely to yield results in terms of eucharistic understanding sufficient to justify the effort. In this case, as in so many others where theological explanations have become embedded in decrees of the ecumenical councils of the Church, Trent in fact imposes little as to what one should believe, much about what one should not believe: which is why the rhetorical formulas employed by the medieval and later councils are all expressed in negations. They do not insist on what you must say. They insist on what you must not deny. Hence, a twenty-first-century account of the real change of the bread and wine into the body and blood of Christ, even one fully and formally consistent with Thomas's account, need not be set out in terms of a transubstantiation, just so long, that is, that any account now given is not *in*consistent with that formula of the Council of Trent. That formula does this much work at least: it declares to be the true faith of Christians that what happens upon the utterance of the words of consecration is really and truly a change, by which, of course, its intention is to deny that the bread and wine are by the divine power annihilated and replaced by the body and blood of Christ—no change there. And if it is truly a change, it is not just a subjective change in the minds of the communicants, choosing to see things that way. If therefore it is a *real* change in what there is, it is not a change of that sort whereby one kind of thing becomes another kind of thing by some natural process, amenable to analysis in terms of natural causes. Put together the conjunction of all these affirmations and negations and you have that event to which Thomas gives the name "transubstantiation," whereby through the words of consecration what was before correctly described as bread and wine are now correctly described as the body and blood of the risen Christ. There is a variety of ways of construing all the data of eucharistic faith otherwise than, but consistently with, that Tridentine doctrine of transubstantiation, and they, rather than this rather unsatisfactory, quasi-mechanistic account of the *process* of eucharistic change, constitute the heart of Thomas's eucharistic theology.

ANOTHER WAY OF PUTTING IT

What is missed when Thomas's doctrine of transubstantiation gets treated as a curiously mystical form of bad chemistry is what matters to him most theologically about the sacramental presence of the risen Christ in the Eucharist. And that is that in this "sacred feast," in which Christ is our food, not only is there the "memorial of his passion" which fills the soul with present grace; there is also given to us "a pledge of eternal glory." In short, gathered into this eucharistic act of the Church is at once a memory of a past, a presence of what is now, and a promise of what is to come, a single event in which "time present and time past / Are both . . . present in time future,"[16] all this gathered up into a meal, and, being there gathered, instantly redeemed by the food that Christians eat.

Something happens. Something deeply paradoxical happens. For what happens is that the work of creation is done, then a fall, a promise is made of a new creation, the promise is fulfilled, and the Church celebrates the reality of salvation history wrapped up in a fragile fragment of bread and a tiny drop of wine, that is to say, in the most elementary forms of organic life, the taking and sharing of bread and wine. And so it is that the meaning of world history is contained in the simplest and most common of meals. What happens here is a change, but what changes is not chemistry. What changes is meaning. If, as I said earlier in this essay, central to Thomas's philosophy of mind and body is the idea of "matter articulate," then we can see why central to his theological perspectives is the Eucharist. For if ever matter were made articulate, if ever there could be a limit case of matter bearing meaning and becoming what it declares, if ever there were an ultimate possibility of bodily presence through sign, it will be if so elementary a form of life-giving matter as bread and wine can be made to carry the meaning of the whole of salvation history, of the past as memory, of the present as grace, and the future glory as pledge, the resurrection of Jesus contained in human life at its most material, in the form of food.

How, then, are we to understand what happens, the nature of the change, if not in terms of, still at least consistently with, the teaching of transubstantiation? Consider the (almost certainly apocryphal) legend of the invention of the game of rugby in 1823 by, it is said, one William Webb Ellis, at Rugby School in the East Midlands of England. In the course of a soccer match, becoming impatient with the pace of a game prohibiting the use of the hands as a form of contact with the spherical ball, Ellis picked up the ball and ran in the direction of the opposing team's goal line as if attacking it. Whereupon a member of the opposing team, angered at this flagrant disregard for the rules of soccer, flung himself at Ellis's legs, pulling him to the ground as if defending his team's goal line from invasion, and between the two of them—according to the legend—in this way was invented the game of rugby.

Apocryphal as the legend no doubt is, it is illuminating. There are, as we now know by hindsight, two distinct narratives of one and the same set of events, yielding quite incompatible descriptions thereof. The first is soccer's narrative, within which what happen are two destructive and disruptive acts, fouls, identified as such by the rulebook of soccer, the foul of handling the ball and the foul of pulling down an opposing player. As such, these fouls achieve nothing but a tiresome interruption of the flow of the sport, an uncreative spoiling of the "beautiful game." If all you want is soccer, blow the whistle and call a foul—they are, of course two a penny, and they create nothing new. They are routinely dealt with by the police action of the game's referee.

But in Rugby School in 1823 something different happened, something entirely new: soccer fouls *became* rugby ploys. Those same two events, handling the ball and tackling, not different in any respect from the fouls that within the rules of soccer are routinely penalized, were, within the narrative of rugby, its invention, inventing, that is, a whole new world of meaning, inventing, therefore, not just a new game, but with it, a new language game.

Two things are of the utmost importance in the account of the relationship between these differing descriptions of the same events. The first is that a real change has taken place such that the first description, "soccer fouls," is true of the initial state of affairs, and the second description, "legitimate rugby moves" is true of the subsequent state of affairs. For the events to be described as "fouls" you need to presuppose the rules of soccer that prohibit them. To describe them as legitimate moves, you need to presuppose the game of rugby that they invent. There is real change here: the soccer foul of handling the ball *becomes* the rugby move of passing it from hand to hand; the soccer foul of tripping an opposing player *becomes* the legitimate ploy of tackling.

But if there is real change here it is not of the sort where one event causes another within a common context of meaning, as the causal mechanics of the cow's digestive system cause grass to become beef. Grass and beef belong to the same world of organic matter and organic change. What changes when rugby is invented out of soccer are, far more radically, the worlds of meaning to which the events in 1823 belong. If, as I have put it, soccer and rugby are not just games, they are languages, then what happened in Rugby School in 1823 was that one and the same set of actions, falling under one set of descriptions, was wholly transformed, "really changed," by virtue of its coming to fall under a wholly new set of descriptions: a new language, a new set of meanings, is invented by the events they redescribe. Soccer passes away, and as it does so the language in terms of which Ellis's actions were fouls ceases to have purchase on what happened; a new language, that of rugby, reveals to us what those actions really are, as they find their place within the new game that they invent.

The analogy is obviously weak and partial. Nonetheless, it is in some such terms that Thomas understands eucharistic change: ordinary events that get their meanings from the common human practices of eating and drinking are completely transformed in their significance by their being brought into a wholly new and profoundly revolutionary context of meaning, which is the resurrection, so they realize now that kingdom into which, through his resurrection, Christ has entered and of which he now rightfully has taken possession. The food and drink that we in our mortal bodies bring to the table, and in human communities feast upon, are transformed by their being brought into communion with the risen body of Christ, they are retold by an entirely new story that they also inaugurate. For Thomas, the Eucharist is the future kingdom enacted now, the solution to the problem of history in the form of an event within history; it is eating bread and drinking wine in the deepest meaning that food and drink can have: the raised body of Christ present to our bodies in their unraised condition. The Eucharist is the eating and drinking in which Christ is present to us on condition that, as at Emmaus, he disappears from sight (for "sight, touch and taste are in thee deceived") and is real to us only in the word of faith ("only hearing may be believed"). What for Thomas the "real presence" of Christ in the Eucharist most fully means is that in the bread we break and the wine we pour is the "memorial of his passion," a memorial that is a present grace with which the soul is filled, and a pledge of future glory. This, then, for Thomas, is what food *really* is, this is the true life of which the Eucharist is the *true* bread, the "living bread that has come down from heaven," the "bread of angels," the *panis angelicus*, as Thomas puts it, that has become bread for the human race, the *panis hominum*, food breaking out into wholly unexpected realms of meaning, once again the thing through the divine action being called upon to surpass itself, food supererogatorily being called upon to mean more than you can possibly say. Thus it is that for Thomas in the Eucharist is to be found all the work done which there is for the theologian to do. Thomas the theologian is, then, both the grammarian of a *res mirabilis*, and a saint, a *pauper servus et humilis*, whose last word is to be lost for words before the power of the mystery of faith.

The Secret of Saint Thomas

Thomas thought that etymologically the Latin *sacramentum* derived from the conflation of *sanctum* and *secretum*: a sacrament, he says, is a hidden holiness. "Godhead here in hiding, whom I do adore"—thus does Hopkins translate the first line (as we now have it) of "Adoro te devote, latens deitas," one of Thomas's Eucharistic hymns. You wouldn't have known that mere bread and wine could bear such weight of meaning, for basic human food is the last place you would guess to be the point of entry into the mystery of the world's creation out of nothing and its trajectory through history to its final end in the eternal love that created it. For Thomas it is all there in the meaning of eating and drinking. And it should not surprise us that all the meaning of all the world is contained and hidden in that holy hiddenness. If it is a cause of surprise that theology should culminate there, in Christ's followers eating and drinking together, then there is still something to learn from Thomas.

It is, for sure, no overstatement to say that for Thomas theology is but an extended meditation on the meaning of bread and wine, a reflection on what they *really* are. If so much meaning is "here in hiding" it is because it has that strangest form of the unseen that consists in being all too obvious, too visible to be noticed. I promised the reader that our Thomas would be a caricature, though no more so than any other profile that I have read, whether ancient and hagiographical or modern and scholarly, whether pedantically accurate and tedious or, like Chesterton's, historically carefree and uncannily illuminating. I also promised that my caricature would turn out to be that of a materialist whose respect for matter, being theologically motivated, is such as to reveal in the material world far more power of significance than is allowed by the dull, flat, and unprofitable materialism of today's atheistic fashion. Thomas's matter speaks, it overflows with meaning. For what are human beings but matter articulate, animals that in speaking make sounds utter, and in writing make literate shapes? And how do human beings differ from other species of their genus but in their freedom from a selectively adapted environment, in only a universe being enough for them? For it is not anything in particular, but only everything whatsoever that will yield the meaning that is at once hidden and palpably "charged with the grandeur of God."

Articulate animals that we are, our bodies speak to one another, and through word and gesture we share in friendship the universe we inhabit. And it is through that same materiality of speech that the body of Christ is in converse with the world, the Word spoken to us as food and food given to us as Word spoken, as body speaks to body, as friend speaks to friend.

So it is no surprise for Thomas that matter is made supremely articulate through the body of Christ in the Eucharist: it doesn't surprise him that matter could bear such weight of meaning, for he is, after all, a materialist. Nor, conversely, does it surprise Thomas that the solution to the riddle of existence should be found so easily and so obviously, a heaven in the ordinariness of eating and drinking together, matter shot through with divine meaning.

But here also, in the theology that tells us of this hidden obviousness, is fat Thomas, the man as gross in girth as an ox, the teacher invisible, standing out of the light himself that others might see. And though as vast in output of words as he was in girth, vastest of all was he in his finally falling silent so that others might hear. Thomas stops short so that it would be not *his* word that his readers heard, but what in that silence he himself was always listening for, the Word of God in the matter that articulates it.

From the outset I have commented on Thomas's disappearing act, on the Thomas "here in hiding": again and again his theology serves the purpose that he, the person, and especially the saint, escapes our attention. But try as he might, the very trying gives him away. There is, after all, a secret of Saint Thomas. It lies at the intercrossing of the theologian, the Dominican, and the saint. But that intersection does not occur in some hidden place. The truth is exactly the contrary. The secret of Thomas's holiness is hard to see not because it is hidden somewhere, but because it is every-where obvious in the Dominican theologian, so that were you to look for it here rather than there, the holiness in one place, the theology in another, you would miss both. The holiness of Thomas is a theologian's holiness, the holy teacher invisible otherwise than in the holy teaching itself. And that, if there is one, is the secret of Saint Thomas—quite the most obvious thing about him.

Notes

ONE. A DOMINICAN

1. *ST* 2–2ae, q26 a11 *corp.*

2. 2 Thess. 3:10.

3. "When they live by the labor of their hands, as our fathers and the apostles did, then they are really monks." *Rule of St. Benedict*, 48:8.

4. Guigo II, *Scala Claustralium*, in *Guigo II: The Ladder of Monks and Twelve Meditations*, trans. Edmund Colledge and James Walsh (Garden City, N.J.: Doubleday, 1978).

5. Genesis 28:12.

6. Mark Jordan, "Ideals of *Scientia Moralis* and the Invention of the *Summa Theologiae*," in *Aquinas's Moral Theory: Essays in Honor of Norman Kretzmann*, ed. Scott MacDonald and Eleonore Stump (Ithaca: Cornell University Press, 1999).

7. *De unitate intellectus contra Averroistas*, 5: para 124, trans. *On the Uniqueness of the Intellect Against the Averroists*, www.geocities.com/CapitolHill/8246.

8. Bonaventure, *The Journey of the Soul into God*, chapter 5, Works of St. Bonaventure, volume 1, *Bonaventure Texts in Translation Series*, translation, introduction, and commentary by Philotheus Boehner and Zachary Hayes, OFM, 2002.

9. Ibid.

10. In the Vulgate numbering; it is 102 in the Hebrew.

11. *Verbum supernum prodiens*, a hymn composed for the office of Lauds on the feast of Corpus Christi (see Chapter 6 below).

TWO. A MATERIALIST

1. *ST* 1a, q13 a2 ad2.

2. *ST* 1a, q2 a2 ad2.

3. *Confessions*, 7, 17.

4. Bonaventure, *The Journey of the Soul into God*, 5.1, p. 81.

5. *Meditations on First Philosophy*, edited and translated by John Cottingham (Cambridge: Cambridge University Press, 2002).

6. Not everyone would agree with the sharpness with which Thomas makes this distinction between human and animal behavior. Courtney Palmbush has pointed out to me that to use a tool to achieve a purpose is to act "for a reason." And there is some evidence that some animals use tools for purposes, intentionally. Thomas knew nothing of this evidence, which may require us to soften or even erase the boundary line that for him is drawn so sharply between rational and nonrational animals in favor of something more like a graded continuum of rationalities.

7. "Si . . . animal non esset totum quod est homo, sed pars eius, non praedicaretur de eo, cum nulla pars integralis de suo toto praedicetur." (If being an animal were not what a human being is as a whole, but only a part, it would not be predicated of [any human], for no integral part is predicated of the whole.) *De ente et essentia*, 2.

8. This is why, for Thomas, an animal is not related to a vegetable as species to genus. An animal possesses all the forms of life that a

vegetable possesses, but all the same is not a species of vegetable. There are no "animal vegetables" as there are rational animals.

9. This puzzles some. Are not angels rational? Is not God? Thomas's answer is no they are not. As we will see, reason is simply the form that intellect takes in an animal—and it is the lowest form of intellect possible.

10. "Sic ergo genus significant indeterminate totum id quod est in specie, non enim significant tantum materiam; similiter etiam differentia significant totum et non significant tantum formam." (And so it is that the genus [animal] signifies indeterminately everything that is specific [rational animal], it does not signify what is material only; in the same way the difference [rational] signifies the whole, and not just the formal principle [rationality].) *De ente et essentia*, 2. What Thomas means is that being rational is one way, but not the only way, of being an animal, "animality" being indeterminate between animals of either sort. Hence, to describe a living being as an animal *might be* to describe a human being. It *can't be* to describe an angel. Likewise, the description of a living being as rational *is* to describe a kind of animal, and *cannot be* to describe an angel of any kind.

THREE. THE SOUL

1. *Super I ad Corinthios*, 14, 5.

2. "If the resurrection of the body is denied it is no easy matter, indeed it is difficult to defend the immortality of the soul. For it is undeniable that the natural condition of the soul is to be united to the body and to be separated from it is against its nature, something that just happens to it [*per accidens*]. For this reason a soul disengaged from the body is imperfect just inasmuch as it is thus disengaged. But it is impossible that what is natural and intrinsic to a thing should be in such a way limited and, as it were, as if nothing to it; just as [it is impossible] that what is against a thing's

nature and just as it happens, should be its unqualified condition, as would be so were the soul to endure for ever without a body. It is for this reason that the Platonists, who affirm immortality, postulate a reincarnation, granted that this postulation is heretical: and therefore, if the dead will not rise again, we will have assurance of this life alone." Ibid.

3. P. T. Geach, "Immortality," in *God and the Soul* (London: Routledge, 1978), pp. 27–28.

4. *ST* ia, q13 a12 ad3.

5. *On There Being One Intellect Against the Averroists*, 1:23–24.

6. Ibid., 5:124.

7. The objects of Thomas's anger were evidently the chief representatives of what was known as "Latin Averroism" in the University of Paris in 1270, namely Siger of Brabant and Boethius of Dacia. Although Thomas never mentions them by name, it was probably Siger and Boethius he had in mind when insisting that you cannot consistently have Averroës and maintain Christian teaching about personal identity and immortality of persons.

FOUR. GOD

1. *ST* ia, q1 a7 *corp.*

2. The United States being the unlucky exception.

3. *ST* ia, q1 a7 *corp.*

4. See Karl Rahner, *The Trinity*, trans. Joseph Donceel, introduction, text, and glossary by Catherine Mowry LaCugna (New York: Crossroad, 1997), pp. 15–21.

5. It is true that the chapter of his *Proslogion* in which the argument is introduced is in the form of a prayer. But when Gaunilo responds "on behalf of the fool" he attacks Anselm's case in respect of validity, a property the possession or absence of which is relevant only to what is offered as proof. Anselm responds not by saying that such attacks are

irrelevant to what was never intended as proof in the first place, but by attempting to shore up the faults of inference that Gaunilo identifies— that is to say, he accepts that the case stands or falls by the standards required of formal proof. Anselm clearly thinks that by those standards his "argument" stands. It *is* a valid argument; it is sound: it is a proof. Thomas too thinks that it is intended as a proof, and that it is *as such* that it fails.

6. The problem with unsound arguments is not that they will get you nowhere. The problem is that they will get you anywhere, including, at their most misleading, to true conclusions. The following is a valid argument entailing a true conclusion: "All rubber conducts electricity; all metal is rubber; therefore all metal conducts electricity." One would be ill advised, however, to offer this syllogism, valid as it is, in a physics exam. It is unsound, the premises both being false.

7. *ST* 1a, q2 a3.

8. John Milbank, "Intensities," in *Modern Theology* 15, no. 4 (1999): 455.

9. Thomas describes his arguments as five ways whereby *Deum esse probari potest*. There is no good English translation of Thomas's *probari* that weakens the force of "strictly and formally proves."

10. See *ST* 1a, q11 a3 *corp.*, where Thomas says that to be God and to be this God are identical.

11. *ST* 1a, q3 a.

12. *ST* 1a, q11 a3 ad2.

13. *Divine Names*, 5, 817D, p. 98.

14. *Divine Names*, 5, 824B, p. 101.

15. It is, however, important to note an asymmetry here: "There are two Gods" is simply false. "There is one God" is not false, it is true, but the oneness of God is beyond our comprehension. That is why the manner in which "There is one God" excludes "There are two Gods" is

not the same as the manner in which "There is one pie for lunch" excludes "There are two pies for lunch."

16. Augustine, *On the Trinity*, 7.3; Thomas, *ST* 1a, q2 a3.

17. Boethius, *Liber de Persona et Duabus Naturis*, ch. 3.

18. Augustine's Latin of which I have given this circumlocutory translation is *ego animus*. Augustine is usually careful to distinguish *animus*, generally synonymous with *spiritus, intellectus*, and a variety of other literal and metaphorical terms, from *anima*, in that the latter informs and is intrinsically connected with the body, whereas the former is the highest part of the human *mens* which in some way overlaps with the divine nature: it is there in my most spiritual being that my identity is to be found, not in that dimension of my being that informs and is limited by my body.

19. *Confessions*, 10.9.

20. *The Five Ways: St. Thomas Aquinas' Proofs of God's Existence*, Anthony Kenny, *Studies in Ethics and the Philosophy of Religion* 5 (London: Routledge, 2002).

21. *A Revelation of Love*, chapter 5, in *The Writings of Julian of Norwich*, ed. Jacqueline Jenkins and Nicholas Watson (University Park: Pennsylvania State University Press, 2006), p. 139.

FIVE. FRIENDSHIP AND GRACE

1. *ST* 1–2ae, q38 a2 *corp.*

2. *ST* 1–2ae, q38 a3 *corp.*

3. *ST* 1–2ae, q38 a4 *corp.*

4. *ST* 1–2ae, q38 a5 *corp.*

5. There are a few others, especially the twelfth-century Cistercian monk Aelred of Rievaulx, whose *On Spiritual Friendship* is perhaps the more remarkable exception in that he was a friend personally of Bernard of Clairvaux, who must be the champion among monks of the model of the love of God as *eros*.

6. I am much indebted to Elizabeth Trang for pointing to the need for some important nuances in this connection. It is of course true, as she suggested in a comment on an earlier draft, that it would be a mistake to set the erotic and the friendship models of Christian love in opposition to one another, and it is fair to say that in the context of his theology of marriage Thomas by no means does so: friendship, Thomas says, should be the context in which husbands and wives love each other erotically. Nonetheless, in terms of more general literary and theological styles, Thomas's choice is for the model of friendship, because erotic love is one-to-one and exclusive, whereas friendship is inclusive of many, and so seems the better to express the multiple solidarities of *caritas*.

7. *In librum B. Dionysii De divinis nominibus expositio*, cap. 4, lectio 9.

8. *Nicomachean Ethics*, 8:12, 1161a30–b10.

9. *ST* 1–2ae, q112 a1 *corp*. That friendship on equal terms between God and human beings should be a pure gift of an infinite creator to a finite creature is, in my view, a lovely paradox. It is not an oxymoron.

10. I have benefited much from (amicable) disagreements with T. J. Dumansky, a Ph.D. student in theology at Yale, on the subject of Thomas and Aristotle on friendship.

11. *ST* 1–2ae, q111 a1 *corp*.

12. *ST* 1–2ae, q113 a3 *corp*.

13. *ST* 1–2ae, q112 a3 *corp*.

14. *ST* 1–2ae, q113 a7 *corp*.

15. *Paradiso* 3, 85.

16. Thus a residual Catholic triumphalism.

17. "Interior intimo meo," *Confessions*, 3:6, 11.

18. Comments on an earlier draft by Elizabeth Trang cause me to add the following important clarification. Friendship between two human creatures is possible on the basis only of an already existing

equality between them, as Aristotle says. There is no existing equality between God and creatures on which their friendship can be based. Friendship between God and creatures is a gift offered by God to creatures, a gift that creates the equality on condition of which that friendship is possible. As it is with grace, so it is with friendship. As grace creates the freedom with which we consent to it, so grace creates the equality to which we are invited by the divine offer of friendship.

19. *ST* 2–2ae, q17 a8 *corp.*

20. John Donne, *The Extasie.*

21. *Sentences*, I, d.17, 1, 1: *Cum ergo de dilectione diligimus fratrem de Deo diligimus fratrem.* See Fergus Kerr's discussion of the development of Thomas's ideas on charity as friendship, "Charity as Friendship," in *Language, Meaning, and God: Essays in Honour of Herbert McCabe, O.P.,* ed. Brian Davies (London: Geoffrey Chapman, 1987), pp. 1–23.

22. *Golden Epistle*, 1.169, trans. Theodore Berkeley, OCSO, *The Works of William of St. Thierry*, Cistercian Fathers Series 12 (Kalamazoo: Cistercian Publications, 1980), p. 67.

23. *Golden Epistle*, II.

24. "Unus spiritus," *Golden Epistle*, III.

25. *On the Trinity* XV, 17.

26. *ST* 2–2ae, q23 a2 obj.1.

27. *ST* 2–2ae, q23 a2 ad1.

28. *ST* 1a, q6 a4 *corp.*

29. *ST* 1a, q6 a4, ad1.

30. *ST* 1a, q6 a2 ad3.

31. *Mystical Theology*, 1.

32. *Tractatus Logico-Philosophicus.*

SIX. GRACE, DESIRE, AND PRAYER

1. William of Tocco, unpublished fourteenth-century life of Thomas, quoted in Torrell, *Saint Thomas Aquinas*, vol. 1, pp. 284.

2. *ST* 3a, q21 a4 *corp.*

3. *ST* 3a, q21 a1 *corp.*

4. For all this, see *ST* 1–2ae, qq1–5.

5. *ST* 3a, q21 a2 *corp.*

6. *Enarrationes in Psalmis*, Psalm 32:1, *Patrologia Latina*, 36, p. 277.

7. For what ensues in the rest of this paragraph, see *ST* 1–2ae, q94 a2 *corp.*

SEVEN. CHRIST

1. See Torrell's account of this dispute in *Saint Thomas Aquinas*, vol. 1, pp. 184–87.

2. *ST* 1a, q46 a2 *corp.*

3. *ST* 1a, q46 a3 ad3.

4. *ST* 1a, q19 a3 *corp.*

5. *ST* 1a, q49 a2 *corp.*

6. *ST* 3a, q1 a3 *corp.*

7. *ST* 3a, q1 a1.

8. *ST* 3a, q46 a1 *corp.*

9. *ST* 3a, q1 a1 *corp.*

10. Nicholas Love, *The Mirrour of the Blessed Lyf of Jesu Christ*, I, ed. James Hogg and Lawrence F. Powell, Analecta Cartusiana 91 (Salzburg: Institut für Anglistik un Amerikanistik, 1989), pp. 13–19. Love's *Mirrour* is a translation and adaptation of a Latin work of the thirteenth century, *Meditationes vitae Christi*, the author being unknown, though in the Middle Ages the work was mistakenly attributed to Bonaventure.

11. *ST* 1a, q44 a4 ad1.

12. *ST* 1a, q21 a4 *corp.*

13. *ST* 1a, q21 14 *corp.*

14. "Mercye and sothefastnesse metten louely to gidere; Rightwisnes and pees hauen kissed." *Love*, p. 19.

15. *ST* 3a, q1 a1.

16. For an extended discussion of the logic of Julian's "behovely," see my *Julian of Norwich, Theologian* (New Haven: Yale University Press, 2011), pp. 32–67.

17. *ST* 3a, q1 a1 *corp.*

18. *Divine Names*, 4.

19. *De trinitate*, XIII, 17.

20. I am grateful to Evan Morse for correcting an error of interpretation of ST 3a, q1 a1 that I had included in an earlier draft of this paragraph.

21. *In Librum De divinis nominibus*, cap. 4, lect. 1.

22. *Divine Names*, 4.

23. See Sermon 49, in Meister Eckhart, *The Essential Sermons, Commentaries, Treatises, and Defense*, ed., introduction, and trans. Bernard McGinn and Edmund Colledge, Classics of Western Spirituality (London: SPCK, 1981).

24. "Et in mundo conversatus / sparso verbo semine" (and scattering the word like a seed, it was within the world that he spoke it), from the hymn *Pange lingua gloriosi*, composed by Thomas for the office of the newly established feast of *Corpus Christi* in 1264.

25. *ST* 3a, q40 a1 ad2.

26. *ST* 3a, q40 a2 *corp.*

27. *ST* 3a, q40 a2 ad3.

28. *Contra impugnantes*, 6.

29. *ST* 3a, q40 a3 *corp.*

30. *ST* 2–2ae, q188 a7 *corp.*

31. *ST* 2–2ae, q188 a7 *corp.*

32. *ST* 2–2ae, q188 a7 *corp.*

33. *ST* 2–2ae, q188 a7 ad1.

34. *ST* 2–2ae, q188 a7 *corp.*

35. *Republic*, I.

36. *Republic*, VII.

37. *The Myth of God Incarnate*, ed., John Hick (London: SCM Press, 1977), p. 178.

38. Of course I can always produce a state of affairs in which as a matter of fact all the circles are yellow and all the squares are green. In that state of affairs it will always be false that there is a yellow square. But even in that state of affairs it would never be contradictory to describe one of the squares as yellow.

EIGHT. THE EUCHARIST AND ESCHATOLOGY

1. "O sacrum convivium, in quo Christus sumitur, recolitur memoria passionis eius. Mens impletur gratia, futurae gloriae nobis pignus datur." Antiphon to the *Magnificat*, Vespers for the feast of *Corpus Christi*.

2. *Super Evangelium S. Matthaei lectura*, cap. 26, lectio 3.

3. "Sacramenta novae legis efficiunt quod signant," *Super Evangelium S. Matthaei lectura*, cap. 26, lectio 3.

4. I am grateful to Elizabeth Trang for alerting me to this reference.

5. *ST* 3a, q78 a5 *corp.*

6. *ST* 3a, q78 a5 *corp.*

7. Ulrich Zwingli, *On the Lord's Supper*, in *Zwingli and Bullinger*, ed. and trans. G. W. Bromiley, Library of Christian Classics 24 (London: SCM Press, 1954), p. 188.

8. See the excellent discussion of the debates on the Eucharistic presence at Trent in Edward Schillebeekx's *The Eucharist* (New York: Continuum, 2002), part 1.

9. *ST* 3a, q40 a1 *corp.*

10. *ST* 3a, q76 a6 *corp.* There is nothing strange about this. If standing just here I am thinking about what to eat for lunch, and, pacing as I think, I move six feet to the left, we are not inclined to say

that my thinking what to have for lunch has just moved six feet to the left.

11. I am grateful to Elizabeth Trang for this reference.

12. *Super Evangelium S. Ioannis lectura*, cap. 20, lect. 4:

Per nullam autem proprietatem corporis gloriosi possent removeri dimensiones a corpore, natura corporis remanente. Et ideo dicendum est, quod hoc miraculose Christus fecit virtute suae divinitatis; et quandocumque in sanctis simile contingeret, miraculosum esset, et per novum miraculum fit. Et hoc expresse dicunt Augustinus et Gregorius. (There is nothing in the nature of a glorified body that can deprive it of its dimensive properties consistently with its nature as a body. And so the conclusion to draw is that Christ [walked through the locked door] miraculously and by the power of his Godhead; and whenever the same was to happen from time to time with the saints it would likewise have to be a miracle, and a new miracle to boot. Both Augustine and Gregory expressly affirm this.)

13. See Fra Angelico's fresco *Noli Me Tangere* in the Convent of San Marco, Florence, 1440–41.

14. *In Joannem*, cap. 20, lectio 4. The rest of the passage in Thomas's *Reportatio* is worth quoting for other reasons, not strictly relevant to the issues here:

And then he gives [her] positive instructions, saying "but go to my brethren," that is, to the apostles ["and say to them: I am ascending to my Father and yours"], . . . and here we should take note of a threefold privilege accorded to Mary Magdalene. The first of these is prophetical, in that she was rewarded with the sight of the Angels, for a prophet mediates between the Angels and the people. Secondly she is credited with the high standpoint of the Angels, in as much as she sees Christ, upon whom the Angels desired to gaze. Thirdly, she is appointed to an apostolic responsibility, in fact she is made to be the woman who is apostle to the apostles in that to her is given the responsibility of announcing the resurrection of the Lord to the disciples: so that just as it was a woman who first uttered the words of death to a man, so it is a woman who is first to announce the words of life.

15. The popular Latin hymn attributed to Thomas speaks of a *latens deitas*. Dom Wilmart has shown that the original text of this hymn (which on grounds that Torrell rejects Wilmart denies to Thomas's authorship) begins: *Adoro te devote, latens veritas.* See Torrell, *Saint Thomas Aquinas*, vol. 1, pp. 132–35.

16. T. S. Eliot, "Burnt Norton," in *Four Quartets*, ll. 1–2.

Further Reading

Rather than providing within the text of this book detailed annotation of the works of Thomas relevant to the issues raised, here I provide references to the more limited primary sources on which I have relied in writing it. I include but few references to secondary material. This is not because I have not needed them myself in the past, but because in my view it is far better to consult such works having engaged in a first encounter with the primary sources directly rather than as mediated through the filter of (often contentious and always contended) interpretations. And in that class of interpretations I of course include my own.

REFERENCING THE WORKS OF THOMAS AQUINAS
The works of Thomas on which I have drawn in writing this work are of four general kinds: systematic and comprehensive treatises, for example the *Summa Theologiae*; collections of "questions" disputed in the university and formally written up, including the *Disputed Questions on*

Virtue in General; polemical works, such as *On the Unity of the Intellect Against the Averroists*, and *On the Eternity of the World*; and scriptural commentaries, such as the so-called *Reportatio* on the gospel of John, so-called because it is a record of Thomas's lectures on John's gospel delivered in the University of Paris, taken down by students and (in this case partially) edited by Thomas himself. References to these works take the following forms.

1. *Summa Theologiae*. This work (abbreviated for reference purposes as *ST*) is divided into three parts, of which the second part is further divided in half, the work being usually published therefore as four volumes: the first part (in Latin, "Prima pars" shortened for reference purposes to 1a), the first part of the second part ("Prima secundae," or 1–2ae), the second part of the second part ("Secunda secundae," or 2–2ae), and the third part ("Tertia pars," or 3a).

Each part is divided in turn into a series of "questions" or topics, of which there are, for example, some 102 in the first part, and 114 in the first part of the second part—thus question 109 of the first part of the second part ("On the necessity of grace") is referenced as *ST* 1–2ae, q109.

These questions are subdivided into a series of articles, the article being the basic unit of substantive theological discussion. Thus, within question 109 of the Prima secundae, there are 10 articles, reference to which takes the form of *ST* 1–2ae, q109 a1, or a2 or a3 and so forth. Every article is headlined by a question in the form "Whether it is the case that . . ." followed by a theological statement with which Thomas either agrees or disagrees. Thus, *ST* 1–2ae, q109 a1 is headed by the question: "Whether it is the case that there is no knowledge of truth without grace," to which Thomas's answer will turn out to be that genuine knowledge is possible without grace—but his answer is hard won and not arrived at before he has gone through an elaborate process of dialectical debate, the structure of which is as follows.

First Thomas sets out in a series of arguments—commonly, as in this case, three but sometimes as many as four or five—the case for the opinion on the question to hand to which he is opposed, the so-called "objections." Next, he declares in a single statement his opposed opinion ("sed contra," or "but as against this view"), supported usually by a quotation from some major authority, theological or philosophical. In 1–2ae q109 a1 the appeal is to the *Retractions* of Augustine. There follows the main part or body of the article (corpus in Latin, abbreviated to "corp.") in which Thomas sets out his own opinion together with accompanying arguments in its favor, followed by responses in turn to the "objections" put forward in support of the opposed view. Each of these responses begins "with reference to the first objection [or second or third as the case may be] it should be said that . . ." (in Latin, ad primum dicendum est). Hence the reference to the main part of Thomas's argument about grace and knowledge of the truth takes the form: *ST* 1–2ae, q109 a1 *corp.* When Thomas responds to the second of the three objections to his own view the reference takes the form: *ST* 1a–2ae, q109 a1 ad2.

Disputed questions. These are collections of questions, subdivided into articles, each of which is structured as above but devoted to a single general topic, such as the collections "On Truth" or "On Evil." Most such compilations gather together questions and articles composed over a long period of time and are not written through as a single continuous treatise. References to these questions take the form of *Disputed question on truth* (in Latin *Quaestio disputata de veritate*) q2 a2 *corp.*

Polemical works. These are generally written through in more recognizable and less dialectical modern form as longer or shorter monographs, divided into parts and chapters, as in the case of *On there being one intellect*. Modern editions and translations will often add line or paragraph numbering.

Biblical commentaries. The chief biblical commentary referred to in this monograph is Thomas's *Commentary on John's Gospel,* which is organized on a typically medieval principle of subdivision of the text. In Thomas's time the numbering of verses of Scripture had not yet been standardized, though chapter divisions roughly corresponding with modern ones were more or less universally accepted. Commentaries such as Thomas's on John further subdivide chapters into small units of two or three verses at a time, and the commentary is organized as a series of lecturae ("readings") on these groupings of verses.

SOURCES BY CHAPTER

Chapter One

Having emphasized the primacy of reading Thomas in primary sources and not as mediated through secondary works, it makes very little sense to read the early hagiographical material about Thomas except out of interest in hagiography itself as a genre. Better is to consult a good secondary source containing what concerning Thomas's life can now be established as fact, such as the work on which I have relied, Jean-Pierre Torrell's two volumes, *Saint Thomas Aquinas: Person and His Work,* trans. Robert Royal (Washington, D.C.: Catholic University of America Press, 1996), and *Saint Thomas Aquinas: Spiritual Master* (2003). G. K. Chesterton's work, written in great haste in the 1920s, is obviously very dated, and is not to be relied upon to have distinguished successfully between fact and legend. Nonetheless, somehow Chesterton gets to the man and his mind in a way that few others do whose scholarship is more to be trusted. I first read Joseph Pieper's *The Silence of St. Thomas* more than forty years ago and it did for me what did Hume did for Kant, in that it "awoke me from my dogmatic slumber" and disclosed for me a living mind hidden behind versions of Thomas's thought that amounted to but dead dogma. Pieper's own short work is probably the best introduction to the theologian, though it is worth noting that he himself says that Chesterton's is the best short account of the man and his thought. The influence of the late Herbert McCabe on my reading of Thomas will be obvious to all who know his work, and those who do not know it ought to. Otherwise, a first read for absolute neophytes who want a short, sharp, clear, and accessible tour of Thomas's thought will find it in Fergus Kerr's *Thomas Aquinas, a Very Short Introduction* (Oxford: Oxford University Press, 2009), though for those looking for something at once relatively brief but more technically detailed perhaps the best of combination of the two available in English is Simon Tugwell's introduction to the selected works of Thomas in English translation contained in the volume *Albert and Thomas, Selected Works* in the series *Classics of Western Spirituality* (New Jersey: Paulist Press, 1989).

Chapters Two and Three

Punchily polemical, conceptually clear (though it is far from an easy read and not recommended for beginners), Thomas's *Aquinas Against the Averroists: On There Being Only One Intellect*, ed. and trans. Ralph McInerney (Indiana: Purdue University Press, 1993) is probably the best short account of his views on the nature of the human soul, the human body, and their relation. It is also the most compendious philosophical exposition of the consequences of his account for the defense of personal immortality. Much easier for nonspecialists (and intended for them) are chapters 75–94 on the soul and chapters 151–63 on the resurrection of the body in Thomas' *Compendium Theologiae*, published in translation by Cyril Vollert as *Light of Faith, The Compendium of Theology* (Manchester, N.H.: Sophia Institute Press, 1993). The defense of the corresponding doctrine of bodily resurrection in its biblical sources is to be found in the English translation of the Commentary on 1 Corinthians 15, 12–19, lecture 2, para. 924. See the parallel Latin and English versions done by

Fabian Larcher, O.P., and Daniel Keating, in the online version edited by Joseph Kenny, O.P.

Chapter Four

No one should be encouraged to read Thomas's famous "five ways" of proving there to be a God (*ST* ia, q2 a3) who is not as strongly encouraged to read *ST* ia, q3, especially the prologue to that question, which tells us that no proof of God's existence can answer the question of what God is, for there is no such answer. Otherwise the best way into Thomas's understanding of God in general is through his account of the creation of all things out of nothing in *ST* ia, qq44–46, which notably follows his discussion of God's Trinitarian nature (*ST* ia, qq27–43). Only when all three discussions have been read together can you get the hang of Thomas's method, which is to conduct every theological discussion in the light of the unknowable mystery of God at once as incomprehensibly one as incomprehensibly three. Again, a simpler read of Thomas's doctrine of God, one and three, is to be found in the *Compendium* (*Light of Faith*, chapters 3–67).

Chapters Five and Six

For Thomas's discussion of Aristotle on friendship see ST 1–2ae, qq26–28, and Book 8 of his *Commentary on the Nicomachean Ethics of Aristotle*, translated by C. I. Litzinger, O.P. (Chicago: Henry Regnery, 1964), 2 volumes. For a more theological discussion of charity as friendship see *ST* 2a-2ae, qq23–46, and *Commentary on the Gospel of John*, chapter 15, lecture 3, in the translation by James A. Weisheipl and Fabian R. Larcher, with introduction and notes by Daniel Keating and Matthew Levering, 3 vols., *Thomas Aquinas in Translation* (Washington, D.C.: Catholic University of America Press, 2010). On grace, see *ST* 1–2ae qq 109–13 (*Compendium*, chapters 143–50). On the prayer of Jesus see *ST* 3a, q 21; on happiness as the final end, see *ST* 1–2ae, qq1–5 (*Compendium*, chapters 100–107); on natural inclinations, see *ST* 1–2ae, q94 a2 *corp.*

Chapter Seven

On the act of creation, *ST* 1a, qq 44–46 (*Compendium*, chapters 68–74); on the vexed question of eternity of the world, see *Compendium*, chapters 95–99; more technical is Thomas's polemic on the eternity of the world, found online as Medieval Sourcebook: Thomas Aquinas: *On the Eternity of the World*, http://www.fordham.edu/halsall/basis/aquinas-eternity.asp, translation © 1991, 1997 by Robert T. Miller. On the logic of the incarnation, see *ST* 3a, qq1–7, though this is seriously technical theology; again, without patronizing oversimplification, a much more straightforward read is found in the *Compendium*, chapters 198–219. On prayer (and its foundation in the theological virtue of hope) see the incomplete Part II of the *Compendium*—it breaks off at midpoint of chapter 10. An excellent extract on the relation between prayer and providence translated from the *Summa contra Gentiles* is in Simon Tugwell's *Albert and Thomas* (see above). Specifically on Jesus' prayer in Gethsemane, see *ST* 3a, q21. On the issue of Dominican poverty, see *Liber contra impugnantes Dei cultum et religionem*, translated by John Procter, O.P., in *An Apology for the Religious Orders* (London: Sands, 1902), English updated, many corrections, and chapters renumbered according to Latin, and html-edited by Joseph Kenny, O.P., online at: http://josephkenny.joyeurs.com/CDtexts/ContraImpugnantes.htm.

Chapter Eight

For the liturgical texts (in Latin with English translation) of the feast of Corpus Christ composed by Thomas in 1264, see http://josephkenny.joyeurs.com/CDtexts/CorpusChristi.htm#1. The antiphon *O sacrum convivium* composed by Thomas for the liturgy of that feast is a poetic resume of *ST* 3a, q60 a3 *corp*. On transubstantiation and the real presence of Christ in the Eucharist, see *ST* 3a, q75. On sacraments in general, see *ST* 3a, q60, especially aa 1 and 2; on eschatology and its relation to the Eucharist, see the *Commentary on the Gospel of John*, chapter 20, lecture 4.

Index

Abstraction, Locke on, 85–87, 234–35; and the concrete, 90. *See also* Meaning

Adam, his sin, 186–87

Albert the Great, Saint, 5–6, 20, 21, 47, 91

Alexander of Hales, 21

Anselm of Canterbury, Saint: the logic of the Incarnation, 198; ontological argument, 107–8

Apophaticism, 42–44, 126, 142–43

Aquinas, Thomas. *See* Thomas Aquinas, Saint

Aristotle, 32, 35; Arabic translations of, 114; Averroist reading of, 92–96; on the eternity of the world, 189–93; the "good man," 187; *Nicomachean Ethics*, 179; Thomas's indebtedness to, 112–14

Augustine, Saint, 4, 36–38, 69–71; charity and the Spirit, 162; contingency, 133; God and creation, 133–34; prayer of Christ, 181; on the Trinity, 123–26, 142. *See also* Platonism (medieval)

Averroës (Ibn Rushd), 92

Avicenna (Ibn Sina), 114

Barth, Karl, 105, 118

Benedict, Saint, 10, 15

Benedictines, 9

Bonaventure, Saint, 3, 4, 23, 36–37; on the eternity of the world, 190; knowledge of God, 54–55; more spiritual than Thomas, 48; Platonist on soul and body, 56–57, 59; three human souls, 65–66

Brain, not the organ of thought, 83

Catherine Earnshaw, 227

Chalcedon, Council of, 219, 224, 228

Charity. *See* Love

Chesterton, G. K., 288

Christ, 100–106; divinity of, 224–28; humanity of, 187, 219, 223–24; poverty of, 14, 211–18, 223–24, 228–29; prayer of, 181; sinlessness of, 219–24

Christology, 6, 166; Christ's full humanity, 219–24; conflict impossible between humanity

and divinity of Christ, 224–28; full divinity, 224–28; Hick on the incarnation, 224–25. *See also* Chalcedon, Council of

Cologne, 19

Compendium theologiae, 20, 26–27, 289

Condemnations, Paris and Oxford (1277), 23–24, 58

Contemplation, 6–7; as cure for sadness, 146; monastic, 16–17; Thomas and, 45–46

Contingency: argument from, 134–39; Augustine, 133

Contra impugnantes dei cultum et religionem, 280n28, 290

Creation: distinction between creature and Creator, 163; distinction not disjunction, 153, 164–66; *ex nihilo*, 140–44; grace as new creation, 185; no creation of matter without form, 50

Dante, 2, 52, 222

Davies, Brian, O.P., 278n21

Dawkins, Richard, 106

Democritus, 51

Denys, Pseudo-, 147, 166–67, 205–7, 209

Desire: for happiness, 177–80; and natural law, 181–85; not knowing what you want, 179–80; prayer and desire (will), 172, 174–81; and self-deception, 176–77

Determinism, Calvinist, 154

Dominic, Saint, 8, 10, 14; idea of holiness, 17–18, 45

Dominicans, 8; begging, 17; manual labor, 17; no Dominican stereotype, 47; poverty, 11–12, 18, 210–19, 224; preaching, 13–14, 17–18, 33, 216–19; school of holiness, 18

Donne, John, interinanimation, 161–62, 226–27

Dumansky, T. J., 277n10

Eckhart, Meister, 4, 47, 48, 64, 209

Eliot, T. S., 283n16

Empedocles, 51

De ente et essentia, 272n7, 273n10

Eucharist, 98, 166, 230–66; Council of Trent on, 243–44; eating and drinking the human basis of, 235–36; the eschatological meaning of eating and drinking, 235–37, 261, 265–68; feast of *Corpus Christi*, 233–34; Luther and, 240; real change in, 239–46; and resurrection, 246–54; Thomas and signs which effect, 242–46; transubstantiation, 254–65; Zwingli and presence in the sign only, 243–45, 255

Fall, 169–71

Fallacies: Composition, 138–39; Quantifier Shift, 135–38

Francis of Assisi, 11

Franciscans, 3, 48. *See also* Bonaventure, Saint

Freedom: free-will defense, 154–60, 165–66; and grace, 154–60, 164–65

Friars, 14–18

Friendship. *See* Grace; Love

Geach, Peter, 77

Giles of Rome, 21; condemnation in Paris, 49

Glossa ordinaria, 21–22

God, 6; Bonaventure on, 54; Creator *ex nihilo*, 140–43; Descartes on, 55; formal object of theology, 101–2; foundationalism, 103–6; Muslims and Jews on oneness, 111, 122, 125–26; no number in God, 121; not in any genus, 165; not first object of human mind, 52–55; not opposed to creatures, 153–55; not a person, 124–25; number and the Trinity, 122–31; oneness of, 111; oneness incomprehensible, 130–31; ontological argument (*see* Anselm of Canterbury, Saint); of the philosophers, 104, 111; proofs of the existence of, 105–6, 108–12, 115–17; the silence of, 42; the "third way," 131–39; uniqueness of, 119–21; unknowability of, 42–44, 126, 142–43

Grace: and desire, 171–72; effective, 151–54; equality with God, 149–50; free will and, 150–60, 167–68; ground of friendship with God, 152, 160–69, 187; and justification, 150; and merit, 150; and nature, 169–70; as new creation, 185–86; and prayer, 172; and sanctification, 150; supererogatory, 171

Guigo II, the Carthusian, 11, 15

Heathcliff, 227
Henry of Ghent, 21
Hick, John, 224–25, 227
Hobbes, Thomas, 223
Homer, 2
Hopkins, Gerard Manley, translation of *Adoro te devote*, 242, 267
Hugh of St. Victor, 16
Human beings: not souls, 58–69; wholly animal, 56–58, 62–65, 132; wholly rational, 68–69
Hume, David, 88

Ibn Rushd (Averroës), 92
Ibn Sina (Avicenna), 114
Incarnation: as *conveniens*, 201–4; Nicholas Love on, 199–204; source of grace, 150; as supererogatory, 204–10
Immortality: Aristotle on, 76; Averroist intellect and, 93–99;

Fifth Lateran Council on, 76; problem for Thomas, 72–75; and resurrection of the body, 74–76

In librum B Dionysii De divinis nominibus, 277n7, 280n21

Intellect, 82–90; immateriality of, 88–90; Latin Averroists on, 91–99

Interinanimation, 161–62, 226–27

John of San Giuliano, 8, 18

John XXII, Pope, 34, 46

Jordan, Mark, 30–31

Julian of Norwich, 139–41

Kant, Immanuel, 109–12, 131

Kerr, Fergus, O.P., 278n21, 289

Kilwardby, Robert, 48–51, 97

Knowledge: and light, 37–39; of self, 38–39

Love: as *amicitia*/friendship, 147; as *amor*/*eros*, 147–48, 162–63; charity, as *agape*, 147–48; created and uncreated, 163; Donne, interinanimation and, 161–62; and equality, Aristotle on, 148; gift of the Holy Spirit, 161; not identical with Holy Spirit, 162–63; of parents, 13; singleness of will, 161; Thomas on, 148–50

Luther, Martin, Eucharist and companation, 240

McCabe, Herbert, O.P., 13, 278n21

McCosker, Philip, 153

Materialism: and the Eucharist, 237–38, 269; Thomas accused of, 50; Thomas's distinct from modern forms, 47–69, 72, 96–98. *See also* Dawkins, Richard

Meaning: Locke, 85; and matter, 91–99, 268–69; and naming, 85–86; Swift, 85. *See also* Abstraction

Milbank, John, 275n8

Mind: immateriality of, 89–90; matter the natural object of, 52–54

Monks, 14–18; ladder of, 15; manual labor, 15–16; silence, 15; singing, 14–15; stability of place, 14

Monte Cassino, monastery of, 9, 13, 16–18

Mozart, Wolfgang Amadeus, Requiem unfinished, 232

Naples, University of, 8, 17, 19
Natural law: and divine will, 184–85; and grace, 187–88; and "real wants," 181–85; rooted in human nature of Christ, 187–88; and sin, 183, 185–88
Nicholas Love, the logic of the incarnation, 199–204

Palmbush, Courtney, 272n6
Paris, Faculty of Arts in, 19, 35, 92
Paul, Saint, 4, 15, 75, 246–47
Pecham, John, 190, 191
Personal identity, 77–78
Persons of Trinity. *See* Trinity
Peter Lombard, *Sentences*, 20–23, 162–63, 231–32
Pieper, Joseph, 288–89
Plato, 2, 56, 60, 70–71, 75, 147; and Thrasymachus, 222
Platonism (medieval), 52, 56, 75, 92–98
Poverty, 31–33, 40–46; of Christ, 223–24; and the Incarnation, 228–29; and theology, 229

Prayer: act of intellect, 174; as discovery of true desire, 172–81, 185; Jesus' prayer, 181; petitionary, 174; Thomas's prayer, 172–74
Preaching: Dominicans and, 13–14, 17–18, 33; poverty and, 31–33

Quaestio disputata de veritate, 287

Rahner, Karl, 105, 118–19, 122, 128, 131
Reginald of Piperno, 41
Reincarnation, 75
Reportatio in Joannem, 27, 148, 282–83n14
Resurrection: of the body, 74–78; of Christ, post-resurrection appearances, nature of, 246–54; in the Eucharist, 250–54; to Mary Magdalene, 252–54; to Thomas Apostle, 252. *See also* Immortality

Sacra doctrina, 18
Sacraments: performative character of, 239–42; and signs, 244–45

Sadness, cures for, 145–46

Schillebeekx, Edward, 281n8

Schopenhauer, Artur, 141

Scotus, John Duns, 21, 48

Semmelweis, Ignaz, virus as explanatory hypothesis, 257–59. *See also* Eucharist: transubstantiation

Senses of the body, 79–82

Sentences (Peter Lombard), 20–23, 162–63, 231–32

Shakespeare, William, 2, 7

Sin: *Letter to the Hebrews* and the sinlessness of Christ, 219–24; sin and loss of humanity, 221–24

Song of Songs, 147

Soul: Aristotle on, 71; form of the body, 56–68, 70–72; human souls are animal, 56–58; I am not my soul, 56–68; are immaterial, 79–83; are immortal, 72–76; not part of human person, 61–62, 64–65; only one intellectual soul, 50, 62–69; principle of life, 56, 60; separated soul, 79

Summa contra gentiles, 26

Summa theologiae, 20, 25–33; incompleteness of, 41–46, 230–33; structure of, 31–33, 103, 286–87

Supererogation, incarnation as, 204–10

Super Evangelium S Matthaei lectura, 281n3

Super I ad Corinthios, 273n1, 273–74n2, 289–90

Tempier, Stephen, 48–51, 59, 97

Theological language: Nietzsche, 167; and transcendence, 166–67

Theology: Catholic and Protestant, 153–54; *convenientia* and the logic of theology, 201–4; designed for preachers, 29; as *disciplina* or *scientia*, 28–29, 193–99; monastic, 16–17; theological propositions rationally undecidable, 194–99; Thomas's methodological pluralism, 26–27; university, 19–24

Thomas Aquinas, Saint: anger of, 35–36, 91–92; appearance, 35, 269; Benedictine oblate, 9–10; canonization of, 34; condemnations of Tempier and Kilwardby, 48–51, 59, 97; Dominican, 7, 19, 47, 270; death at Fossanova, 147; the dumb ox, 5–6; holiness, 2–7, 270; humility, 3–4, 34–40; lucidity, 36–40; parents, 10, 12; prayer, 172; preacher, 2–7, 19; preaching and poverty, 31–32; reform of Dominican syllabus, 25–33; silence, 40–46, 269; teacher, 2–7, 19–25, 36, 270; theologian, 2–7; travels, 3

Thomas of Lentini, 8, 18

Torrell, Jean-Pierre, 288

Trang, Elizabeth, 103, 277n6, 277–78n18, 281n4, 282n11

Transubstantiation, 254–60; comparison with invention of rugby, 261–65; comparison with Semmelweis, 257–61; Council of Trent on, 256–61

Trinity, 102, 111, 118, 122–31; incomprehensibility of, 130–31;

persons of Trinity as relations, 126–31; persons really distinct, 129. *See also* God: oneness of

Tri-theism, 122–24

Tugwell, Simon, O.P., 289

De unitate intellectus contra Averroistas, 35, 274n5, 289

Verbum supernum prodiens, 43

Virtues, theological, 161–62

Will, 161, 163, 175–85

William of St Thierry, 162

William of Tocco, 172

Wittgenstein, Ludwig, 85, 167

Word, and silence, 41–44

World: creation of, 189–92; creation of the world in time according to Pecham, 189–90; eternity of demonstrable according to Aristotle, 192; the question demonstrably undecidable according to Thomas, 192–93

Wuthering Heights (Brontë), 226–27

Printed and bound by CPI Group (UK) Ltd, Croydon, CR0 4YY

25/11/2024

14598461-0001